*Bloom's Shakespeare Through the Ages*

*Bloom's Shakespeare Through the Ages*

# THE COMEDY OF ERRORS

*Edited and with an introduction by*
## Harold Bloom
Sterling Professor of the Humanities
Yale University

*Volume Editor*
Janyce Marson

BLOOM'S
LITERARY CRITICISM
*An imprint of Infobase Publishing*

**Bloom's Shakespeare Through the Ages: The Comedy of Errors**

Copyright © 2010 by Infobase Publishing
Introduction © 2010 by Harold Bloom

Bloom's Literary Criticism
An imprint of Infobase Publishing
132 West 31st Street
New York NY 10001

**Library of Congress Cataloging-in-Publication Data**
The comedy of errors / edited and with an introduction by Harold Bloom ; volume editor, Janyce Marson.
    p. cm. — (Bloom's Shakespeare through the ages)
  Includes bibliographical references and index.
  ISBN 978-1-60413-720-0 (hardcover)
  1. Shakespeare, William, 1564–1616. Comedy of errors.  I. Bloom, Harold.
  II. Marson, Janyce.
  PR2804.C65 2010
  822.3'3—dc22                                    2010001313

Bloom's Literary Criticism books are available at special discounts when purchased in bulk quantities for businesses, associations, institutions, or sales promotions. Please call our Special Sales Department in New York at (212) 967-8800 or (800) 322-8755.

You can find Bloom's Literary Criticism on the World Wide Web at
http://www.chelseahouse.com

Text design by Erika A. Arroyo
Cover design by Ben Peterson
Composition by IBT Global, Inc., Troy NY
Cover printed by IBT Global, Inc., Troy NY
Book printed and bound by IBT Global, Inc., Troy NY
Date printed: June 2010
Printed in the United States of America

10 9 8 7 6 5 4 3 2 1

This book is printed on acid-free paper.

All links and Web addresses were checked and verified to be correct at the time of publication. Because of the dynamic nature of the Web, some addresses and links may have changed since publication and may no longer be valid.

# CONTENTS

❦

# SERIES INTRODUCTION

Shakespeare Through the Ages presents not the most current of Shakespeare criticism, but the best of Shakespeare criticism, from the seventeenth century to today. In the process, each volume also charts the flow over time of critical discussion of a particular play. Other useful and fascinating collections of historical Shakespearean criticism exist, but no collection that we know of contains such a range of commentary on each of Shakespeare's greatest plays and at the same time emphasizes the greatest critics in our literary tradition: from John Dryden in the seventeenth century, to Samuel Johnson in the eighteenth century, to William Hazlitt and Samuel Coleridge in the nineteenth century, to A. C. Bradley and William Empson in the twentieth century, to the most perceptive critics of our own day. This canon of Shakespearean criticism emphasizes aesthetic rather than political or social analysis.

Some of the pieces included here are full-length essays; others are excerpts designed to present a key point. Much (but not all) of the earliest criticism consists only of brief mentions of specific plays. In addition to the classics of criticism, some pieces of mainly historical importance have been included, often to provide background for important reactions from future critics.

These volumes are intended for students, particularly those just beginning their explorations of Shakespeare. We have therefore also included basic materials designed to provide a solid grounding in each play: a biography of Shakespeare, a synopsis of the play, a list of characters, and an explication of key passages. In addition, each selection of the criticism of a particular century begins with an introductory essay discussing the general nature of that century's commentary and the particular issues and controversies addressed by critics presented in the volume.

Shakespeare was "not of an age, but for all time," but much Shakespeare criticism is decidedly for its own age, of lasting importance only to the scholar who wrote it. Students today read the criticism most readily available to them, which means essays printed in recent books and journals, especially those journals made available on the Internet. Older criticism is too often buried in out-of-print books on forgotten shelves of libraries or in defunct periodicals. Therefore, many students, particularly younger students, have no way of knowing that some of the most profound criticism of Shakespeare's plays was written decades or centuries ago. We hope this series remedies that problem, and more importantly, we hope it infuses students with the enthusiasm of the critics in these volumes for the beauty and power of Shakespeare's plays.

# Introduction by
# Harold Bloom

At the close of Plato's *Symposium*, just before Aristophanes and Agathon, the young tragic dramatist, pass out from too much wine, Socrates wickedly expounds the thesis that the same playwright should be equally accomplished at comedy and tragedy. Only Shakespeare more than fulfills this admonition of Socrates. Still, *Titus Andronicus* (unless it is a deliberate outrage) does not show Shakespeare as a tragic genius. *The Comedy of Errors*, one of his earliest plays, already reveals Shakespeare's magnificence at the art of comedy. It is as perfect a work as ever he crafted.

Every performance I have seen of *The Comedy of Errors* was played at too slow a pace. It ought to go at an outrageous speed, forcing us to catch up as best we can. Phantasmagoria suits Ephesus, city of magicians and charlatans, where the surprisingly complex and subtle Antipholus of Syracuse seems to be living a dream.

The play is his quest-romance. He finds his lost brother, father, and mother but that is far less important than his instant falling in love with his brother's sister-in-law, Luciana. His declaration to her is more Hermetic than Christian:

Are you a god? would you create me new?
Transform me then, and to your power I'll yield.

That centers the play: He does not drink of Circe's cup but of the fountain of Hermes, mercurial god of metamorphoses. One doubts that he and his Ephesian brother ever will have much to say to each other, unlike the Dromios who will delight each another as they do us. What the quester requires is a wife so vitalizing that all loss falls away, and he finds her in Luciana.

*The Comedy of Errors* wildly blends knockabout farce with visionary romance. Shakespeare went on to compose the finest comedies in Western history: *A Midsummer Night's Dream, As You Like It, Twelfth Night*. Extraordinary as they are, *The Comedy of Errors* presages them in the depth of character of Antipholus of Syracuse and even more in his personality. His tentative inwardness and deep yearning for completion break the bounds of genre, as we perpetually learn and expect of Shakespeare.

# Biography of
# William Shakespeare
❦

WILLIAM SHAKESPEARE WAS born in Stratford-on-Avon in April 1564 into a family of some prominence. His father, John Shakespeare, was a glover and merchant of leather goods, who earned enough to marry the daughter of his father's landlord, Mary Arden, in 1557. John Shakespeare was a prominent citizen in Stratford, and at one point, he served as an alderman and bailiff.

Shakespeare presumably attended the Stratford grammar school, where he would have received an education in Latin, but he did not go on to either Oxford or Cambridge universities. Little is recorded about Shakespeare's early life; indeed, the first record of his life after his christening is of his marriage to Anne Hathaway in 1582 in the church at Temple Grafton, near Stratford. He would have been required to obtain a special license from the bishop as security that there was no impediment to the marriage. Peter Alexander states in his book *Shakespeare's Life and Art* that marriage at this time in England required neither a church nor a priest or, for that matter, even a document— only a declaration of the contracting parties in the presence of witnesses. Thus, it was customary, though not mandatory, to follow the marriage with a church ceremony.

Little is known about William and Anne Shakespeare's marriage. Their first child, Susanna, was born in May 1583, and twins, Hamnet and Judith Shakespeare, in 1585. Later on, Susanna married Dr. John Hall, but the younger daughter, Judith, remained unmarried. When Hamnet died in Stratford in 1596, the boy was only eleven years old.

We have no record of Shakespeare's activities for the seven years after the birth of his twins, but by 1592 he was in London working as an actor. He was also apparently well known as a playwright, for reference is made of him by his contemporary, Robert Greene, in *A Groatsworth of Wit*, as "an upstart crow."

Several companies of actors were in London at this time. Shakespeare may have had connection with one or more of them before 1592, but we have no record that tells us definitely. However, we do know of his long association with the most famous and successful troupe, the Lord Chamberlain's Men. (When James I came to the throne in 1603, after Elizabeth's death, the troupe's name changed to the King's Men.) In 1599, the Lord Chamberlain's Men provided the financial backing for the construction of their own theater, the Globe.

The Globe was begun by a carpenter named James Burbage and finished by his two sons, Cuthbert and Robert. To escape the jurisdiction of the Corporation of London, which was composed of conservative Puritans who opposed the theater's "licentiousness," James Burbage built the Globe just outside London, in the Liberty of Holywell, beside Finsbury Fields. This also meant that the Globe was safer from the threats that lurked in London's crowded streets, like plague and other diseases, as well as rioting mobs. When James Burbage died in 1597, his sons completed the Globe's construction. Shakespeare played a vital role, financially and otherwise, in the construction of the theater, which was finally occupied some time before May 16, 1599.

Shakespeare not only acted with the Globe's company of actors, he was also a shareholder and eventually became the troupe's most important playwright. The company included London's most famous actors, who inspired the creation of some of Shakespeare's best-known characters, such as Hamlet and Lear, as well as his clowns and fools.

In his early years, however, Shakespeare did not confine himself to the theater. He also composed some mythological-erotic poetry, such as *Venus and Adonis* and *The Rape of Lucrece*, both of which were dedicated to the earl of Southampton. Shakespeare was successful enough that in 1597 he was able to purchase his own home in Stratford, which he called New Place. He could even call himself a gentleman, for his father had been granted a coat of arms.

By 1598, Shakespeare had written some of his most famous works, *Romeo and Juliet*, *The Comedy of Errors*, *A Midsummer Night's Dream*, *The Merchant of Venice*, *Two Gentleman of Verona*, and *Love's Labour's Lost*, as well as his historical plays *Richard II*, *Richard III*, *Henry IV*, and *King John*. Somewhere around the turn of the century, Shakespeare wrote his romantic comedies, *As You Like It*, *Twelfth Night*, and *Much Ado about Nothing*, as well as *Henry V*, the last of his history plays in the Prince Hal series. During the next ten years he wrote his great tragedies, *Hamlet*, *Macbeth*, *Othello*, *King Lear*, and *Antony and Cleopatra*.

At this time, the theater was burgeoning in London; the public took an avid interest in drama, the audiences were large, the plays demonstrated an enormous range of subjects, and playwrights competed for approval. By 1613, however, the rising tide of Puritanism had changed the theater. With the desertion of the theaters by the middle classes, the acting companies were compelled to depend more on the aristocracy, which also meant that they now had to cater to a more sophisticated audience.

Perhaps this change in London's artistic atmosphere contributed to Shakespeare's reasons for leaving London after 1612. His retirement from the theater is sometimes thought to be evidence that his artistic skills were waning. During this time, however, he wrote *The Tempest* and *Henry VIII*. He also wrote the "tragicomedies," *Pericles, Cymbeline*, and *The Winter's Tale*. These were thought to be inspired by Shakespeare's personal problems, and have sometimes been considered proof of his greatly diminished abilities.

However, so far as biographical facts indicate, the circumstances of his life at this time do not imply any personal problems. He was in good health, financially secure, and enjoyed an excellent reputation. Indeed, although he was settled in Stratford at this time, he made frequent visits to London, enjoying and participating in events at the royal court, directing rehearsals, and attending to other business matters.

In addition to his brilliant and enormous contributions to the theater, Shakespeare remained a poetic genius throughout the years, publishing a renowned and critically acclaimed sonnet cycle in 1609 (most of the sonnets were written many years earlier). Shakespeare's contribution to this popular poetic genre are all the more amazing in his break with contemporary notions of subject matter. Shakespeare idealized the beauty of man as an object of praise and devotion (rather than the Petrarchan tradition of the idealized, unattainable woman). In the same spirit of breaking with tradition, Shakespeare also treated themes that hitherto had been considered off limits—the dark, sexual side of a woman as opposed to the Petrarchan ideal of a chaste and remote love object. He also expanded the sonnet's emotional range, including such emotions as delight, pride, shame, disgust, sadness, and fear.

When Shakespeare died in 1616, no collected edition of his works had ever been published, although some of his plays had been printed in separate unauthorized editions. (Some of these were taken from his manuscripts, some from the actors' prompt books, and others were reconstructed from memory by actors or spectators.) In 1623, two members of the King's Men, John Hemings and Henry Condell, published a collection of all the plays they considered to be authentic, the First Folio.

Included in the First Folio is a poem by Shakespeare's contemporary Ben Jonson, an outstanding playwright and critic in his own right. Jonson paid tribute to Shakespeare's genius, proclaiming his superiority to what previously had been held as the models for literary excellence—the Greek and Latin writers. "Triumph, my Britain, thou hast one to show / To whom all scenes of Europe homage owe. / He was not of an age, but for all time!"

Jonson was the first to state what has been said so many times since. Having captured what is permanent and universal to all human beings at all times, Shakespeare's genius continues to inspire us—and the critical debate about his works never ceases.

# SUMMARY OF
## *THE COMEDY OF ERRORS*
❧

*The Comedy of Errors* opens in Ephesus, a prosperous, cosmopolitan, and culturally diverse city, the third largest within the Roman Empire. Because of its associations of urban sophistication, Ephesus also became associated with the occult, superstition, and witchcraft. Significantly, it is also where Paul lived and conducted his missionary work. Thus, Ephesus was an important center to early Christianity. According to the *Book of Acts*, Luke's narrative of Paul's missionary work in Ephesus (ca. A.D. 53). The town was where he spread the Christian gospel, preaching to the citizens and attempting to dissuade them from pagan worship, for Ephesus was also the locale of the great temple of Artemis, built in 560 B.C. to honor the Greek goddess of that name. In Greek mythology, Artemis, whose name means "virtuous," was a virgin goddess and the twin sister of Apollo. She was known as the goddess of hunting and the protectoress of young women, childbirth, and nature and was often depicted as a huntress carrying a bow and arrows. Her marble temple in Ephesus was one of the seven wonders of the ancient world. When Paul took up a three-year residence in the city, his message about the Christian God was initially met with resistance and disbelief. Paul would ultimately sway the populace, the practitioners of exorcism burning their books and extolling Jesus after witnessing the miracles performed by Paul. Many critics have written of the significance of Shakespeare setting *The Comedy of Errors* in Ephesus as his deliberate intention to Christianize the story. In many instances, they use this choice on the playwright's part as the basis for their contention that the play contains an unmistakable spiritual message.

*The Comedy of Errors* is one of Shakespeare's earliest comedies and is based closely on the plots of two Latin plays by Plautus. The first and major source is the *Menaechmi,* a play about long-separated twins who are mistaken for each other and are eventually reunited. The secondary source is found in the *Amphitruo,* a play in which masters are confused for servants and vice versa. Among the many changes made, Shakespeare added an additional set of twins, this time twin servants to their twin masters, thus complicating the plot from the start. Despite some of its less favorable reviews, *The Comedy of Errors* has proved enormously entertaining with its elements of farce, improbable plot development, and slapstick gestures.

# Act 1

Act 1, scene 1: *The Comedy of Errors* opens in the city of Ephesus, with Solinus, the duke of Ephesus, leading an elderly merchant, named Egeon, who is under arrest and facing imminent execution. Egeon is the unwitting victim of hostilities between Ephesus and Syracuse, having broken a law forbidding commerce and travel between the two cities. The only way for the old man to avoid his terrible fate is to raise a vast sum of money, a thousand marks, a sum that he neither possesses nor has the means for acquiring. From his entrance and initial lines in the play, Egeon is portrayed as an elderly, pathetic, and deeply wronged merchant, accepting of the fate that awaits him for having unintentionally entered into a hostile world. For his part, Solinus, who has arrested him, appears wholly unsympathetic to Egeon's dire circumstances. "Merchant of Syracuse, plead no more. / I am not partial to infringe our laws." Instead, Solinus presents himself as a cold-blooded administrator who blames the Syracusans of being "seditious countrymen" who have, by decree, decided to prohibit all commerce between the two towns. Thus, in retaliation, the Ephesian law demands that anyone from Syracuse who breaches the border will be killed, with the individual's goods becoming the property of the duke. "Therefore by law thou are condemned to die." In response, Egeon can find consolation only in knowing that his suffering will soon end at sundown when he is executed.

When Solinus next asks Egeon about the circumstances that led him to the Ephesian shore, Egeon responds with a heartrending tale, describing the "griefs unspeakable" of his sad personal history caused through no fault of his own but, rather, by an accident of nature leaving him and his family the victims of a shipwreck. Egeon begins with a description of his separation from his wife, a happy and prosperous marriage until he left home on one of his many voyages to the neighboring town of Epidamnum because his associate there had died, leaving the business in disarray. Egeon tells the duke that he regrets this last voyage that "[d]rew me from kind embracements of my spouse" who was, at that time, pregnant and that she, in turn, was compelled to leave home to join her husband. While in Epidamnum, Egeon's wife gave birth to a set of identical male twins, "the one so like the other / As could not be distinguished but by names." As it happened, through sheer coincidence, an extremely poor woman staying at the same inn as Egeon and his wife, also gave birth to a set of male twins, whom Egeon and his wife bought from the impoverished mother with the intention of raising them to work as servants to their two sons.

Once everything had been arranged, Egeon's wife made an urgent request that they return home to Syracuse. Egeon relates to the duke the details concerning their premature departure from Epidamnum despite adverse weather. As a result of their untimely sailing, we learn that they became the victims of a storm that struck at night, making any hope of rescue nearly futile. Though Egeon would have readily accepted the ostensible death sentence such a predicament imparts, his wife's insistent pleadings for the lives of the family compelled him to find a means of saving them from drowning. A group of sailors hoping to find safety in Egeon's boat abandoned the family's sinking ship instead once they saw the hopelessness of the situation. Following this unfortunate desertion, Egeon tells us that his wife came up with an alternate, albeit perilous, plan to save the family by tying herself with one son and one slave to one of the masts while Egeon did the same with his other twin son and twin slave to the other mast of the nearly destroyed boat. Egeon's family floated for a time, during which the sea grew calm. They then spotted two ships coming toward them from the distance—one from Corinth and the other from Epidaurus. At this juncture, Solinus, who has been listening with rapt attention, encourages Egeon to continue his sad tale, though promising no pardon for his violation of Ephesian law.

As Egeon continues his saga, we learn that yet another unfortunate turn of events had taken place, for before the ships could reach them, Egeon's family ran into a rock that split the wreckage in two, carrying Egeon in one direction and his wife in the other. "Our helpful ship was splitted in the midst; / So that in this unjust divorce of us / Fortune had left to both of us / What to delight in, what to sorrow for." Eventually, his wife and the two children appeared to be rescued by an Epidauran ship, but the slow boat was unable to catch up with Egeon and the two children with him.

As Solinus continues to encourage Egeon in his story, the old man relates how, 18 years later, his youngest son and his young servant both wished to seek out their twin brother counterparts; so the two young men set off in search of their missing family. Egeon eventually followed suit and wandered for five summers through Greece until he ultimately found himself in Ephesus. Though the threat of execution is imminent, Egeon's love for his family is so great that he is willing to withstand whatever misfortune awaits him in this alien land, if only he can confirm that they are alive and well. "But here must end the story of my life, / And happy were I in my timely death / Could all my travels warrant me they live." The duke is deeply moved by Egeon's story though insists that he still cannot suspend the death sentence unless Egeon can find someone to ransom his life. "Now trust me," Solinus says, "were it not against our laws. . . . My soul should sue as advocate for thee," though he offers Egeon a day of freedom to find someone to give him the requisite money. The stay of execution does little to dispel Egeon's despair, since the task seems hopeless. Nevertheless, Egeon is determined to persevere against the odds and canvass the city in search of his family.

Act 1, scene 2 begins with Antipholus of Syracuse, his servant, Dromio and the First Merchant onstage together, though they are unaware that Antipholus's father is in Ephesus, just as Egeon is oblivious to their presence. In addition, the passage of time has brought changes to their respective appearances that later make identification and recognition difficult. The kind Merchant warns Antipholus of their risky situation, given the law against Syracusans being in the city. The man informs Antipholus that another Syracusan has been arrested and fears for his life. The merchant advises Antipholus to pretend that he is from some other place. "Therefore give out you are of Epidamnum / Lest your goods too soon be confiscate." Antipholus then directs Dromio of Syracuse to bring his money to the Centaur, the inn where they are staying, and cautions his servant to wait there while Antipholus familiarizes himself with the town and observes the workings of its traders. Antipholus then states that he will go lose himself in the city, a telling statement since his whole history is predicated on being lost, a condition that he seems painfully aware of. "I to the world am like a drop of water / That in the ocean seeks another drop, . . . So I, to find a mother and a brother, / In quest of them unhappy, lose myself." Dromio of Ephesus then enters, and Antipholus of Syracuse immediately mistakes him for his own Dromio, the man he has just sent to the inn. Hoping that this is his true servant, a man who shares his history, "the almanac of my true date," Antipholus expresses surprise at Dromio's rapid return, while Dromio of Ephesus in turn responds that he has actually arrived too late. He has come to summon Antipholus home to dinner and grows agitated as he describes the circumstances of the meal and the domestic uproar that accompanies it. "The capon burns, the pig falls from the spit. / The clock hath stricken twelve upon the bell; / My mistress made it one upon my cheek." Clearly, Antipholus of Ephesus is in trouble, for his wife is furious that he is not home and his servant has been beaten through no fault of his own. Antipholus of Syracuse, of course, is baffled by this demand to come home and instead wants to know what his servant has done with the money entrusted to him. The servant, for his part, knows nothing of the money and makes a trite remark: "O sixpence that I had a-Wednesday last. / To pay the saddler for my mistress' crupper." An argument ensues with Dromio insisting that Antipholus of Syracuse return home for dinner and expressing fear that he will once again be struck by his angry mistress. Antipholus tries to reason with Dromio, still believing his servant is deliberately joking with his master, and attempts to bring him back to his senses, but to no avail. Antipholus of Syracuse becomes increasingly frustrated and threatens Dromio with violence. "In what safe place have you bestowed my money, / Or I shall break that merry sconce of yours." Dromio still insists that Antipholus's wife awaits him at the Phoenix (apparently the name of the Ephesian domicile), stating that she will continue to fast until his return. Antipholus strikes Dromio, observing that Ephesus is reputed to be populated by tricksters and deceivers and that his servant has somehow hoodwinked him and stolen the money. "The villain is o'er-raught of all my money. / They way this town is full of cozenage, / As nimble jugglers that deceive the eye, / Dark-working sorcerers that change the mind, / . . . And many suchlike liberties of sin." The scene ends with Antipholus resolving to go to the Centaur to ascertain whether he has been robbed. All of this action takes place while Antipholus of Syracuse is unaware that his twin brother is a prosperous and well-respected citizen of Ephesus, a favorite of the duke, with a servant also named Dromio and a wife named Adriana.

## Act 2

In scene 1, the venue shifts to the home of Antipholus of Ephesus, where his wife, Adriana, and her sister, Luciana, are engaged in a conversation as to the whereabouts of Adriana's errant husband. Luciana tries to offer some theories as to why he might be delayed, such as a dinner with a merchant. Beyond these excuses, however, Luciana proceeds to rebuke her sister for her impatience, counseling instead that a dutiful wife should meekly accept her subservient position to her husband. "A man is master of his liberty; / Time is their master, and when they see time / They'll go or come. If so, be patient, sister." Adriana protests this interpretation, as Luciana continues to explain that men are superior by divine decree. "There's nothing situate under heaven's eye / But hath his bound in earth, in sea, in sky. / . . . Man, more divine, the master of all these, / . . . Are masters to their females, and their lords." Adriana responds that Luciana lacks the experience to offer any insight on such matters and that she will adopt a different perspective once she finds a mate who causes her grief. Adriana even attributes Luciana's unmarried status to this distorted way of thinking: "This servitude makes you to keep unwed." As the two continue to debate, Dromio of Ephesus returns home and reports that his master has abused him by striking his ears (the man referred to actually being Antipholus of Syracuse, whom he mistook for his master). Dromio proceeds to declare his master to be insane in his obsessive babbling about misplaced money and his insistence that he has no wife. "'I know,' quoth he, 'no house, no wife, no mistress.'" Despite Dromio's accurately relating what happened, he must withstand Adriana's fury, as she threatens to beat him unless he brings her husband back. "Back, slave, or I will break thy pate across." A few lines later, Adriana delivers on her threat as a reluctant Dromio sets out to confront his supposed master once again and comments on the endless succession of beatings that await him:

"You spurn me hence, and he will spurn me hither. / If I last in this service you must case me in leather." Once he is gone, Adriana launches into further speculations as to her husband's whereabouts, including the anxiety that the ravages of time have stolen her beauty. When Luciana responds that her sister is indulging in self-created jealousy, Adriana imagines that her husband has now taken a lover. "I know his eye doth homage otherwhere; / Or else what lets it but he would be here?" Finally, she makes a melodramatic statement concerning a bejeweled chain that Antipholus has promised her and has not yet delivered. "Since that my beauty cannot please his eye, / I'll weep what's left away, and weeping die." Luciana insists that all of her sister's grievances are merely the product of unchecked jealousy.

Scene 2 begins with Antipholus of Syracuse, who has gone to the Centaur to confirm that his gold is safe, returning to the marketplace where his slave, Dromio of Syracuse, appears. Antipholus encourages Dromio to drop his joke about a wife waiting for him to return home to dinner, asking him if he was in his right mind when he made these statements. Dromio of Syracuse, of course, knows nothing about the previous exchange between his master and Dromio of Ephesus. When Dromio insists that he has no idea what his master is referring to, Antipholus once again grows angry, calling Dromio a villain for denying possession of the gold he was entrusted with, and proceeds to strike the poor man. Dromio, however, manages to deflect Antipholus's anger by engaging in a long, involved joke about baldness. According to Dromio's reasoning, men should welcome going bald and, although the lost hair cannot be replaced or regrown, Father Time himself is in the same exalted condition: "Time himself is bald, and therefore to the world's end will have bald followers."

Following this interlude between the Syracusans, Adriana and Luciana enter and confront the two men before them, mistakenly thinking that they are Antipholus of Ephesus and his slave, Dromio. Adriana immediately accuses Antipholus of Syracuse of infidelity and chastises him for violating their marriage. She begins by expressing her anger at his denial that he even has a wife and, after reminding him of his former devotion, launches into allegations of betrayal. "The time was once when thou unurged wouldst vow / That never words were music to thine ear, / . . . Unless I spake, or looked, or touched, or carved to thee." She adds her suspicions that he has been unfaithful. Antipholus of Syracuse can only counter these false accusations by pleading with her that he has no wife and has only recently arrived in the city, an explanation that is incomprehensible to Adriana: "In Ephesus I am but two hours old, / As strange unto your town as to your talk." Luciana next adds her disbelief by railing against Antipholus's perceived deception: "Fie, brother, how the world is changed with you. / When you were wont to use my sister thus?" After this last comment, Dromio of Syracuse joins the fracas by denying that he ever met Adriana. Antipholus, however, thinking of his conversation with Dromio of

Ephesus, brands the servant an abject liar, though he is amazed that Adriana, whom he has never met before, mysteriously knows his name. The confusion only increases Adriana's indignation, as she accuses him of further mocking her: "How ill it agrees with your gravity / To counterfeit thus grossly with your slave, / Abetting him to thwart me in my mood." Adriana is so adamant in her stand that Antipholus of Syracuse begins to wonder if he was betrothed to her in some dream, which is only now coming back to him in a waking moment. Even Dromio begins to think he is in the land of make-believe where impish sprites will attack them if they do not come to dinner as commanded. Meanwhile, Antipholus, in an aside, continues to question the validity of what is unfolding: "Am I in earth, in heaven, or in hell? / Sleeping or waking? mad or well advised?" Thus, the group goes home with Adriana, and Dromio is charged with guarding the gate while they eat.

## Act 3

In scene 1, the location shifts to the home of Antipholus of Ephesus. During the dinner interval at which his long-lost brother is dining upstairs, Antipholus of Ephesus returns home from the marketplace, accompanied by Dromio of Ephesus, Angelo the goldsmith, and Balthasar the merchant, anticipating in advance his wife's angry response to his lateness and her expected rudeness toward his guests. It is, in fact, a preemptive apology in which Antipholus of Ephesus seeks their cooperation in supporting the excuse he is about to give, namely that he lingered too long in Angelo's shop to oversee the making of her necklace. Antipholus then observes his slave's bizarre behavior in denying that he had a wife or insanely stating that Dromio accused him of having handed over a thousand gold marks for safekeeping. For his part, Dromio of Ephesus stands firm about what has transpired: "Say what you will, sir, but I know what I know: / That you beat me at the mart I have your hand to show." His master can only respond that his Dromio is an ass to which the clever slave answers by turning the tables on his master: "Marry, so it doth appear / By the wrongs I suffer, and the blows I bear. / I should kick, being kicked, and, being at that pass, / You would keep from my hells, and beware of an ass." This dialogue transpires while Balthasar and the goldsmith are waiting to come, Antipholus of Ephesus becoming increasingly embarrassed by this completely inhospitable reception. To further his sense of embarrassment, when Antipholus knocks at the gate, Dromio of Syracuse refuses to let the company in, instead mocking and abusing them: "Dost thou conjure for wenches, that thou call'st for such store, / When one is one too many? Go, get thee from the door." Nevertheless, Antipholus of Ephesus violently pounds on the door while shouting furiously, which brings Luce, his maid, to the door. She inquires as to the cause of the uproar. Meanwhile, Dromio of Ephesus commands Luce to let them in, but to no avail. When Adriana next appears at the door and hears the absurd request to let her husband in, while she is dining upstairs with the twin brother she believes to be her husband, she summarily sends the man away. When Antipholus of Ephesus continues to threaten violence, Balthasar counsels discretion when faced with an impossible situation. He advises Antipholus against any act of violence that would reflect badly on him or his wife's reputation, adding that Adriana will not hesitate to explain, to her own advantage, why she denied her husband admittance to his own home: "A vulgar comment will be made of it, / And that supposed by the common rout / Against your yet ungallèd estimation / That may with foul intrusion enter in / And dwell upon our grave when you are dead." Though still enraged, Antipholus leads his friends away, resolving to dine with the Courtesan at her house, the Porpentine, while asking Angelo to fetch a gold chain, recently made, that he had promised to his wife. In a mood of vindictiveness for Adriana's behavior, Antipholus intends to give the gold chain to the Courtesan instead.

Scene 2 shifts the action to inside the house, where Luciana and Antipholus of Syracuse are alone together. Luciana, believing that the man before her is really her brother-in-law, delivers an eloquent lecture and reprimand to Antipholus for having ignored his responsibilities toward Adriana. Indeed, Luciana runs through a definitive list of questions in regard to Antipholus's true motives for marrying her sister, displaying both her fine oratorical skills and ability to play the devil's advocate: "If you did wed my sister for her wealth, / Then for wealth's sake use her with more kindness; / Or if you like elsewhere, do it by stealth, / Muffle your false love with some show of blindness; / Let not my sister read it in your eye, / Be not thy tongue thy own shame's orator." Though Luciana admonished her sister for having jealous suspicions about Antipholus's infidelity, she now appears to accept that he may have actually taken another lover and advises him accordingly to use discretion and deception. Under the pretense of wanting to spare her sister any unnecessary hurt, Luciana becomes a fellow accomplice to her supposed brother-in-law by turning the concept of virtue on its head as she encourages discretion in any adulterous liaisons he may be involved in: "Apparel vice like virtue's harbinger. / Bear a fair presence, though your heart be tainted, / Teach sin the carriage of a holy saint." In sum, Luciana is taking her advice to her sister—about the husband's mastery in the household—to an extreme through her admission that women are to be pitied and deserve compassion since they are helpless to change their diminished status: "Alas, poor women, make us but believe."

In another turn of events, Antipholus of Syracuse, who continues to protest that he is not Adriana's husband, now professes his great love for Luciana: "Teach me, dear creature, how to think and speak, / Lay open to my earthly gross conceit, / Smothered in errors, feeble, shallow, weak, / The folded meaning of your words' deceit." By declaring his love in such terms, Antipholus of Syracuse proves himself to be a romantic and sentimental presence while also displaying a degree of urbanity and self-awareness of his own precarious status. For Luciana's part, she is shocked by what she perceives to be such an indecent and misguided proposal on her brother-in-law's part, ordering him to refocus his attention on Adriana: "Gaze where you should, and that will clear your sight."

When Dromio of Syracuse enters to joins his master, Antipholus inquires why he has moved with such speed, a question that prompts Dromio to launch into a hilarious account of Nell, the obese and insincere kitchen maid who mistook him for her own husband. According to Dromio, Nell has claimed him for her own and intends to treat him as her chattel and extend the same respect to him as she would to an animal, despite her own bestial associations: "Marry, sir such claim as you would lay to your horse; and she would have me as a beast—not that, I being a beast, she would have me, but that she, being a beastly creature, lays claim to me." Antipholus and Dromio continue to have fun at Nell's expense, as Dromio presents a description of Nell's body that is best characterized as a cartographic rendition of her physical attributes. All the while, Antipholus eggs him on in creating this irreverent portrait: "No longer from head to foot than from hip to hip. She is / spherical, like a globe; I could find out countries in her." While this banter continues, the scene begins to wind down with Antipholus of Syracuse telling his slave that he intends to depart from Ephesus immediately, for it is a dangerous and formidable place they must leave before anyone discovers them. Antipholus is so desperate to leave that he vows to board the first boat that appears. Dromio, thrilled to find a means of escaping the amorous Nell, is ready to flee on a moment's notice: "As from a bear a man would run for life, / So fly I from her that would be my wife." Antipholus agrees with the urgent need to flee, for he is faced with his own domestic drama, having succumbed to the enchantments of Luciana while simultaneously being pronounced the husband of a woman he never met before coming to Ephesus. He declares Ephesus to be a city where mischief abides in the form of the mermaid's song. Accordingly, he sends Dromio to the harbor to book their passage. However, Angelo the goldsmith appears bearing the chain commissioned by Antipholus of Ephesus, which, of course, his Syracusan brother knows nothing about and states that he never requested. Angelo, believing that he is speaking to Antipholus of Ephesus, responds that indeed Antipholus has been relentlessly pursuing the chain for his wife. Antipholus then accepts the chain while Angelo says he will wait for payment until dinner that evening. Once again, though baffled by the circumstances, Antipholus of Syracuse displays an extraordinary sensitivity for a beautiful token of love: "What I should think of this I cannot tell. / But this I think, there's no man is so vain / That would refuse so fair an offered chain."

## Act 4

Scene 1 opens with the Second Merchant, who has brought an officer with him, ready to arrest Angelo the goldsmith unless he pays his debt. The Merchant is getting ready to sail for Persia and claims that, though he has been owed money since Pentecost, he has not pressured Angelo until now to make good on his debt. The goldsmith promises to collect the sum from Antipholus of Ephesus, whom he plans on meeting that evening, when Angelo discovers both Antipholus and Dromio of Ephesus leaving the Courtesan's house, making Angelo's five o'clock meeting unnecessary. As Antipholus approaches, he orders his slave to go and purchase "a rope's end," which he intends to use on his household in retribution for having locked him out. Antipholus then addresses Angelo, stating that he never received the chain and quips that perhaps the goldsmith's delay in delivering the jewelry can be attributed to his having relied too heavily on their friendship: "Belike you thought our love would last too long / If it were chained together, and therefore came not." For his part, Angelo thinks his friend is speaking in jest since he has recently delivered the necklace in question and produces a note detailing the weight of the gold down to the precise karat and amount due, a sum that is more than he owes the Merchant. Angelo expects to pay the Merchant in full, but since Antipholus does not have the money with him, he requests that the officer take them to his house where his wife will pay the sum after receiving the chain. Angelo, however, no longer has the necklace, and Antipholus of Ephesus never received it. Instead, his Syracusan brother is in possession of the item. A quarrel then erupts between Angelo and Antipholus, each blaming the other of denying possession. While Angelo reiterates the Merchant's urgency, Antipholus accuses the goldsmith of breaking his promise. The two are left in an irresolvable quagmire. Since the item cannot be produced, there is no other choice than to have Antipholus of Ephesus arrested by the officer who will then bring him before the duke. During the arrest, Angelo again expresses his concern for his professional reputation and informs Antipholus that he will see justice done: "Sir, sir, I shall have law in Ephesus, / To your notorious shame, I doubt it not." While the allegations fly between Antipholus and Angelo, Dromio of Syracuse returns from the dock to announce that there is a ship about to set sail for Epidamnum. Of course, this Dromio believes he is speaking to his true master while, in fact, it is the Ephesian Antipholus whom he addresses. He explains that he has already taken care of their luggage and is very much looking forward to their imminent departure from the city: "The oil, the balsamum, and aqua-vitae. / The ship is in her trim; the merry wind / Blows fair from land." With the expectation of perfect weather conditions, the ship is merely waiting for the Syracusans to board. Nevertheless, despite Dromio's excitement in having accomplished his mission, Antipholus of Ephesus is further infuriated by this ridiculous and insane behavior on the part of the man he believes to be his slave: "Why, thou peevish sheep, / What ship of Epidamnum stays for me?" Antipholus accuses Dromio of being drunk, because he has not purchased the requested rope. Antipholus of Ephesus instructs Dromio to return home and bring the money to secure his release. Apparently, Adriana knows that there is money hidden in a desk "covered o'er with Turkish tapestry," and he trusts that she will relinquish the money when she learns that her husband has been arrested. Dromio leaves on this new mission, musing that he returns to the house where he previously dined with his Syracusan master, though he is not yet aware that there are in fact two Antipholuses. He also remembers Nell, referring to her as "Dowsabel"—an ironic nickname since the appellation is the English form of a French feminine name, Dulcibella, generally used in reference to a sweetheart.

In scene 2, Luciana reveals to Adriana all the details of the Syracusan Antihpolus's amorous overtures to her, seductive words which they both assume were adulterously uttered by Adriana's real husband. Adriana is shocked by this disclosure, wanting to know how her husband looked and sounded during this shameful display: "What observation mad'st thou in this case / Of his heart's meteors tilting in his face?" As Luciana responds with great care, she is also mindful to state that she did nothing to encourage his advances. Adriana, however, grows increasingly impetuous, casting all manner of aspersions on her husband, attacking him from every vantage point she can imagine: "He is deformed, crooked, old, and sere; / Ill-faced, worse-bodied, shapeless everywhere; / Vicious, ungentle, foolish, blunt, unkind, / Stigmatical in making, worse in mind." He is, she believes, a villain who deserves to be publicly branded as such. Nevertheless, despite her relentless cursing, Adriana is forced to admit that she still bears some love for Antipholus: "Ah, but I think him better than I say."

Dromio of Syracuse suddenly appears to report, rather dramatically, that Antipholus has been arrested and needs money: "[H]e's in Tartar limbo, worse than hell. A devil in an everlasting garment have him, / . . . A hound that runs counter, and yet draws dryfoot well; / One that before the Judgment carries poor souls to hell." Hearing such disturbing news, Adriana directs Luciana to fetch the money, though she cannot comprehend why her husband should be in debt. Dromio assures her that her man is indeed a thief. She then orders him to go immediately and bring her master home from prison.

Scene 3 begins with Antipholus of Syracuse exploring the city while he wears the chain about his neck. He finds it remarkable that everyone who greets him acts as though they are well acquainted with him and, moreover, that he is accorded such great respect: "There's not a man I meet but doth salute me / As if I were their well-acquainted friend, / . . . Even now a tailor called me in his shop / And showed me silks that he had bought for me." Obviously, the citizens of Ephesus believe this to be their own prosperous Antipholus and not his identical twin brother. Dromio of Syracuse dashes up to him, carrying the gold that Adriana sent to free Antipholus of Ephesus from jail. This Antipholus, of course, has no clue as to why his servant is bringing him money and is totally bewildered by Dromio's explanation. For his part, Dromio, believing he has done his master's bidding (and not realizing that he now addresses a different Antipholus, indeed his own Antipholus of Syracuse), insists on returning the pressing issue at hand, namely securing his master's release from jail. Antipholus demands to know whether their ship is ready to set sail from Ephesus. Dromio reminds his master that he had already made arrangements when their plans were thwarted by the alleged arrest, "hindered by the sergeant to tarry for the hoy Delay." In response to this preposterous story, Antipholus can only conclude that they are both addled and perplexed as a result of their sojourn in a topsy-turvy world where appearances cannot be trusted. The Courtesan then enters. It is at her home, of course, that Antipholus of Ephesus had dined and, thus, the Syracusan master and slave who stand before her know nothing of this previous engagement. Since she approaches Antipholus with great informality, "[w]ell met, well met, Master Antipholus," the typically reserved Syracusan responds rudely to her inappropriate forwardness from a woman of her disreputable stature: "Satan, avoid! I charge thee, tempt me not." For her part, the Courtesan is insistent that they return her diamond ring or at least exchange it for the golden necklace promised her by Antipholus of Ephesus. Dromio thinks she is unduly greedy as he and his master exit while telling her to fly away. The Courtesan remains alone onstage and now admits her own utter confusion at their response, as they know they have her ring, worth 40 ducats, and surely must remember their promise to deliver the necklace. Reviewing the events of the day, she concludes that the two are insane in looks and demeanor. "Besides this present instance of his rage, / Is a mad tale he told today at dinner / Of his own doors being shut against his entrance." Nevertheless, his lunacy notwithstanding, the Courtesan states that she cannot afford to forfeit the price of the ring and will instead head straight to his house to seek recompense, while at the same time exposing Antipholus of Ephesus's wrongdoing to his wife.

Scene 4 opens with Antipholus of Ephesus arriving in the custody of an officer and assuring the latter that he will not attempt to escape. Antipholus understands that his situation is highly precarious, and the money he requested from home is far from being assured given these uncertain circumstances. In describing Adriana's mood as "wayward," Antipholus acknowledges that she could very well act contrary to his wishes and, furthermore, may not believe Dromio's words: "I tell you, 'twill sound harshly in her ears."

Following this brief interlude, Dromio of Ephesus returns with the rope that Antipholus had previously requested. However, other priorities now take precedence and, rather than being interested in a rope with which to take revenge on his household, Antipholus of Ephesus desperately needs the funds to buy his way out of jail. Dromio, however, returns only with a rope. When asked to what purpose he thinks he was sent home, the slave responds that he spent the money on a rope, believing that he is delivering precisely what was asked for. "To a rope's end, sir, and to that end am I returned." Antipholus, infuriated with Dromio's ineptitude and taunting, begins to beat the servant, at which point the officer attempts to intercede on Dromio's behalf. Dromio assures the officer that he lives in a state of "adversity" and bears the blows with patience, though he hopes the officer can ultimately talk his master out of this attack. When Antipholus calls Dromio a "senseless villain," the slave adeptly turns the accusation to his own advantage, by stating that he wishes he were truly "senseless," unconscious, and thus impervious to the assaults. This exchange between master and servant accelerates when Antipholus calls Dromio an ass. To this, Dromio responds by agreeing that he is indeed an ass, because he has been treated like an animal from the start and has the scars to prove it: "You may prove it by my long ears. I have / served him from the hour of my nativity to this instant, and have / nothing at his hands for my service but blows. . . . I bear it on my shoulders, as a beggar wont her brat, and / I think when he hath lamed me I shall beg with it from door to door." It is important to note the verbal dexterity displayed by the slave in comparison to Antipholus's perverse way of expressing his feelings, both in words and actions. It is equally important to note that for a significant length of time in the play, Antipholus of Ephesus has been perceived by others to be an upright citizen. Nonetheless, the abuse stops when Adriana suddenly appears along with her sister, Luciana, the Courtesan, and a would-be exorcist named Dr. Pinch.

Antipholus's initial response to these newly arrived visitors is to send Dromio away, but Dromio remains and instead issues a warning to his mistress, telling her to beware of Antipholus's intention to beat her as well. Antipholus once again strikes Dromio, which prompts the Courtesan to ask Adriana whether this indeed proves her husband's insanity. Adriana agrees, "[h]is incivility confirms no less," and immediately orders Dr. Pinch to set to work restoring Antipholus's sanity. Luciana then adds to the chorus of condemnation, remarking that Antipholus looks "fiery" and "sharp," while the Courtesan makes note of his agitated state, "how he trembles in his ecstasy." Antipholus only grows increasingly enraged and strikes Dr. Pinch, who in return attempts to perform an exorcism: "I charge thee, Satan, housed within this man, / To yield possession to my holy prayers." The "ceremony" is, unsurprisingly, a sham performed by a ridiculous charlatan. Antipholus of Ephesus recognizes Pinch for what he is: "Peace, doting wizard, peace. I am not mad," but Pinch will not waver from his diagnosis. Speaking to the Courtesan, he asks whether Dr. Pinch is one of her customers and suggests that perhaps he enjoyed a great feast at Antipholus's home, a celebration to which the master of the house was denied entrance. This, of course, sounds ridiculous to Adriana, since she believes the man who actually dined with her was her own husband: "Where would you have remained until this time, / Free from these slanders and this open shame." An argument erupts between Antipholus and his wife, the former protesting that he was forced to wait outdoors, spurned and enraged. Dromio attempts to confirm his master's story, since he knows they were forced to dine elsewhere, with the Courtesan. Dromio once again proves his integrity and reliability by undertaking to supply eyewitness testimony. At the same time, Dromio does not miss an opportunity to highlight his master's abusive personality: "In verity you did. My bones bears witness, / That since have felt the vigour of his rage." Witnessing this exchange, Dr. Pinch suggests that Dromio is merely placating his master, whose mental state he correctly surmises. In saying this, Dr. Pinch invalidates the servant's honest testimony: "The fellow finds his vein, / And yield to him humours well his frenzy." When Antipholus then accuses Adriana of encouraging the goldsmith to have him arrested, Adriana protests that she sent the requisite money to secure his release to which Dromio chimes in to the contrary: "Heart and good will you might, / But surely, master, not a rag of money." Instead, Dromio insists that he was sent to fetch a rope. Dr. Pinch declares both men insane, dangerous, and in need of physical restraint: "I know it by their pale and deadly looks. / They must be bound and laid in some dark room." Adriana, nevertheless, continues to deny that she locked her husband out, and Dromio continues to assert that he never received any gold. Once again, Antipholus of Ephesus vents his violent temper, this time at his wife: "But with these nails I'll pluck out these false eyes / That would behold in me this shameful report."

As Antipholus makes threatening motions toward Adriana, several officers arrive on the scene to bind him, while all in attendance agree with this measure, including Dr. Pinch, who declares, "[t]he fiend is strong within him." Dromio is likewise subject to the same restraint. However, Adriana surprisingly intervenes and states that she will pay the debt, requesting that Dr. Pinch escort him home. Apparently, Dromio of Ephesus is likewise released under a torrent of abuse from Antipholus. With Antipholus, Dromio, and Pinch gone, Adriana and the other visitors remain. She inquires of the jailer how this debt to the goldsmith came to be incurred. The officer responds that the debt is from a chain her husband had requisitioned. The Courtesan then relates how Antipholus, infuriated, came to her house and took her ring. As she is requesting an audience with the goldsmith, Antipholus of Syracuse arrives with his own Dromio, and Luciana exclaims that the pair have not only broken loose from their chains but have come prepared to do violence with their swords. Everyone flees in fear, except for Antipholus and Dromio of Syracuse, while the master comments that the city is bewitched and their only hope is to board a ship straightaway. Dromio of Syracuse protests with this assessment of Ephesus as a world gone insane, noting that they were given gold. Nonetheless, he is happy to leave to escape the attentions of Nell: "Methinks they are such a / gentle nation that, but for the mountain of mad flesh that claims / marriage of me, I could find it in my heart to stay here still, and turn / witch." His master wants to set sail immediately, ordering Dromio to collect their things and bring them onboard.

# Act 5

Act 5 is unique in *The Comedy of Errors* in that it consists of one long scene made up of heightened tensions, threatened violence, and accusations of thievery and insanity until the abbess, Egeon's long-lost wife, enters and begins to restore calm and order. Ultimately, through her wise and spiritual offices, the requisite peace and tranquility finally prevail, allowing for the unraveling of a multitude of mysteries and errors. It is a potentially dizzying task to follow the untangling of the increasing confusion, as there is a consistent and breathless cross-referencing of the Antipholi, the brothers caught up in a web of unjust indictments and misapprehensions about their alleged crimes. The charges of bad behavior and insanity are leveled at such a rapid pace that we, too, are genuinely relieved at the final establishment of true identities and the reconciliations that occur among the characters assembled.

Act 5 opens with the entrance of the Second Merchant and Angelo the goldsmith. While Angelo insists that Antipholus of Syracuse (whom he mistakes for the Ephesian brother) has robbed him of his chain, the Second Merchant questions how so upright as citizen as Antipholus of Ephesus could commit such as shameful act. Angelo can only validate this public assessment of Antipholus of Ephesus's spotless reputation: "Of credit infinite, highly beloved, / Second to none that lives here in the city." The two stop conversing between themselves as Antipholus of Syracuse and his servant approach, while Angelo vows to make him answer for the chain he is wearing. Face to face with Antipholus, Angelo states that he cannot possibly understand how the former can deny having stolen the necklace, which he so brazenly wears in public: "I wonder much / That you would put me to this shame and trouble, / And not without some scandal to yourself, / . . . This chain, which now you wear so openly." Antipholus of Syracuse can only respond that he never denied possessing it, but the Merchant backs up Angelo's contention, stating that he heard Antipholus of Syracuse deny possession of the item. For this accusation, Antipholus calls the Merchant a villain and vows to prove his integrity, whereupon they prepare for a fight, as Adriana, Luciana, the Courtesan, and others enter. Adriana immediately orders Antipholus of Syracuse and his servant to be held as madmen. Dromio of Syracuse advises his master to run, and the two of them flee to the priory.

The abbess next enters; it will soon be revealed that she is Egeon's long-lost wife. As she approaches, she puts an abrupt end to the scuffling and arguing, counseling everyone to be still: "Be quiet people. Wherefore throng you hither?" Adriana is the first to speak, as she explains that she is attempting to retrieve her strangely afflicted husband, who apparently has sought sanctuary at the abbey. She also believes that, in order to get him home, he must be physically restrained, so she requests the help of the others. Surprisingly, some of the hostility begins to abate at this point, with Angelo stating that he believes Antipholous (of Syracuse) to be not of his right mind and the Second Merchant likewise expressing compassion, suggesting that perhaps his pressuring him for the money worsened his already unstable mental condition: "I am sorry now that I did draw on him." Listening to these comments on Antipholus's volatility, the abbess wants to know how long he has been in such a state. Although Adriana observes that Antipholus (whom she all the while mistakes as her husband, Antipholus of Ephesus) has been in ill humor for the past week, she makes especial mention of this particular afternoon when he seemed to have taken complete leave of his senses: "But till this afternoon his passion / Ne'er brake into extremity of rage." The abbess, however, is not ready to confirm Antipholus of Syracuse's insanity and, instead, asks some important and perceptive questions that the others have failed to consider. She wonders if he has lost a large sum of money, lost a dear friend, or is perhaps grieved at having been unfaithful to his wife: "A sin prevailing much in youthful men / Who give their eyes the liberty of gazing." Of all the possible reasons listed by the abbess, Adriana will only allow for the last, since she has long suspected her husband of being unfaithful to her.

Following this last statement by Adriana, the abbess questions how Adriana has handled the situation and suggests that she should have privately rebuked her husband in the strongest terms. Unfortunately, Adriana, who is impetuous in her own right, admits that she has even rebuked her husband in the company of others, all the while maintaining that she never missed an opportunity to confront his infidelity. It is the beginning of an incisive interrogation and highly stylized debate between the abbess and Adriana concerning the latter's methods of confronting her husband. The abbess launches into a stern lecture on the evil engendered by acting out feelings based on jealous assumptions: "The venom clamours of a jealous woman / Poisons more deadly than a mad dog's tooth." She then proceeds to catalog the disturbances caused by Adriana's behavior, including indigestion, insomnia, passions running amok, and an inability to enjoy sports and "sweet recreation." The abbess suggests that Antipholus's equilibrium and happiness have been altered, producing illness and distemper instead: "In food, in sport, and life-preserving rest / To be disturbed would mad or man or beast." In the face of this chiding, Luciana is quick to defend her sister to the abbess, stating that "[s]he never reprehended him but mildly," and just as quickly turns to her sister to ask why she bears these insults in silence. Adriana can only answer that the abbess has cleverly turned the tables on her own argument and shown her the error of her ways in dealing with her husband: "She did betray me to my own reproof. / Good people, enter, and lay hold on him." Nevertheless, Adriana is finally willing to seize control of the situation and have her husband let out of the abbey in shackles. The abbess, however, adamantly objects to releasing Antipholus (of Syracuse), for it would be a violation of the law regarding the granting of sanctuary. She adds that she will succeed in bringing him back to his senses no matter the cost or outcome. Unlike Dr. Pinch, the abbess does not hold herself up to be a conjurer of evil spirits. Instead, as a devout member of the church, she pledges she will do her best to bring about a cure, an attempt that she acknowledges she is not wholly assured of: "Till I have brought him to his wits again, / Or lose my labour in assaying it." Adriana protests this decision and insists that she will "diet his sickness," for as his wife she is the appropriate person to come to his aid. The abbess can only counsel patience for Adriana, for she has no intention of relenting on her decision to keep him and use the remedies available to someone in her position to restore his sanity: "With wholesome syrups, drugs, and holy prayers, / To make of him a formal man again/ . . . A charitable duty of my order." With this last proclamation, the abbess departs, despite Adriana's protests, advising her once again to remain quiet and accept her decision. Luciana suggests that Adriana seek remedy from the duke, and she agrees, adding that she will humbly beg for the release her husband, undermining the abbess's authority by taking violent measures: "And never rise until my tears and prayers / have won his grace to come in person hither / And take perforce my husband from the Abbess." The Second Merchant then reminds them that since it is five o'clock, the appointed hour of Egeon's execution, he is sure that the duke is already on his way to carry out the deed, which is to take place somewhere behind the abbey. When Angelo asks whom he refers to, the Second Merchant exclaims it is Egeon who has violated the law by entering the town and, accordingly, is to be "[b]eheaded publicly for his offense."

The duke then enters with Egeon, who is bareheaded and accompanied by a headsman and two other officers. The duke once again appears reluctant to carry out the sentence and again implores the crowd to come forward with the ransom money and thus save Egeon's life: "If any friend will pay the sum for him, / He shall not die, so much we tender him." The duke's use of the word *tender* is a pun, for while it refers to the funds needed to save his life it is, simultaneously, an expression of great affection for the old man. Adriana, for her part, is oblivious to what is taking place before her and has not heard a word of the duke's plea. Instead, she can only cast blame on the abbess, who she believes has performed a great injustice. The duke does not agree and cannot possibly believe the abbess capable of any wrongdoing or unfairness: "She is a virtuous and reverend lady." Nevertheless, Adriana will not be deterred in pursuing her case against the abbess, despite the duke's deference to the holy woman. Adriana begins to make her case by first attempting to persuade the duke of her obedience to his laws in making her husband lord and master over her and their possessions and, having stated her faithfulness to his authority, explains that her husband and his servant, both having lost their minds, have exhibited the most bizarre and inexplicable behavior. Adriana crafts her argument in the most extreme terms to demonstrate that there are social implications to the alleged insanity, since they are disturbing the citizens of Ephesus by running through the streets, entering people's homes, and grabbing their jewels or any other items that please them: "A most outrageous fit of madness took him, / That desp'rately he hurried through the street, / With him his bondsman all as mad as he, / Doing displeasure to the citizens / By rushing into their houses." She further explains to the duke that she had Antipholus and his servant placed in shackles and brought home but that Antipholus and Dromio (of Syracuse) mysteriously managed to break free from the guards and, with swords drawn, came after Adriana and her attendants, chasing her away: "Each one with ireful passion, with drawn swords / Met us again, and, madly bent on us, / Chased us away." However, as Adriana continues to solicit the duke's sympathy, she explains that she came back and made another brave effort to have Antipholus and Dromio (of Syracuse) restrained, only to have the pair seek sanctuary inside the abbey. Adriana contends that, with the abbess's refusal to allow her into the abbey, she is left with no other recourse but to seek the duke's intervention. In response, the duke shows himself to be respectful to all parties concerned and, his deference to the abbess's spiritual authority notwithstanding, he acknowledges Antipholus's civic service to Ephesus—"[l]ong since thy husband served me in my wars"— while remembering his wedding promise to Adriana "[t]o do him all the grace and good I could." Thus, the duke resolves to summon the abbess and endeavor to serve as a mediator in this predicament.

A messenger enters to warn Adriana of the imminent danger she faces from Antipholus and Dromio (of Ephesus), who have broken loose, "beaten the maids a-row," and gone so far as to physically restrain Dr. Pinch, the sham exorcist. According to the messenger's report, their treatment of Dr. Pinch has turned especially violent and abusive; they have set his beard ablaze and then extinguished the flames with some form of muddy debris: "Whose beard they have singed off with brands of fire, / And ever as it blazed they threw on him / Great pails of puddle mire to quench the hair." The messenger has come to enlist Adriana's help in saving Dr. Pinch, but Adriana responds that he is a fool and bears false report, for she knows that Antipholus and Dromio are inside the abbey. The frightened messenger advises her otherwise, explaining that she is about to meet the same fate as the conjurer: "He cries for you, and vows, if he can take you, / To scorch your face and to disfigure you." To this last piece of alarming news, the duke orders his guards to be ready, assuring Adriana she has nothing to fear, as she watches her husband approach. She is completely baffled, however: "Witness you / That he is borne about invisible. / . . . And now he's there, past thought of human reason." Antipholus of Ephesus, who has managed to break free, and his servant, Dromio, then make their entrance.

Antipholus of Ephesus makes his own appeal to the duke for justice, reminding his commander of the brave military service he has done him in the past, "[w]hen I bestrid thee in the wars, and took / Deep scars to save thy life." In the meantime, in an aside, Egeon tells the audience that he believes he recognizes his long-lost twin son and servant. Antipholus of Ephesus continues his petition to the duke, explaining that Adriana, the same woman whom he gave in marriage, has abused him of late and caused him great public shame: "Beyond imagination is the wrong / That she this day hath shameless thrown on me." When the duke asks for specifics, Antipholus of Ephesus explains that she locked him out of his house while choosing to dine with "harlots," meaning villainous or roguish men. Adriana categorically denies this last accusation: "So befall my soul, / As this is false he burdens me withal." Luciana confirms Adriana's story. Undeterred by his witnesses, including Angelo the goldsmith who speaks in an aside, Antipholus of Ephesus continues to set forth his case that he is neither drunk nor the victim of his own wild imagination, though making it clear that others have certainly given him ample cause to become enraged beyond endurance: "Neither disturbed with the effect of wine / Nor heady-rash provoked with raging ire, / Albeit my wrongs might make one wiser mad." He then proceeds to enumerate all his grievances, stating that he was indeed locked out of the house and that the goldsmith is in league with Adriana, as otherwise he would have admitted that he was there when Antipholus was denied admittance to his own home. Antipholus of Ephesus further charges Angelo with failing to bring the gold chain to the Porpentine, where Antipholus was forced to dine that evening. Thus, he explains, he had to pursue the goldsmith on his own: "I went to seek him. In the street I met him, / And in his company that gentleman / There did this perjured goldsmith swear me down." This, Antipholus of Ephesus explains, is the chronology of events and the chain of false allegations that have led to his arrest, a situation that he tried to resolve by having his servant get the necessary funds from home to secure his release, although to no avail, since Dromio returned without the money. Following this disappointing result, Antipholus then relates how he persuaded the officer to accompany him home while, along the way, they were beset by Adriana, Luciana, and the revolting Dr. Pinch. Antihpholus's description of Dr. Pinch is a hilarious portrait of a fraud perpetrated on the gullible citizens of Ephesus: "They brought one Pinch, a hungry, lean-faced villain, / A mere anatomy, a mountebank, / A threadbare juggler and a fortune-teller, / A needy, hollow-eyed, shar-looking wretch, / A living dead man." As Antipholus continues to declaim on his moral outrage at being diagnosed as a man possessed by evil spirits by an unqualified quack, he makes a convincing argument for the indignities and outrageous behavior he has been subject to: "And in a dark and dankish vault at home / There left me and my man, both bound together, / Till, gnawing with my teeth my bonds in sunder, / I gained my freedom." Thus, he stands before the duke to seek justice and, in the first sign that the truth will at last begin to surface, Angelo confesses that he was with Antipholus of Ephesus when he was locked out of his home. Yet, there still remains the question of the chain that Angelo insists was around Antipholus's neck (actually worn by Antipholus of Syracuse), which the Second Merchant confirms. In an aside to Antipholus of Ephesus, the Merchant implies that he is an outright liar: "Besides, I will be sworn these ears of / mine / Heard you confess you had the chain of him / After you first forswore it on the mart." The Merchant believes that when he confronted Antipholus (who was in actuality the Syracusan twin) and threatened violence, the latter fled to the abbey rather than relinquish the necklace. Antipholus of Ephesus, who of course has no knowledge of these events, adamantly denies ever entering the abbey, being threatened by the Merchant's sword, or even having seen the necklace he allegedly possesses: "And this is false you burden me withal." The duke can now only state what a remarkable and fantastical impasse they have reached, noting that a madman could never fashion such an eloquent and orderly defense of his innocence. At this, Dromio of Ephesus tells the duke that they dined with the Courtesan at the Porpentine and that they have her ring in their possession. In response, the Courtesan swears to the duke that she saw the pair (whom she believes were the Ephesians) enter the abbey. The duke is utterly perplexed at this point and thinks them all insane. Accordingly, he tells a messenger to summon the abbess.

While the abbess is being summoned, the humble and deferential Egeon requests permission to speak, for he recognizes that his long lost son, Antipholus of Ephesus, is the man standing before him and that he will ultimately save his father's life: "Haply I see a friend will save my life / And pay the sum that may deliver me." The duke is at first confused by Egeon's statement, but the old man asks whether the proper names of the man and servant before him are Antipholus and Dromio and then states that he is assured they will remember their father. Dromio of Ephesus is the first to speak and, not recognizing Egeon, wonders if the old man has lately been one of Dr. Pinch's victims. Egeon becomes distressed at this last question, for he now fears that the passage of time has aged him beyond recognition and that his situation is again hopeless: "O, grief hath changed me since you saw me last, / And careful hours with time's deformèd hand, / That written strange defeatures in my face." Antipholus of Ephesus likewise denies recognition of his father. Egeon, for whom the stakes are so high, nonetheless continues to engage the long-lost twins in an effort to bring about the critical moment of identification. He asks whether the sound of his voice can possibly bring back memories of their younger days. As soon as he asks the question, however, Egeon immediately despairs of this hopeful approach, noting that time has brought the same alteration to the sound of his voice: "O time's extremity, / Hast thou so cracked and splitted my poor tongue / In seven short years that here are my only son / Knows not my feeble key of untuned cares?" While the Ephesian twins continue to protest that they have never met the old man, Egeon reminds them that they are originally from Syracuse and perhaps are ashamed to admit knowing him. The duke supports the twins' contention that they were never in Syracuse and instead attributes the mistake to Egeon's senility: "I see thy age and dangers make thee dote."

Following this depressing interlude, the abbess arrives with Antipholus and Dromio of Syracuse and declares to the duke that, while Egeon is a man who has been deeply wronged, there are in truth two sets of twins. Finally, the duke understands the source and reason for the mistaken identities but does not yet realize that all the errors resulted from the foursome's presence: "One of these men is genius to the other; / And so, of these, which is the natural man, / And which the spirit?" Antipholus of Syracuse is the first to recognize his father, followed by Dromio of Syracuse: "Egeon, art thou not? or else his ghost?" With these finally dawning recognitions, the abbess vows to liberate Egeon from his wrongful imprisonment and, most importantly, recognizes the old man is her long-separated husband and she his lawful wife, Aemilia: "Whoever bound him, I will loose his bonds, / And gain a husband by his liberty." At last, the duke finally understands that there are in fact two men named Antipholus and two Dromios. The Ephesian twins, it is revealed, were originally rescued by a fisherman of Corinth and then made their way to Ephesus "by that most famous warrior / Duke Menaphon," the duke's revered uncle. In the wake of these positive identifications, Adriana inquires which of the brothers dined with her that day, to which Antipholus of Syracuse responds in the affirmative and explains that he is definitely not her husband. Always the romantic sentimentalist, Antipholus of Syracuse hastens to address Luciana and express his sincere hope that she will take his previous overtures seriously: "What I told you then / I hope I shall have leisure to make good, / If this be not a dream I see and hear."

As to the contentious necklace, Angelo now understands why Antipholus of Syracuse has it in his possession and why Antipholus of Ephesus believes he has been hoodwinked, for it was actually Dromio of Syracuse who received the money from Adriana. Accordingly, Antipholus of Ephesus hands the money over to the duke in order to secure his father's freedom, but the duke refuses to take payment for Egeon's wrongful captivity. For the Courtesan's part, the diamond ring is returned to her by Antipholus of Ephesus, now a thoroughly happy man: "There, take it, and much thanks for my good cheer." With all the errors satisfactorily explained, the abbess invites all assembled for a celebratory feast in with abbey: "The Duke, my husband, and my children both, / And you, the calendars of their nativity, / Go to a gossips' feast, and go with me / After so long grief, such nativity." So, the play concludes with the two Dromios embracing each other and walking off arm in arm to their special dinner. As they discuss which of the two is truly the eldest, Dromio of Ephesus declares they are equals and thus they should enter the abbey together: "We came into the world like brother and brother / And now let's go hand in hand, not one before another."

# Key Passages in
## The Comedy of Errors

### Act 1, 1, 1–154

*Egeon:* Proceed, Solinus, to procure my fall,
And by the doom of death end woes and all.

*Duke of Solinus:* Merchant of Syracuse, plead no more;
I am not partial to infringe our laws:
The enmity and discord which of late
Sprung from the rancorous outrage of your duke
To merchants, our well-dealing countrymen,
Who wanting guilders to redeem their lives
Have seal'd his rigorous statutes with their bloods,
Excludes all pity from our threatening looks.
For, since the mortal and intestine jars
'Twixt thy seditious countrymen and us,
It hath in solemn synods been decreed
Both by the Syracusians and ourselves,
To admit no traffic to our adverse towns Nay, more,
If any born at Ephesus be seen
At any Syracusian marts and fairs;
Again: if any Syracusian born
Come to the bay of Ephesus, he dies,
His goods confiscate to the duke's dispose,
Unless a thousand marks be levied,
To quit the penalty and to ransom him.
Thy substance, valued at the highest rate,
Cannot amount unto a hundred marks;
Therefore by law thou art condemned to die.

*Egeon:* Yet this my comfort: when your words are done,
My woes end likewise with the evening sun.

27

*Duke Solinus:* Well, Syracusian, say in brief the cause
Why thou departed'st from thy native home
And for what cause thou camest to Ephesus.

*Egeon:* A heavier task could not have been imposed
Than I to speak my griefs unspeakable:
Yet, that the world may witness that my end
Was wrought by nature, not by vile offence,
I'll utter what my sorrows give me leave.
In Syracusa was I born, and wed
Unto a woman, happy but for me,
And by me, had not our hap been bad.
With her I lived in joy; our wealth increased
By prosperous voyages I often made
To Epidamnum; till my factor's death
And the great care of goods at random left
Drew me from kind embracements of my spouse:
From whom my absence was not six months old

. . . . .

There had she not been long, but she became
A joyful mother of two goodly sons;
And, which was strange, the one so like the other,
As could not be distinguish'd but by names.
That very hour, and in the self-same inn,
A meaner woman was delivered
Of such a burden, male twins, both alike:
Those, for their parents were exceeding poor,
I bought and brought up to attend my sons.
My wife, not meanly proud of two such boys,
Made daily motions for our home return:
Unwilling I agreed.
Alas! too soon, we came aboard.
A league from Epidamnum had we sail'd,
Before the always wind-obeying deep
Gave any tragic instance of our harm:
But longer did we not retain much hope;
For what obscured light the heavens did grant
Did but convey unto our fearful minds
A doubtful warrant of immediate death;
Which though myself would gladly have embraced,
Yet the incessant weepings of my wife,

Weeping before for what she saw must come,
And piteous plainings of the pretty babes,
That mourn'd for fashion, ignorant what to fear,

                    . . . . .

*Duke Solinus:* Nay, forward, old man; do not break off so;
For we may pity, though not pardon thee.


*Egeon:* O, had the gods done so, I had not now
Worthily term'd them merciless to us!
For, ere the ships could meet by twice five leagues,
We were encounterd by a mighty rock;
Which being violently borne upon,
Our helpful ship was splitted in the midst;
So that, in this unjust divorce of us,
Fortune had left to both of us alike
What to delight in, what to sorrow for.
Her part, poor soul! seeming as burdened
With lesser weight but not with lesser woe,
Was carried with more speed before the wind;
And in our sight they three were taken up
By fishermen of Corinth, as we thought.
At length, another ship had seized on us;
And, knowing whom it was their hap to save,
Gave healthful welcome to their shipwreck'd guests;
And would have reft the fishers of their prey,
Had not their bark been very slow of sail;
And therefore homeward did they bend their course.
Thus have you heard me sever'd from my bliss;
That by misfortunes was my life prolong'd,
To tell sad stories of my own mishaps.


*Duke Solinus:* And for the sake of them thou sorrowest for,
Do me the favour to dilate at full
What hath befall'n of them and thee till now.


*Egeon:* My youngest boy, and yet my eldest care,
At eighteen years became inquisitive
After his brother: and importuned me
That his attendant—so his case was like,
Reft of his brother, but retain'd his name—
Might bear him company in the quest of him:

Whom whilst I labour'd of a love to see,
I hazarded the loss of whom I loved.
Five summers have I spent in furthest Greece,
Roaming clean through the bounds of Asia,
And, coasting homeward, came to Ephesus;
Hopeless to find, yet loath to leave unsought
Or that or any place that harbours men.
But here must end the story of my life;
And happy were I in my timely death,
Could all my travels warrant me they live.

*Duke Solinus:* Hapless Egeon, whom the fates have mark'd
To bear the extremity of dire mishap!
Now, trust me, were it not against our laws,
Against my crown, my oath, my dignity,
Which princes, would they, may not disannul,
My soul would sue as advocate for thee.
But, though thou art adjudged to the death
And passed sentence may not be recall'd
But to our honour's great disparagement,
Yet I will favour thee in what I can.
Therefore, merchant, I'll limit thee this day
To seek thy life by beneficial help:
Try all the friends thou hast in Ephesus;
Beg thou, or borrow, to make up the sum,
And live; if no, then thou art doom'd to die.

---

The first scene of *The Comedy of Errors* is significant for several reasons. First, in the context of the ensuing farce, with its rapid rush of dizzying events and mistaken identities, Egeon's opening statement to the duke provides a coherent narrative to explain past events and his current predicament as he faces the death penalty. Egeon's story also injects, from the outset, a sense of tragedy and pathos into a plot that will soon become increasingly incredible and often hilarious. Nevertheless, it is important to recognize that, despite the comedic situation that is about to unfold in subsequent scenes, the sense of sorrow and impending violence introduced in this opening scene remains throughout the play, even if typically manifest in a more lighthearted manner. Egeon, however, is anything but optimistic and at no time is his demeanor blithe and cheery. Instead, he is a man who passively accepts the fate that awaits him, with no other desire or concern for his own well-being. He remains steadfast in his wish to find his family and know that they are safe. Confronted with insurmountable obstacles, Egeon is portrayed as a suffering and selfless hero willing to sacrifice his own life for the sake of those he loves so dearly. He like-wise establishes himself as a world traveler having wandered through Greece and Asia in search of his family. In his explanation to the duke, Egeon demonstrates a genuine concern for his reputation and desire to be known as one who lives by a moral code, as he states that the accident that separated him from his family was a natural one and not the result of any baseness of character: "Yet, that the world may witness that my end / Was wrought by nature, not by vile offence." Even in his melancholy description of the beloved wife he initially left behind, Egeon manifests a spiritual dimension to his character as he describes the "kind embracements" he misses. Egeon welcomes an end to his agony and, as he relates, had it not been for his devotion to his wife, he would easily have forfeited his own life on the night of the shipwreck. "A doubtful warrant of immediate death; / Which though myself would gladly have embraced, / [but for] the incessant weepings of my wife." Moreover, in expressing a concern for his own code of honor, Egeon establishes an ethical center within *The Comedy of Errors*, namely the redemptive power of love and forgiveness that will eventually bring the play to its happy conclusion.

In contrast to the sympathetic portrayal of Egeon's character is the duke of Solinus who, though not dismissive of the circumstances surrounding Egeon's death sentence in Ephesus, at first appears rigid and unyielding in his belief that he must uphold the punitive laws of his city that "Excludes all pity from our threatening looks." Instead, the duke is wholly concerned with upholding the law as dictated by the warlike conditions he believes the Syracusans have initiated, with their "rigorous statutes" that strictly prohibit any commerce or travel between the two cities. Thus, he explains to Egeon that he has no other choice than to execute Egeon unless he find someone to provide the ransom. However, as soon as Solinus starts to hear Egeon's sad tale, the duke slowly begins to equivocate, at first stating that he is sympathetic to the old man's plight but without recourse to change the punishment. By the end of the scene, the duke has grown increasingly compassionate toward Egeon's plight, seeing him as a "hapless" victim of bad luck. He yields as far as he believes the law will allow in granting the old man a day in which to find someone who will ransom his life. The duke is ultimately sincere in stating that he feels dishonored and shamed in having to deal with such an unjust law.

⚜ ⚜ ⚜

# Act 1, 2, 33–40

*Antipholus Syracuse:* He that commends me to mine own content
Commends me to the thing I cannot get.
I to the world am like a drop of water
That in the ocean seeks another drop,
Who, falling there to find his fellow forth,

Unseen, inquisitive, confounds himself.
So I, to find a mother and a brother,
In quest of them, unhappy, lose myself.

---

In making an astute analysis of his predicament in this passage, Antipholus of Syracuse establishes his sensitivity and keen awareness of his surroundings. He is clearly a man given to careful consideration of his situation and, moreover, displays a talent for poetic expression. Conscious of the enigmatic web in which he is entangled, Antipholus compares himself to a mere drop of water in search of its likeness in a vast expanse of ocean. Thus, Antipholus appears to suggest that his mission is doomed to failure before he even begins.

A mythological reference can be inferred in the passage, namely the myth of Narcissus, most fully told in Ovid's *Metamorphoses*, the story of a beautiful young man who fell in love with his own reflection in the water, though he had been advised never to do so. As a result of his abiding self-love, he was unable to respond to his lover, Echo, and was instead transformed into a flower bearing his name. Narcissus's punishment was never to know or receive the love of another since he was infatuated with himself alone. Like Narcissus's predicament, Antipholus here astutely refers to his anxiety that in his search for one who looks exactly like him, he will have no basis for distinction. In modern psychoanalytic terms, a narcissist is one who is preoccupied with himself, and several twentieth-century critics have commented on this phenomenon in *The Comedy of Errors*. Ironically, the interrogating and sensitive mind of Antipholus of Syracuse is an important distinction that will later become more distinct when we are introduced to and observe the unquestioning and irascible behavior of his Ephesian brother.

## Act 1, 2, 95–102

*Antipholus Syracuse:* Upon my life, by some device or other
The villain is o'er-raught of all my money.
They say this town is full of cozenage,
As, nimble jugglers that deceive the eye,
Dark-working sorcerers that change the mind,
Soul-killing witches that deform the body,
Disguised cheaters, prating mountebanks,
And many such-like liberties of sin:
If it prove so, I will be gone the sooner.
I'll to the Centaur, to go seek this slave:
I greatly fear my money is not safe.

---

Ancient Ephesus was associated with an abundance of evildoers who subjected the vulnerable citizenry to deception and trickery. This passage recites many of the crimes perpetrated by those who made a career out of cheating others, including illusionists, conjurers who could physically harm an individual, and, perhaps most insidiously, those who played mind games with their victims. When Antipholus speaks of "prating mountebanks," he is referring to the wandering charlatans who made boastful and outlandish claims to supernatural powers of healing. Antipholus, thus, is commenting on those who deliberately abuse language for their own personal gain and, in making such a reference, presages or anticipates the presence of Dr. Pinch, the fraudulent exorcist encountered in act 5. Additionally, in referring to a town full of "cozenage," one of the major puns in *The Comedy of Errors* is employed, since the entire play is predicated on an endless string of confusion and mistaken identities due to the existence of two sets of identical twins who reside in the same city. The word *cozenage*, which refers to the practice of fraud and cheating, bears an etymological relationship to the word *cousinage*, which refers to kinship and warm mutual relations. Thus, "cozenage" becomes a term that bears multiple meanings, all of which have a direct bearing on the strange circumstances and errors that beset the characters in the play. Additionally, the name of the inn where Antipholus of Syracuse is staying is the Centaur, a reference to the group of Greek mythological creatures which were part human, part horse. Far less threatening than their counterparts, the satyrs, centaurs were a source of amusement and, thus, an inn named after them is apt for a farce such as *The Comedy of Errors*. According to one mythological story, Pirithous, the king of the Lapiths, invited a group of centaurs to his wedding feast, where the half-human creatures became drunk on wine and disrupted the party. In mythology, centaurs were considered a challenge to law and order, since there was no clearly defined or delineated place for them in society.

## Act 3, 2, 29–52

*Antipholus Syracuse:* Sweet mistress, what your name is else I know not,
Nor by what wonder you do hit of mine;
Less in your knowledge and your grace you show not
Than our earth's wonder, more than earth divine.
Teach me, dear creature, how to think and speak;
Lay open to my earthy gross conceit,
Smother'd in errors, feeble, shallow, weak,
The folded meaning of your words' deceit.
Against my soul's pure truth why labour you
To make it wander in an unknown field?
Are you a god? would you create me new?
Transform me then, and to your power I'll yield.
But if that I am I, then well I know
Your weeping sister is no wife of mine,

Nor to her bed no homage do I owe;
Far more, far more to you do I decline;
O, train me not, sweet mermaid, with thy note,
To drown me in thy sister's flood of tears;
Sing, siren, for thyself and I will dote;
Spread o'er the silver waves thy golden hairs,
And as a bed I'll take them and there lie,
And in that glorious supposition think
He gains by death that hath such means to die;
Let Love, being light, be drowned if she sink.

---

As in so many other instances in *The Comedy of Errors*, this passage manifests the high degree of sensitivity and poetic beauty that Shakespeare has so adeptly woven into a fundamentally farcical plot. Here, Antipholus of Syracuse's sophistication and tenderhearted nature is fully demonstrated as he adopts, with complete sincerity, the language of a courtly lover. As will be later revealed, the fact that Antipholus is honest and forthright in his romantic overture to Luciana is of singular importance to recognizing the nobility of his character. At the same time, this passage is also a testament to Shakespeare's deft transformation of a highly conventional literary tradition into an earnest and heartfelt statement of love and spiritual awareness, as Antipholus maintains his "soul's pure truth."

The courtly love tradition is a literary convention that developed during the Middle Ages. These literary works reflect the chivalric ideals of a knight's utter devotion to a noblewoman. His expressions of love are highly idealized, combining propriety with passion. The knight's rhetoric is refined, filled with elaborate metaphors that describe the woman's exalted position in relation to his own diminished status and his wish to become worthy of her love. His speeches are marked with protestations of melancholy and emotional suffering at the hopelessness of his situation. In this manner, the courtly love tradition often becomes a lush indulgence of emotions and an exposition of highly charged imagery, despite the theme of unrequited affection that remains its central defining feature. Furthermore, it should be noted that, within this literary tradition, the romantic liaison between the knight and his lady is often illicit, as the woman is usually married.

Here, Antipholus's solemn affirmation of love for Luciana can be seen as an attempt to counter or subvert conventional notions of the courtly love tradition. Though he employs the complex and highly structured rhetoric of the chivalrous suitor, Antipholus's passion is unaffected, and his intentions are certainly within the realm of possibility. Antipholus's fundamental problem in declaring his love for Luciana is the same issue that besets all of the characters: the impossibility of establishing the identity of the other individuals with whom he comes in contact. While he knows that he is not married to Adriana and is thus a legitimate suitor of Luciana, Antipholus of Syracuse does not yet realize that he is in his brother's household; Luciana likewise does not realize he is her brother-in-law's long lost twin. Thus, his opening lines admit to this problem of not knowing who the person he is addressing truly is. Nevertheless, despite the unusual circumstance and despite admitting the many problems it causes, Antipholus proceeds to implore Luciana to help him understand his predicament, namely why she assumes he is Adriana's husband. Ultimately, he asks her to accept his romantic intentions as legitimate. In his confession of bewilderment at her insistence that he is Adriana's errant husband, Antipholus is humble in asking for Luciana's help. At the same time, he manifests rhetorical finesse in expressing his confusion and misapprehension as a *conceit*, a word that refers both to something conceived by the mind as well as to a complex metaphor of logic whereby dissimilar objects are juxtaposed in an effort to stimulate understanding. Given the succession of errors that plague Antipholus of Syracuse, his use of the word *conceit* in this passage is particularly apt, for he is desperately seeking a way out of this maze of incomprehensibility: "Teach me, dear creature, how to think and speak; / Lay open to my earthy gross conceit, / Smother'd in errors, feeble, shallow, weak."

Antipholus also exhibits a literary sophistication in referring to Luciana as a siren whose enchanting song he longs to hear, an unmistakable allusion to Homer's romantic epic, the *Odyssey*, in which the powerful sorceress Circe lures Odysseus's men into a trap with wine and enchanting music, only to transform them into swine. The beauty of Antipholus's poetry is likewise as enchanting though recited with the most sincere intention. Moreover, he beckons Luciana to become his sorceress: "Far more, far more to you do I decline; / O, train me not, sweet mermaid, with thy note, / To drown me in thy sister's flood of tears; / Sing, siren, for thyself and I will dote." Finally, in stating that he will "dote" on Luciana's song, Antipholus again demonstrates his rhetorical dexterity for though his use of the word is meant as an expression of his affection, to be infatuated is to show an excessive fondness in addition to potentially displaying a deranged state of mind. Antipholus, thus, acknowledges that he is at his wit's end and, in doing so, subverts the original rhetorical agenda of the courtly love tradition, the imagery of which he otherwise easily employs and exploits.

## Act 3, 2, 71–148

*Antipholus of Syracuse:* Why, how now, Dromio! where runn'st thou so fast?

*Dromio of Syracuse:* Do you know me, sir? am I Dromio? am I your man? am I myself?

*Antipholus of Syracuse:* Thou art Dromio, thou art my man, thou art thyself.

*Dromio of Syracuse:* I am an ass, I am a woman's man and besides myself.

*Antipholus of Syracuse:* What woman's man? and how besides thyself? besides thyself?

*Dromio of Syracuse:* Marry, sir, besides myself, I am due to a woman; one that claims me, one that haunts me, one that will have me.

*Antipholus of Syracuse:* What claim lays she to thee?

*Dromio of Syracuse:* Marry sir, such claim as you would lay to your horse; and she would have me as a beast: not that I being a beast, she would have me; but that she, being a very beastly creature, lays claim to me.

*Antipholus of Syracuse:* What is she?

*Dromio of Syracuse:* A very reverent body; ay, such a one as a man may not speak of without he say 'Sir-reverence.' I have but lean luck in the match, and yet is she a wondrous fat marriage.

*Antipholus of Syracuse:* How dost thou mean a fat marriage?

*Dromio of Syracuse:* Marry, sir, she's the kitchen wench and all grease; and I know not what use to put her to but to make a lamp of her and run from her by her own light. I warrant, her rags and the tallow in them will burn a Poland winter: if she lives till doomsday, she'll burn a week longer than the whole world.

*Antipholus of Syracuse:* What complexion is she of?

*Dromio of Syracuse:* Swart, like my shoe, but her face nothing half so clean kept: for why, she sweats; a man may go over shoes in the grime of it.

*Antipholus of Syracuse:* That's a fault that water will mend.

*Dromio of Syracuse:* No, sir, 'tis in grain; Noah's flood could not do it.

*Antipholus of Syracuse:* What's her name?

*Dromio of Syracuse:* Nell, sir; but her name and three quarters, that's
an ell and three quarters, will not measure her from
hip to hip.

*Antipholus of Syracuse:* Then she bears some breadth?

*Dromio of Syracuse:* No longer from head to foot than from hip to hip:
she is spherical, like a globe; I could find out
countries in her.

*Antipholus of Syracuse:* In what part of her body stands Ireland?

*Dromio of Syracuse:* Marry, in her buttocks: I found it out by the bogs.

*Antipholus of Syracuse:* Where Scotland?

*Dromio of Syracuse:* I found it by the barrenness; hard in the palm of the
hand.

*Antipholus of Syracuse:* Where France?

*Dromio of Syracuse:* In her forehead; armed and reverted, making war
against her heir.

*Antipholus of Syracuse:* Where England?

*Dromio of Syracuse:* I looked for the chalky cliffs, but I could find no
whiteness in them; but I guess it stood in her chin,
by the salt rheum that ran between France and it.

*Antipholus of Syracuse:* Where Spain?

*Dromio of Syracuse:* Faith, I saw it not; but I felt it hot in her breath.

*Antipholus of Syracuse:* Where America, the Indies?

*Dromio of Syracuse:* Oh, sir, upon her nose all o'er embellished with
rubies, carbuncles, sapphires, declining their rich
aspect to the hot breath of Spain; who sent whole
armadoes of caracks to be ballast at her nose.

*Antipholus of Syracuse:* Where stood Belgia, the Netherlands?

*Dromio of Syracuse:* Oh, sir, I did not look so low. To conclude, this
drudge, or diviner, laid claim to me, call'd me
Dromio; swore I was assured to her; told me what
privy marks I had about me, as, the mark of my
shoulder, the mole in my neck, the great wart on my
left arm, that I amazed ran from her as a witch.

And, I think, if my breast had not been made of
    faith and my heart of steel,
She had transform'd me to a curtal dog and made me turn
    i' the wheel.

*Antipholus of Syracuse:* Go hie thee presently, post to the road:
An if the wind blow any way from shore,
I will not harbour in this town to-night:
If any bark put forth, come to the mart,
Where I will walk till thou return to me.
If every one knows us and we know none,
'Tis time, I think, to trudge, pack and be gone.

*Dromio of Syracuse:* As from a bear a man would run for life,
So fly I from her that would be my wife.

*Antipholus of Syracuse:* There's none but witches do inhabit here;
And therefore 'tis high time that I were hence.
She that doth call me husband, even my soul
Doth for a wife abhor. But her fair sister,
Possess'd with such a gentle sovereign grace,
Of such enchanting presence and discourse,
Hath almost made me traitor to myself:
But, lest myself be guilty to self-wrong,
I'll stop mine ears against the mermaid's song.

---

This scene serves as an explanation of a variety of puns and as a humorous
example of cartography in the description of Nell. A pun is a playful use of one
or more words in such a way as to suggest two or more simultaneous meanings
or associations, sometimes employing a word with the same sound but with different meanings. Though the word *pun* first appeared in the English language
in 1644, Shakespeare clearly made full and effective use of the device in *The
Comedy of Errors*. In this passage, three initial puns are employed by Dromio of
Ephesus, hinging on the words *besides* and *marry*. The scene involves Dromio

of Syracuse's breathless escape from the clutches of Nell, the servant who has claimed him for a husband. In the first instance, when Dromio states that he is "besides" himself, he describes the core comic device employed in the play: He has been mistaken by Nell for someone else, her husband. Her misidentification of him as her spouse has created yet another layer of confusion and disorientation from which he seeks refuge. Additionally, to be beside oneself is one of the fundamental problems in the play, for it signifies the distress that accompanies an inability to know who one is in reality, an overwhelming quandary that the major characters desperately need to resolve.

In the passage's second significant use of wordplay, in Dromio's initial declaration of revulsion toward Antipholus, his use of the word *marry* is an emphatic expression of outrage and astonishment at Nell's unwanted advances. In yet another instance of punning, Dromio's play on the word *ass* underscores Nell's intention to use him as livestock or a beast of burden and, of course, his fear that her intention to exercise absolute control renders him a fool. As Dromio points out, the irony is that Nell is the true beast both in her unappealing appearance and abhorrent perspective on marriage and husbands.

Another significant aspect of this passage has to do with comparing the overweight Nell's body to an immense map on which countries, even continents, can be identified. In each instance, while comparing aspects of her physical being to various types of challenging terrain, difficult climates, national conflicts, and even biblical prophecies, Dromio—with the enthusiastic encouragement of his master—formulates a series of ingenious puns. When asked where he would locate Ireland on her body, he responds that it would be found by the "bogs," a reference to both the actual soggy, spongy areas composed of decaying vegetation and to the flabby texture of her buttocks. Finally, when asked where he would locate the Netherlands, Dromio punningly transforms the geographic citation into a reference to her genitals: "Oh, sir, I did not look so low." In the end, the description of Nell's uncouth advances toward Dromio, from which he sees no recourse but to leave the city, is in direct opposition to his master's polite and high romantic overtures to Luciana, a relationship Antipholus sincerely and devoutly hopes will come to fruition.

## Act 4, 2, 28–66

*Dromio of Syracuse:* Here! Go—the desk, the purse, sweat, now, make haste.

*Luciana:* How hast thou lost thy breath?

*Dromio of Syracuse:* By running fast.

*Adriana:* Where is thy master, Dromio? Is he well?

*Dromio of Syracuse:* No, he's in Tartar limbo, worse than hell.
A devil in an everlasting garment hath him;
One whose hard heart is button'd up with steel;
A fiend, a fury, pitiless and rough;
A wolf, nay, worse, a fellow all in buff;
A back-friend, a shoulder-clapper, one that countermands
The passages of alleys, creeks and narrow lands;
A hound that runs counter and yet draws dryfoot well;
One that before the judgement carries poor souls to hell.

*Adriana:* Why, man, what is the matter?

*Dromio of Syracuse:* I do not know the matter: he is 'rested on the case.

*Adriana:* What, is he arrested? Tell me at whose suit.

*Dromio of Syracuse:* I know not at whose suit he is arrested well;
But he's in a suit of buff which 'rested him, that can I tell.
Will you send him, mistress, redemption, the money in his desk?

*Adriana:* Go fetch it, sister.
[Exit Luciana]
This I wonder at,
That he, unknown to me, should be in debt.
Tell me, was he arrested on a band?

*Dromio of Syracuse:* Not on a band, but on a stronger thing;
A chain, a chain! Do you not hear it ring?

*Adriana:* What, the chain?

*Dromio of Syracuse:* No, no, the bell: 'tis time that I were gone:
It was two ere I left him, and now the clock
strikes one.

*Adriana:* The hours come back! that did I never hear.

*Dromio of Syracuse:* O, yes; if any hour meet a sergeant, a' turns back for
very fear.

*Adriana:* As if Time were in debt! how fondly dost thou reason!

*Dromio of Syracuse:* Time is a very bankrupt, and owes more than he's
worth to season.
Nay, he's a thief too. Have you not heard men say
That Time comes stealing on by night and day?
If 'a be in debt and theft, and a sergeant in the way,
Hath he not reason to turn back an hour in a day?

[Reenter Luciana with a purse]

*Adriana:* Go, Dromio, there's the money. Bear it straight,
And bring thy master home immediately.
Come, sister, I am pressed down with conceit—
Conceit, my comfort and my injury.

---

Once Dromio of Syracuse enters the scene, we are back in the realm of
his refined imagination, incisive wit, and rhetorical skill for speaking in
puns and riddles. While he has come to get the requisite funds to secure
Antipholus of Ephesus's release from imprisonment, Dromio's responses to
Adriana in regard to her husband's status and the reasons for his predicament are anything but straightforward. When asked if Antipholus is well,
Dromio's reply infers that Antipholus is in a predicament akin to being in the
Greek mythological notion of an infernal underworld—"No, he's in Tartar
limbo, worse than hell"—a place conceived as a terrible chasm, a gloomy and
foreboding abyss in which punishment was meted out and judgment passed
on the souls of the departed. Extending his metaphor, Dromio continues
his dramatic and exaggerated description of Antipholus's situation, speaking
of an unyielding and stone-hearted devil who presides over this domain, a
being whose heart is reinforced with steel, donning "an everlasting garment"
of cruelty. Dromio is uncertain as to whether this evil presence has human
or animal attributes, "a wolf, nay, worse," and in referring to the creature's
fiendish delight in threatening his victims—"a fellow all in buff"—he also
implies the unjustified and random violence he is continuously forced to
endure. Furthermore, in his oblique reference to "a back-friend, a shoulder-clapper," Dromio uses an epithet that is also applied to an arresting
officer and, thus, enigmatically comments on Antipholus's current circumstances. Dromio's final mystifying observation is that the fiend in charge of
Adriana's husband is himself misguided, blindly pursuing unsubstantiated
evidence, like an animal that both pursues as well as turns from the tracks of
its prey: "A hound that runs counter and yet draws dryfoot well; / One that
before the judgement carries poor souls to hell." Dromio's astute observation
of the impulse to rush to judgment based on flimsy and uncertain proof is

an incisive commentary on the exact source of all the errors that have thus far occurred in the play.

Once he has finally told Adriana directly that her husband is under arrest for not paying a debt, Dromio continues to fashion puns connecting debt and time, a concept personified in the dual role of a debtor and a burglar with no compunction about changing the hour of the day for his own advantage: "Time is a very bankrupt, and owes more than he's / worth, to season." When the scene concludes with Adriana correctly perceiving that she has a hyperactive imagination that is inclined to forming rapid and erroneous conclusions—"Come, sister: I am press'd down with conceit—/ Conceit, my comfort and my injury"—a contrast emerges between her character and that of Dromio of Syracuse. In her use of the word *conceit,* Adriana admits that she suffers from a excess of misguided thoughts about her husband's infidelity, while the concept of a "conceit," when applied to Dromio's character, denotes his superb ability to speak in sophisticated metaphors.

---

# Act 5, 1, 38–112

*Aemilia:* Be quiet, people. Wherefore throng you hither?

*Adriana:* To fetch my poor distracted husband hence.
Let us come in, that we may bind him fast
And bear him home for his recovery.

*Angelo:* I knew he was not in his perfect wits.

*Second Merchant:* I am sorry now that I did draw on him.

*Aemilia:* How long hath this possession held the man?

*Adriana:* This week he hath been heavy, sour, sad,
And much different from the man he was;
But till this afternoon his passion
Ne'er brake into extremity of rage.

*Aemilia:* Hath he not lost much wealth by wreck of sea?
Buried some dear friend? Hath not else his eye
Stray'd his affection in unlawful love?
A sin prevailing much in youthful men,
Who give their eyes the liberty of gazing.
Which of these sorrows is he subject to?

*Adriana:* To none of these, except it be the last;
Namely, some love that drew him oft from home.

*Aemilia:* You should for that have reprehended him.

*Adriana:* Why, so I did.

*Aemilia:* Ay, but not rough enough.

*Adriana:* As roughly as my modesty would let me.

*Aemilia:* Haply, in private.

*Adriana:* And in assemblies too.

*Aemilia:* Ay, but not enough.

*Adriana:* It was the copy of our conference:
In bed he slept not for my urging it;
At board he fed not for my urging it;
Alone, it was the subject of my theme;
In company I often glanced it;
Still did I tell him it was vile and bad.

*Aemilia:* And thereof came it that the man was mad.
The venom clamours of a jealous woman
Poisons more deadly than a mad dog's tooth.
It seems his sleeps were hinder'd by thy railing,
And therefore comes it that his head is light.
Thou say'st his meat was sauced with thy upbraidings:
Unquiet meals make ill digestions;
Thereof the raging fire of fever bred;
And what's a fever but a fit of madness?
Thou say'st his sports were hinderd by thy brawls:
Sweet recreation barr'd, what doth ensue
But moody and dull melancholy,
Kinsman to grim and comfortless despair,
And at her heels a huge infectious troop
Of pale distemperatures and foes to life?
In food, in sport and life-preserving rest
To be disturb'd, would mad or man or beast:
The consequence is then thy jealous fits
Have scared thy husband from the use of wits.

*Luciana:* She never reprehended him but mildly,
When he demean'd himself rough, rude and wildly.

Why bear you these rebukes and answer not?

*Adriana:* She did betray me to my own reproof.
Good people enter and lay hold on him.

*Aemilia:* No, not a creature enters in my house.

*Adriana:* Then let your servants bring my husband forth.

*Aemilia:* Neither: he took this place for sanctuary,
And it shall privilege him from your hands
Till I have brought him to his wits again,
Or lose my labour in assaying it.

*Adriana:* I will attend my husband, be his nurse,
Diet his sickness, for it is my office,
And will have no attorney but myself;
And therefore let me have him home with me.

*Aemilia:* Be patient; for I will not let him stir
Till I have used the approved means I have,
With wholesome syrups, drugs and holy prayers,
To make of him a formal man again:
It is a branch and parcel of mine oath,
A charitable duty of my order.
Therefore depart and leave him here with me.

*Adriana:* I will not hence and leave my husband here:
And ill it doth beseem your holiness
To separate the husband and the wife.

*Aemilia:* Be quiet and depart: thou shalt not have him.

---

This passage establishes a striking contrast between two opposing perceptions of
mental instability or illness as reckoned by Adriana and Amelia. The scene also
reveals a fundamental tension expressed throughout the play between those who
rush to rapid and ill-informed judgments and others who demonstrate a slower
and more deliberate process of forming their conclusions. Adriana's character is
obstreperous, given over to rash decisions and passionate arguments in defense
of her unfounded opinions about her husband's inexplicable and uncontrollable
rage. She expresses the problem of his perceived insanity in the most extreme
and violent terms, stating that he is *distracted*, a word that connotes a severe state

of mental confusion and agitation. Without a moment's hesitation, Adriana's immediate solution is to take her husband by force, to "bind him fast / And bear him home for his recovery," although we are left wondering just how she will accomplish this since she offers nothing further than her intention to hold him captive. Moreover, in addition to her loud and insistent complaining that she will seize control of the situation, Adriana also states her unequivocal intention to disregard any legal right he may have to seek sanctuary at the abbey.

Aemilia, on the other hand, has a far more quiet and contemplative approach to Antipholus of Ephesus's agitation. Her method of investigation is interrogative as she poses several questions for Adriana to consider as possible explanations of her husband's irascible behavior. These questions begin a process of assigning responsibility to Adriana, as Aemilia asks if she has observed how long the affliction has gone on. Aemilia also demonstrates the sensitivity that Adriana seemingly lacks when she inquires how acutely aware Adriana is of her husband's feelings, whether he may have received some shocking news, perhaps of a shipwreck or the loss of a dear friend. Aemilia goes so far as to suggest that he may be suffering a guilty conscience from "gazing" at another woman. In her use of the word *gazing*, Aemilia suggests a far less extreme form of losing oneself, more in the sense of being preoccupied for a length of time, here a specific fault for looking in the wrong direction by noticing another woman. Aemilia clearly seeks to discover the process whereby Antipholus became volatile and hot tempered. In rendering a diagnosis, Aemilia adopts a gradual and studied procedure for diagnosing Antipholus's ailment, a line of inquiry that also places her in direct opposition to the rash and incompetent Dr. Pinch. Through her deposition of Adriana, Aemilia arrives at the hypothesis that Antipholus is suffering from a type of distemper because of conditions at home, many of which relate to being a badgered husband: "And thereof came it that the man was mad. / The venom clamours of a jealous woman / Poisons more deadly than a mad dog's tooth. / It seems his sleeps were hinder'd by thy railing." In rendering this opinion, Amelia shows herself to be contemplative, as would be expected of a spiritual caregiver, and prudent in her admission that she may not succeed in bringing about a cure, a modesty wanting in the wife. While Adriana threatens to use force to remove her husband from the abbey, Aemilia exhibits the patience and resolve to heal Antipholus through physical and spiritual intercession: "I will not let him stir / Till I have used the approved means I have, / With wholesome syrups, drugs and holy prayers, / To make of him a formal man again." Thus, while Adriana would remove him in a fragmented, distracted state with no actual plan to restore his mental stability, the abbess means to bring him back to a state of integrity, to make him a "formal," rational, and whole man once again.

# LIST OF CHARACTERS IN
# *THE COMEDY OF ERRORS*

**Antipholus of Syracuse** is the twin brother of Antipholus of Ephesus and the son of Egeon. Unlike his Ephesian brother, Antipholus of Syracuse is curious and hopes to find his long-lost brother, his brother's slave, and his mother, so he travels to Ephesus with his slave, Dromio of Syracuse. Antipholus of Syracuse is by far the more sympathetic and sensitive of the two brothers.

**Antipholus of Ephesus** is the twin brother of Antipholus of Syracuse and the son of Egeon; he is a well-respected merchant in Ephesus and Adriana's husband.

**Dromio of Syracuse** is the bumbling, comical slave of Antipholus of Syracuse who displays a rich sense of humor and a keen intellect. He is the twin brother of Dromio of Ephesus.

**Dromio of Ephesus** is the bumbling, comical slave of Antipholus of Ephesus, though, like his master, not as lighthearted as his twin brother, Dromio of Syracuse.

**Adriana** is the wife of Antipholus of Ephesus; she is both extremely passionate and quick to pass judgment while also a devoted and loving wife, capable of forgiveness.

**Luciana** is Adriana's unmarried sister and the object of Antipholus of Syracuse's affections. Always loyal and well-intentioned toward her sister, she nevertheless functions in a somewhat contrary mode in that she argues two different perspectives on the wife's role in marriage.

**Solinus** is the duke of Ephesus, a just and merciful ruler. Though at first he is emphatic that he will uphold the law against Syracusan trespassers, despite its cruelty and injustice, he nevertheless is a sympathetic figure and, ultimately, a compassionate man of clear ethical principle.

**Egeon** is a Syracusan merchant, husband of the abbess (Aemilia), and the father of the Antipholi. He is a sympathetic character, willing to suffer hardship and even forfeit his own life in his determination to locate his long-lost family members. Egeon's presence in the play adds a tragic element and is the subject of much critical discussion.

The abbess is **Aemilia,** the long-lost wife of Egeon and the mother of the Antipholi. She is revered by all and the agent of redemption in the play through her wise and patient counsel.

**Balthasar** is a merchant in Syracuse.

**Angelo** is a goldsmith in Syracuse and a friend to Antipholus of Ephesus.

The **Merchant** is an Ephesian friend of Antipholus of Syracuse.

The **Second Merchant** is a tradesman to whom Angelo is in debt.

**Doctor Pinch** is a schoolteacher, conjurer, and would-be exorcist. His attempts to intervene in the characters' lives imbue the play with an element of the ridiculous. Though he attempts to diagnose mental illness or instability in others, he eventually is held captive by those he has wrongly accused.

**Luce,** also called Nell in the play, is an overweight, unctuous, and abusive kitchen maid in the Ephesian household of Antihpholus and Adriana. She mistakes Dromio of Syracuse for her own husband while he wants to flee the city in order to escape her clutches.

The **Courtesan** is a well-intentioned friend of Antipholus of Ephesus; her only motivation is to reclaim those items that are rightfully hers.

# CRITICISM THROUGH THE AGES

# THE COMEDY OF ERRORS
# IN THE SEVENTEENTH CENTURY
❧

Although there are no critical assessments of *The Comedy of Errors* in the seventeenth century, there is documentation of two separate early performances of the play, one having occurred at Gray's Hall Inn on Innocents' Day, December 28, 1594, and the other having taken place at the court of King James I on December 28, 1604. The account of the first performance is recorded in the *Gesta Grayorum* (Deeds of Gray) printed in manuscript form in 1688 and containing a narrative of the events that transpired during the Christmas revels by the law students at Gray's Inn in 1594. Gray's Inn, which dates at least from 1370, takes its name from Baron Gray of Wilton; it is on the site of the family home, in the manor of Portpoole. During the fifteenth and sixteenth centuries, Gray's Inn grew steadily, attaining its highest stature during the reign of Queen Elizabeth I, who served as its Patron Lady. Apparently, certain prominent politicians and confidantes of Elizabeth, such as Nicolas Bacon, William Cecil, and Gilbert Gerard, were instrumental in recruiting the most promising young men to join.

Gray's Inn also became well known for the parties and festivals it hosted, where students performed masques and plays for weddings, at times with Elizabeth I in attendance, and held regular banquets and celebrations during various religious holidays. Indeed, at Christmastime, a carnival-like atmosphere prevailed at Gray's Inn, where the students ruled the inn and appointed a Lord of Misrule, called the Prince of Purpoole. Thus, it is easy to imagine how the evening of December 28, 1594, during which far too many people were invited to an evening of feasting, merrymaking, and entertainment (including some notable stage performances), resulted in the guests from the Inner Temple leaving the overcrowded festivities. According to the *Gesta Grayorum*, the scene at Gray's Inn, became one of mayhem when it became apparent that there would not be enough space for the actors to perform. Apparently, the arrival of the invitees from the Inner Temple, including its ambassador, created great excitement, which in turn led to a disorderly throng spilling onto the stage and displacing the actors as the revelers occupied the very space on which the entertainments were to take place. Since the prince and his officers could not effectively restore calm and order, the ambassador and his retinue left. According to the *Gesta*, following their departure, it was thought best to offer some light entertainment and "a Comedy of Errors (like Plautus his Menechmus)" was performed. Thereafter, the evening gained notoriety for its breach of decorum and display of irregular behavior: "So that the night was begun, and continued to the end in nothing but confusion and errors, whereupon it was ever afterwards called *The Night of Errors*."

As an additional irony to both the play and the evening of its intended performance, a mock trial was held the following night during which an inquiry was made into the confusion, and a sorcerer or conjurer (meaning an individual who had been charged with organizing the evening's entertainment) was held responsible for the chaos and accused of introducing a group of ardent partygoers with the purpose of creating disorder and confusion. The "sorcerer" was eventually acquitted, and the offended guests were invited to a lavish musical performance on the theme of amity on January 3. The *Gesta Grayorum* is also important for its unmistakable reference to Shakespeare's acting company, the Lord Chamberlain's Men, and that *The Comedy of Errors* may have been expressly written for the Christmas revels at Gray's Inn, especially given its setting within a carnivalesque world and its focus on such topics as birthrights and family origins.

As to the performance on December 29, 1604, it has been recorded that "The Plaie of Errors" by "Shaxberd" was performed at court and, according to Charles Whitworth, King James, who was fond of Shakespeare, commanded a performance of *The Comedy of Errors* to be included in his entertainment.

Today, Gray's Inn is one of four Inns of Court in London, professional associations which all barristers in England and Wales are required to join. In addition to providing living quarters, dining facilities, libraries, and other professional accommodations, the Inns of Court also exercise supervisory and disciplinary authority over their members. With a church or chapel having been originally attached to each of the inns, these associations effectively became self-contained worlds where lawyers could train for their profession.

## 1602—Joshua Cooke. From *How a Man May Choose a Good Wife from a Bad*

The reference in Cooke's play made to the memorable Dr. Pinch fully accords with his characterization in *The Comedy of Errors* and is evidence that this play, along with other Shakespearean works, had gained currency. In a comedy titled *How a Man May Choose a Good Wife from a Bad*, Joshua Cooke refers to an emaciated, contemptuous, and something other than human "schoole-maister," a caricature of a learned man reminiscent of Shakespeare's conjurer.

When didst thou see the starueling Schoole-maister? That Rat, that shrimp, that spindleshanck, that Wren, that sheep-biter, that leane chittiface, that famine, that leane Envy, that all bones, that bare Anatomy, that Jack a Lent, that ghost, that shadow, that Moone in the waine.

---

## 1688—From the *Gesta Grayorum* (Deeds of Gray)

The next grand night was intended to be upon Innocents-Day at night; at which time there was a great presence of lords, ladies, and worshipful personages, that did expect some notable performance at that time; which, indeed, had been effected, if the multitude of beholders had not been so exceeding great, that thereby there was no convenient room for those that were actors; by reason whereof, very good inventions and conceits could not have opportunity to be applauded, which otherwise would have been great contentation to the beholders. Against which time, our friend, the Inner Temple, determined to send their Ambassador to our Prince of State, as sent from Frederick Templarius, their Emperor, who was then busied in his wars against the Turk. The Ambassador came very gallantly appointed, and attended by a great number of brave gentlemen, which arrived at our Court about nine of the clock at night. Upon their coming thither, the King at Arms gave notice to the Prince, then sitting in his chair of state in the hall, that there was to come to his Court an Ambassador from his ancient friend the State of Templaria, which desired to have present access unto his Highness; and shewed his Honour further, that he seemed to be of very good sort, because he was so well attended; and therefore desired, that it would please his Honour that some of his Nobles and Lords might conduct him to his Highness's presence, which was done. So he was brought in very solemnly, with sound of trumpets, the King at Arms and Lords of Purpoole making to his company, which marched before him in order. He was received very kindly of the Prince, and placed in a chair besides his Highness, to the end that he might be a partaker of the sports intended. But first he made a speech to the Prince, wherein he declared how his excellent renown and fame was known throughout all the whole world; and that the report of his greatness was not contained within the bounds of the Ocean, but had come to the ears of his noble Sovereign, Frederick Templarius, where he is now warring against the Turks, the known enemies to all Christendom; who, having heard that his Excellency kept his Court at Graya this Christmas, thought it to stand with his ancient league of amity and near kindness, that so long had been continued and increased by their noble ancestors, of famous memory and desert, to gratulate his happiness, and flourishing estate; and in that regard, had sent him his Ambassador, to be residing at his Excellency's Court, in honour of his greatness, and token of his

tender love and good will he beareth to his Highness; the confirmation whereof
he especially required, and by all means possible would study to increase and
eternize: which function he was the more willing to accomplish, because our
State of Graya did grace Templaria with the presence of an Ambassador about
thirty years since, upon like occasion.

Our Prince made him this answer: that he did acknowledge that the great
kindness of his Lord, whereby he doth invite to further degrees in firm and
loyal friendship, did deserve all honourable commendations, and effectual
accomplishment, that by any means might be devised; and that he accounted
himself happy, by having the sincere and steadfast love of so gracious and
renowned a Prince, as his Lord and Master deserved to be esteemed; and that
nothing in the world should hinder the due observation of so inviolable a band
as he esteemed his favour and good will. Withal, he entred into commendations
of his noble and courageous enterprizes, in that he chuseth out an adversary
fit for his greatness to encounter with, his Honour to be illustrated by, and
such an enemy to all Christendom, as that the glory of his actions tend to the
safety and liberty of all civility and humanity: yet, notwithstanding that he was
thus employed in this action of honouring us, he shewed both his honourable
mindfulnes of our love and friendship, and also his own puissance, that can
afford so great a number of brave gentlemen, and so gallantly furnished and
accomplished: and so concluded, with a welcome both to the Ambassador
himself and his favourites, for their Lord and Master's sake, and so for their
own good deserts and condition.

When the Ambassador was placed, as aforesaid, and that there was something
to be performed for the delight of the beholders, there arose such a disordered
tumult and crowd upon the stage, that there was no opportunity to effect that
which was intended: there came so great a number of worshipful personages
upon the stage that might not be displaced, and gentlewomen whose sex did
privilege them from violence, that when the Prince and his officers had in vain,
a good while, expected and endeavoured a reformation, at length there was no
hope of redress for that present. The Lord Ambassador and his train thought
that they were not so kindly entertained as was before expected, and thereupon
would not stay any longer at that time, but, in a sort, discontented and displeased.
After their departure, the throngs and tumults did somewhat cease, although
so much of them continued as was able to disorder and confound any good
inventions whatsoever. In regard whereof, as also for that the sports intended
were especially for the gracing the Templarians, it was thought good not to
offer any thing of account, saving dancing and revelling with gentlewomen;
and after such sports, a Comedy of Errors (like to Plautus his Menechmus)
was played by the players. So that night was begun and continued to the end
in nothing but confusion and errors; whereupon, it was ever afterwards called,
"The Night of Errors."

This mischanceful accident sorting so ill, to the great prejudice of the rest of our proceedings, was a great discouragement and disparagement to our whole state; yet it gave occasion to the lawyers of the Prince's Council, the next night, after revels, to read a commission of Oyer and Terminer, directed to certain Noblemen and Lords of his Highness's Council, and others, that they should enquire, or cause enquiry to be made, of some great disorders and abuses lately done and committed within his Highness's dominions of Purpoole, especially by sorceries and inchantments; and namely, of a great witchcraft used the night before, whereby there were great disorders and misdemeanours, by hurly-burlies, crowds, errors, confusions, vain representations, and shows, to the utter discredit of our state and policy.

The next night upon this occasion, we preferred judgments thick and threefold, which were read publicly by the Clerk of the Crown, being all against a sorcerer or conjurer that was supposed to be the cause of that confused inconvenience. Therein was contained, How he had caused the stage to be built, and scaffolds to be reared to the top of the house, to increase expectation. Also how he had caused divers ladies and gentlemen, and others of good condition to be invited to our sports; also our dearest friend the Slate of Templaria, to be disgraced, and disappointed of their kind entertainment, deserved and intended. Also that he caused throngs and tumults, crowds and outrages, to disturb our whole proceedings. And lastly, that he had foisted a company of base and common fellows, to make up our disorders with a play of Errors and Confusions; and that that night had gained to us discredit, and itself a nickname of Errors. All which were against the crown and dignity of our Sovereign Lord the Prince of Purpoole.

Under colour of these proceedings, were laid open to the view all the causes of note that were committed by our chiefest statesmen in the government of our principality; and every officer in any great place, that had not performed his duty in that service, was taxed hereby, from the highest to the lowest, not sparing the guard and porters, that suffered so many disordered persons to enter in at the court-gates: upon whose aforesaid indictments the prisoner was arraigned at the bar, being brought thither by the Lieutenant of the Tower (for at that time the stocks were graced with that name); and the Sheriff impanelled a jury of twenty-four gentlemen, that were to give their verdict upon the evidence given. The prisoner appealed to the Prince his Excellency for justice; and humbly desired that it would please his Highness to understand the truth of the matter by his supplication, which he had ready to be offered to the Master of the Requests. The Prince gave leave to the Master of the Requests, that he should read the petition; wherein was a disclosure of all the knavery and juggling of the Attorney and Solicitor, which had brought all this law-stuff on purpose to blind the eyes of his Excellency and all the honourable Court there, going about to make them think that those things which they all saw and perceived sensibly to be in very deed done, and actually performed, were nothing else but vain illusions, fancies, dreams, and enchantments, and to be wrought and compassed by the means of a poor harmless wretch, that never had heard of such great matters in all his life: whereas the very fault was in the negligence of the Prince's Council, Lords, and Officers of his State, that had the rule of the roast, and by whose advice the Commonwealth was so soundly misgoverned. To prove these things to be true, he brought divers instances of great absurdities committed by the greatest; and made such allegations as could not be denied. These were done by some that were touched by the Attorney and Solicitor in their former proceedings, and they used the prisoner's names for means of quittance with them in that behalf. But the Prince and statesmen (being pinched on both sides by both the parties) were not a little offended at the great liberty that they had taken in censuring so far of his Highness's government; and thereupon the prisoner was freed and pardoned, the Attorney, Solicitor, Master of the Requests, and those that were acquainted with the draught of the petition, were all of them commanded to the Tower; so the Lieutenant took charge of them. And this was the end of our lawsports, concerning the Night of Errors.

When we were wearied with mocking thus at our own follies, at length there was a great consultation had for the recovery of our lost honour. It was then concluded, that first the Prince's Council should be reformed, and some graver conceits should have their places, to advise upon those things that were propounded to be done afterward. Therefore, upon better consideration, there were divers plots and devices intended against the Friday after the New Year's day, being the 3d. of January: and, to prevent all unruly tumults, and former inconveniences, there was provided a watch of armed men, to ward at the four ports; and whifflers to make good order under the four Barons; and the Lord Warden to oversee them all; that none but those that were of good condition might be suffered to be let into the Court. And the like officers were every where appointed.

# *The Comedy of Errors* in the Eighteenth Century

The eighteenth century marked both the beginning and the burgeoning of Shakespeare studies and criticism. The first standard collected edition of Shakespeare's plays was produced by Nicholas Rowe (1709), an editorial work which is also significant in that it provided a biography of Shakespeare, using the scant information available, some of dubious reliability, concerning Shakespeare's life. This was followed by the editions of Alexander Pope (1725), Lewis Theobald (1726), William Warburton (1747), Samuel Johnson (1765–58), George Steevens (1773 and 1778), and many others. The eighteenth century has also been commonly referred to as the neoclassical age, a description that is true only in the general sense that it held to a reverence for and observance of the rules for dramatic writing as set forth by ancient writers, in particular Aristotle. Aristotle's so-called "unities," as interpreted by eighteenth-century critics, decreed that plays should observe the unities of time (take place within a single day), place (happen in one specific place), and action (have one plot and no subplots). It is noteworthy that *The Comedy of Errors* and Shakespeare's last play, *The Tempest*, are the only two plays that strictly adhere to the classical unities.

From the 1787 collected edition of commentary, *Annotations upon the Comedy of Errors*, published by Samuel Johnson and George Steevens, in which several prominent eighteenth-century critics are represented, we can see the beginnings of genuine scholarly research techniques being applied to the understanding of the text and can appreciate the important academic contributions these editors made to the field of Shakespearean studies. Many valuable insights and approaches are offered in the commentaries included in this section. These contributions include discussions of word etymologies and an appreciation of how multiple meanings can lead to varied interpretations, as well as an impressive display on the part of these commentators of their vast knowledge of both classical and English literary texts. Their ability to cite the many sources from which Shakespeare drew inspiration as well as the vast range of subsequent literary masterpieces that were influenced by the playwright had the enormous benefit of applying new avenues of approach to interpreting *The Comedy of Errors*. Additionally, their historical investigations underscored the vastly different contexts by which

Plautus and Shakespeare need to be evaluated. It is also significant to note that in their recognition of various inherent textual contradictions, these editors were creating the foundation for modern Shakespearean criticism. Their understanding of a multitude of ambiguities within all of Shakespeare's works has become the mainstay of late twentieth and early twenty-first century interpretive debates.

Some of the more noteworthy observations and interpretations of enigmatic passages include William Warburton's insights in regard to Egeon's entrance in act 1, scene 1. As Egeon explains to the duke the shipwreck that precipitated his current lamentable situation, Warburton singles out line 34, "Was wrought by nature, not by vile offence," to highlight the difference in audience perceptions between spectators of Plautus as opposed to those of an Elizabethan audience. Warburton states that while Shakespeare's audience would understand that Egeon is not guilty of any personal wrongdoing, the ancient world believed that even unexpected misfortune on Earth was the result of heaven's distribution of justice. Accordingly, Warburton maintains that it is wholly appropriate that Egeon make absolutely clear that his current predicament is an accident of nature and not an act of divine vengeance.

In act 2, George Steevens admires Luciana's wise marital counsel to her sister, Adriana, who states that "There's none but asses will be bridled so," to which Luciana responds, "Why, headstrong liberty is lashed with woe" (ll. 14–15). Steevens is so impressed with Luciana's advice that a woman should be subservient to her husband that he even admits to acquiring a newfound diffidence toward his own wife. Steevens then discusses the multiplicity of meanings that accrue around the word *lash*. First, he takes an etymological approach in equating the word with *lace* (an Old English word for a cord used for fastening) and then extends the implication further in pointing out that lace also specifically refers to women fastening their clothes. For his part, Samuel Johnson sees line 41, in which Adriana responds to her sister ("This fool-begged patience in thee will be left"), as having a derogatory implication. Johnson is of the opinion that "patience" here means an exposure of utter stupidity that will in turn cause others to misrepresent Luciana as an idiot. In line 83, when Dromio of Ephesus protests Adriana's rude treatment of him ("Am I so round with you as you with me"), Steevens once again discusses the multiple meanings of the word *round*, which could signify a spherical shape by which Dromio is referring to his physical bearing or, possibly, his outspoken manner toward his mistress.

In act 3, Johnson notes an important instance of self-contradiction on the part of Dromio of Ephesus in lines 15–16: "Marry, so it doth appear / By the wrongs I suffer, and the blows I bear." Johnson states that, although the assault being visited on him would prove him to be an ass, he immediately invalidates this comment by cleverly adding that if he were truly such an animal, he would have protested such treatment by returning a blow in kind. "I should kick, being kicked, and, being at that pass, / You would keep from my heels, and beware of an ass." Later in the same act, Steevens focuses on line 83 (in modern editions), where Dromio of Ephesus responds to his master's command to bring him a crow with the phrase, "we'll pluck a crow together." Here, Steevens is interested in explaining this line by noting an important historical precedent to be found in Plautus's comedies, namely that in ancient times, both Greek and Roman children of the aristocracy were given different types of birds for their amusement. A little further on, Theobald is of the opinion that Luciana's advice to Adriana has suffered under an interpretive corruption of Shakespeare's intended meaning. Commenting on the architectural conceit in which a wife's "love-springs" are equated with a building gone to decay ("Shall love in buildings grow so ruinate?"), Theobald maintains that the bard simply meant that love, an organic entity, should not rot while it is in the process of growing, "in the spring of love."

In act 4, scene 2, Johnson calls attention to the ambiguities raised by Dromio of Syracuse's enigmatic response to Luciana in regard to his master's whereabouts. Stating that his Antipholus is in dire straits, Dromio likens him to "[a] hound that runs counter, and yet draws dry-foot well" (l. 39). According to Johnson, there is an inconsistency between running counter or backwards (which indicates that one has mistaken the trail of the animal being pursued), while drawing dry-foot means to follow in its tracks carefully. Furthermore, Johnson believes there is an additional play on the word *counter*, since it also serves as a specific reference to a prison in London and the officer or "seargent of the counter" who has taken Antipholus of Ephesus into custody. Later in act 4, scene 4, line 36, Warburton interprets a prophecy within Dromio of Ephesus's warning to his master's wife, Adriana, that she should be vigilant of her own safety. "Mistress, *respice finem*—'respect your end', or rather, to / prophesy like the parrot, 'Beware the rope's end.'" According to Warburton, it was a standing joke that a parrot that had learned to repeat unlucky words to random passersby had been schooled by a wise owner. Finally, in act 5, scene 1, line 170, Steevens states that while the description of the assault on Dr. Pinch is thoroughly ridiculous but entirely appropriate to a farce such as this, its source, which he has traced back to Virgil's *Aeneid*, is entirely improper. Commenting on its unsuitability to the classical epic poem, Steevens argues that it only serves to augment an already horrifying battlefield scene of death and destruction. Further on in line 205, Steevens maintains that Shakespeare's use of the word *harlot*, as in Antipholus's accusation that Adriana has been consorting with unsavory company, is a term of reproach applicable to men as well as women, referring to their being cheats and villains. "While she with harlots feasted in my house." This interpretation accords with the Syracusan visitors who dine at Antipholus of Ephesus's expense as well as the *Oxford English Dictionary*, which records the earliest application of this meaning to the word *harlot* as 1225 in the *Ancren Riwle*, a thirteenth-century anonymous tract written by an English churchman that offered instruction to young women about leading a life of religious seclusion.

Apart from the scholarly approach of these commentators is Charlotte Lennox's appraisal of *The Comedy of Errors*. Her three-volume work, *Shakespeare Illustrated*, from which the selection is drawn, is part of a project she undertook to investigate the stories and histories Shakespeare used as the sources for many of his plays. However, given Lennox's preference for original sources, Shakespeare's adaptations receive highly unfavorable and prejudiced reviews from the outset. In her comparison of *The Comedy of Errors* with Plautus's *Menaechmi*, Lennox begins with a denunciation of the play as an unjust translation. She bases her initial comments on those of another contemporary critic, a Mr. Langbain, who has declared the play a mere paraphrase of its ancient source. Following this assertion, Lennox then states that, since she is not "wholly acquainted with the Latin Tongue," she has instead translated a French version of the *Menaechmi* into English. Moreover, while she admits that her French source is not a literal rendition of the original dialogue, she maintains that it nevertheless follows Plautus so closely in plot and characterization that it suffices to serve as a basis for evaluating Shakespeare. Lennox then proceeds to provide a prosaic scene-by-scene summary of Shakespeare's play, an overview totally devoid of the many passages of poetic beauty found in *The Comedy of Errors*. Among the many faults that Lennox finds in Shakespeare is the utter uselessness of Egeon's character, stating that his sole function is to tell the audience of the strange events that caused him to arrive in Ephesus. She also does not appreciate the many differences in characterization between the two Antipholuses. However, above all other considerations and censure, Lennox appears to disregard the fact that *The Comedy of Errors* is based on an ancient farce. Consequently, her condemnation that the events in *The Comedy of Errors* are ludicrous and improbable, while in the *Menaechmi* all events stem from chance, seems to miss the point of Plautus's play, let alone that of Shakespeare's. Nevertheless, Lennox was not alone among eighteenth-century critics in her contention that Shakespeare was inferior to Plautus, as several commentators seriously doubted the bard's ability to read Latin.

Charles Knight's 1849 essay on *The Comedy of Errors*, included in this volume's selection of nineteenth-century criticism, offers a retrospective summary of this debate concerning whether or not Shakespeare knew enough Latin to read Plautus in the original or, alternatively, knew the play from secondhand sources: either William Warner's 1595 translation of *Menaechmi* (though Warner's manuscript may have been circulated before that year) or an earlier, though inferior, performance of a play similar to *The Comedy of Errors*, namely *The Historie of Error*, performed at Hampton Court on New Year's Day, 1567. Charles Knight takes great exception to these accusations and attributes much of the interest in denying Shakespeare sufficient fluency with Latin to the individual critics' vanity and need to elevate themselves above the esteemed playwright. Knight even offers evidence to refute their various unfounded arguments. Moreover, in rejecting these commentators' hypotheses, Knight expresses a deep appreciation for the ways in which Shakespeare enhanced and augmented Plautus's *Menaechmi*, citing such details as the heartbroken Egeon who elicits sympathy, a feature of *The Comedy of Errors* that distinguishes it from its classical source, for in the earlier play the father is deceased.

## 1753—Charlotte Lennox. "Observations on the Use Shakespear has made of the *Menaechmus* of Plautus, in his *Comedy of Errors*," from *Shakespear Illustrated*

Charlotte Ramsay Lennox (ca. 1730-1804) was a British author, poet, and dramatist, and her work received the acclaim of such leading literary figures as Samuel Johnson and Henry Fielding. She was also associated with Samuel Richardson and Joshua Reynolds. Lennox is the author of *The Female Quixote* (1752), *Poems on Several Occasions* (1747), *Henrietta* (1758), and *Philander: A Dramatic Pastoral* (1758).

*Shakespear's Comedy of Errors* has been generally allowed to be founded on the *Menaschmi* of *Plautus*. Mr. *Langbain*, in his Account of the Dramatic Poets, says that if it be not a just Translation of it, it is at least a Paraphrase, and in his Opinion far beyond a Translation, called *Menachmus*, Printed at *London*, 1593.

From this Translation of *Plautus's Menachmi, Shakespear* certainly borrowed his *Comedy of Errors*; but not being able to procure a Copy of it, and being wholly unacquainted with *the Latin* Tongue, I have turned Monsieur *Gueudiville's French* Translation of the *Meneechmi* into *English*, which although, as I am informed, it be not very literal as to the Dialogue, yet the Plot, the Incidents, and Characters, being exactly the same with the *Latin* Poet's, it will serve to shew how much of the Plot *Shakespear* has borrowed in his *Comedy of Errors*.

That we may be the better able to trace him in his Imitations, it will be necessary to examine the *Comedy of Errors* Scene by Scene, and take the Story a little higher than the Commencement of the Action of the Play.

The Cities of *Syracuse* and *Ephesus* being at War with each other, a Law was made in both, by which it was provided, that if *any Ephesian* Merchant was seen to traffic in *Syracuse*, or any *Syracusan* Merchant in *Ephesus*, his Goods should be confiscated, and himself condemned to Death.

An old Merchant of *Syracuse*, named *Ægeon*, landing at *Ephesus*, is apprehended upon this Law.

Here the Action of the Play begins, as *Ægeon* is leading to Prison, the Duke of *Ephesus* meeting him, demands the Cause of his having left his native Country, and coming to *Ephesus* ; *Ægeon* thereupon gives a long Account of himself and his Family, which, in order to understand well the following Incidents, I will transcribe.

> In *Syracuse* was I born, and wed
> Unto a Woman, happy but for me,
> And by me too, had not our Hap been bad:
> With her I liv'd in Joy, our Wealth increas'd,
> By prosperous Voyages I often made
> To *Epidamnum,* 'till my Factor's Death;

> And he great Store of Goods at random leaving,
> Drew me from kind Embracements of my Spouse;
> From whom my Absence was not six Months old,
> Before herself (almost at fainting under
> The pleasing Punishment that Women bear)
> Had made Provision for her following me,
> And soon and safe arrived where I was.

> There she had not been long but she became,
> A joyful Mother of two goodly Sons;
> And, which was strange, the one so like the other,
> As could not be distinguish'd but by Names.

> That very Hour, and in the self-same Inn,
> A poor mean Woman was deliver'd
> Of such a Burthen, Male-Twins both alike:
> Those (for their Parents were exceeding poor)
> I bought, and brought up to attend my Sons.

> My Wife, not meanly proud of two such Boys,
> Made daily Motions for our home Return:
> Unwilling I agreed, alas! too soon!
> We came aboard.

> A League from *Epidamnum* had we fail'd,
> Before the always-Wind-obeying Deep,
> Gave any tragic Instance of our Harm;
> But longer did we not retain much Hope:
> For what obscured Light the Heavens did grant,
> Did but convey unto our fearful Minds,
> A doubtful Warrant of immediate Death;

Which though myself would gladly have embrac'd,
Yet the incessant Weeping of my Wife,
Weeping before for what she saw must come,
And piteous Plainings of the pretty Babes
That mourn'd for Fashion, ignorant what to fear,
Forc'd me to seek Delays for them and me:
And this it was (for other Means were none)
The Sailors fought for Safety by our Boat,
And left the Ship then sinking-ripe to us;
My Wife, more careful for the elder born,
Had fasten'd him unto a small spare Mast,
Such as Sea-faring Men provide for Storms;
To him one of the other Twins was bound,
Whilst I had been like heedful of the other.

    The Children thus dispos'd, my Wife and I
Fixing our Eyes on whom our Care was fixt,
Fasten'd ourselves at the End of either Mast,
And floating streight, obedient to the Stream,
Were carry'd towards *Corinth*, as we thought.

    At length the Sun gazing upon the Earth,
Disperst those Vapours that offended us;
And by the Benefit of his wish'd Light,
The Seas wax'd calm, and we discover'd
Two Ships from far making amain to us;
Of *Corinth* that, of *Epidauris* this;

    But ere they came—Oh! let me say no more;
Gather the Sequel by what went before.

    Duke.
Nay, forward, old Man, do not break off so,
For we may pity, tho' not pardon thee.

    Ægeon.
    Oh! had the Gods done so, I had not now
Worthily term'd them merciless to us;
For ere the Ships could meet by twice five Leagues,
We were encounter'd by a mighty Rock;
Which being violently borne upon,
Our helpless Ship was splitted in the midst:

So that in this unjust Divorce of us,
Fortune had left to both of us alike
What to delight in, what to sorrow for.

Her Part, poor Soul! seeming as burden'd
With lesser Weight, but not with lesser Woe,
Was carry'd with more Speed before the Wind,
And in Our Sight they three were taken up.
By Fishermen of *Corinth*, as we thought.

At length the other Ship had seiz'd on us,
And knowing whom it was their Hap to save,
Gave helpful Welcome to their shipwreck'd Guests,
And would have reft the Fishers of their Prey,
Had not their Bark been very flow of Sail;
And therefore homeward did they bend their Course.

Thus have you heard me sever'd from my Bliss.
Thus by Misfortunes was my Life prolong'd,
To tell sad Stories of my own Mishaps.

Duke.
And for the Sakes of them thou sorrow'st for,
Do me the Favour to dilate at full
What hath befall'n of them and thee till now.

Ægeon.
My youngest Boy, and yet my eldest Care,
At eighteen Years became inquisitive
After his Brother, and importun'd me
That his Attendant, (for his Case was like,
Reft of his Brother, but retain'd his Name,)
Might bear him Company in quest of him:
Whom whilst I labour'd for a Love to see,
I hazarded the Loss of whom I lov'd.

Five Summers have I spent in farthest *Greece*,
Roaming clean through the Bounds of *Asia*,
And coasting homeward, came to *Ephesus:*
Hapless to find, yet loth to leave unsought,
Or that, or any Place that harbours Men.

But here must end the Story of my Life;
And happy were I in my timely Death,
Could all my Travels warrant me they live.

Here ends the first Scene; the Appearance *of Ægeon* is of no other Use than to tell the Spectators several Circumstances antecedent to the Action of the Play, which it is necessary they should be acquainted with; this *Plautus* does in his Prologue.

The Story, though borrowed from *Plautus*, is yet very different; the Circumstance of two Brothers being so extremely like each other, that it was impossible to distinguish them, is highly improbable in the *Latin* Poet.

*Shakespear* however doubles the Miracle and preients us with two Pair of Twins instead of one, with the same wonderful Resemblance.

*Plautus* accounts very naturally for the Brothers having both the same Name; the Grandfather upon the Loss of the eldest, whom he loved best, to preserve the Remembrance of him, gives his Name to the youngest.

*Shakespear*, without assigning any Reason for it, makes the Twin Sons of *Ægeon* be both called *Antipholis*, and the Twin Brothers, their Slaves, both *Dromio*.

The Separation of the Husband and Wife, and their Children, from whence all the diverting Mistakes in the *Comedy of Errors* arise, is brought about without the least Regard to Probability.

*Ægeon* sails from *Syracuse* to *Epidamnum*, to settle his Affairs there, which were left in Confusion by the Death of his Factor, and his Wife, though near the Time of her Lying-in, follows him, for no Reason indeed but to be delivered at an Inn, where a poor Woman, who like her, having born two Male Twins, she may buy them for Slaves to her own Sons; and that returning to *Syracuse* they may be shipwrecked, and separated from each other.

When the Storm arises the Merchant and his Wife, who, as it shou'd seem, have a view to the diverting Perplexities which are to follow, fasten one *Antipholis*, and one *Dromio* together, so when the Ship splits they are very conveniently separated. Had they, like other fond Parents, been more sollicitous for the Preservation of their own Offspring than their little Slaves, and used their joint Endeavours for that Purpose only, the Father and Mother, and their Twin Sons, might have been taken up together by *the Corinthian* Vessel, but thus equally dividing their Affection between their Children and their Slaves, and that excellent Contrivance of fastening a Twin of each Sort together, occasioned their falling into different Hands, and gave to each *Antipholis* his *Dromio*, for the future Business of the Play.

The Mother and the elder *Antipholis* being separated, he and his little Slave *Dromio* are carried to *Ephesus* where in Process of Time he is married to a rich Lady, and settles there: Here the younger *Antipholis* comes to seek for his Brother, and his Father afterwards for him; the old Man is immediately seized, and condemned to die, as has been mentioned, but the Duke respites him for the Space of one Day, in order to try if he can raise the Sum of one Thousand Marks to buy his Life.

In the second Scene *Antipholis* of *Syracuse* makes his Appearance with the Merchant of the City, who informing him of what had happened to the *Syracusan* Merchant, advises him to give out that he came from *Epidamnun*.

*Antipholis* of *Syracuse* sends his Man, *Dromio*, with a Thousand Marks to lay up safe at his Inn, and being left to himself, declares the Cause of his wandering about the World to be the Hopes of finding his Mother and Brother, whose Loss he deplores. While he is standing in the Street, *Dramio* of *Ephesus* comes up to him, and taking him for his Master, tells him his Dinner is ready, and that his Wife waits for him.

*Antipholis*, deceived by the Resemblance, supposes this *Dromio* to be his Slave, reproves him for his ill timed Jests, and asks him where he had left his Money. *Dromio* talks of Sixpence he had given him two or three Days ago.

*Antipholis* asks for his Thousand Marks. *Dromio* tells him of his Dinner, his House, his Wife, and presses him to come home. *Antipholis* at last, in a Fury, strikes him, *Dromio* runs off, and *Antipholis*, full of Uneasiness about his Money, returns to his Inn to look after it.

In the second Act the Scene is the House of *Antipholis* of *Ephesus*, his Wife complains to her Sister of her Husband's long Stay, and wonders why the Slave she sent for him is not returned. *Dromio* then enters, and humorously repeats what had past between his supposed Master and him, declaring that he believes him to be mad, the Wife frets, and orders him to go back again and fetch him.

The Scene changes again to the Street, *Antipholis* of *Syracuse* enters, and informs the Audience that his Money is safe, and adds,

"By Computation, and mine Host's Report
I cou'd not speak with *Dromio* since at first
I sent him from the Mart."

Yet notwithstanding this Reflexion, the Moment his own Slave, *Dromio* of *Syracuse* appears, he reproaches him with his having denied receiving his Gold, and with talking to him about his Wife, and a Dinner; and though the poor Fellow assures him that he never spoke such Words to him, and had not seen him since he sent him to the Inn till now, yet *Antipholis* falls into a Rage, and beats him.

A Dialogue of Puns and Quibbles ensues between the Master and Man, which is interrupted *by* the Entrance of *Adriana*, the Wife of *Antipholis* of *Ephesus*, and her Sister.

*Adriana*, taking this *Antipholis*, and this *Dromio*, for her Husband and his Slave, reproaches him with his Neglect of her, and intreats him to come home to dinner.

*Antipholis* protests he does not know her, and that he is but just arrived at *Ephesus*; the Sister chides him, and tells him his Wife had sent for him home to Dinner by *Dromio*. *Dromio* is surprised, and denies it. *Antipholis* who had had that Message delivered to him by the other *Dromio*, storms at the Slave for lying, the Fellow assures him he had never seen her. *Antipholis* asks how she could be acquainted with their Names if he had not seen her before, and informed her of them. *Adriana*, vexed at this Jesting, as she thinks it, intreats *Antipholis* to go home with her, and charges *Dromio* to keep the Gate for that Day, and let no one in to interrupt them.

*Antipholis*, though amazed to the last Degree at all this, resolves at last to

"Say as they say, and persevere so,
And in this Mist at all Adventures go."

In the third Act, the Scene is the Street before the House of *Antipholis* of *Ephesus*. *Antipholis* of *Ephesus*, and his Slave *Dromio*, with a Merchant and a Goldsmith, whom *Antipholis* has invited to dine at his House enter.

*Antipholis*, fearing lest his Wife should be angry at his long Stay, desires the Jeweller to excuse it, by saying that he lingered at his House seeing the making of her Bracelet, and chides his Man for having dared to tell him he miet him on the Mart, and charged him with a Thousand Marks in Gold, and with having denied his Wife and House. He then knocks at his Door, but is refused Entrance.

*Adriana*, who supposes her Husband Is dining with her above, is surprised at the Fellow below, who calls her Wife, and insists upon Admittance, and renews her Orders to *Dromio* of *Syracuse* to keep the Door shut.

A smart Dialogue follows between the two *Dromios*, the one within Doors and the other without; the Husband and his Guests not being suffered to enter, he resolves to go and dine with a Courtezan at the *Porcupine*, and desires the Jeweller to bring the Gold Chain, thither to him, that as he says, he may, to spight his Wife, bestow it upon the Courtezan, and accordingly they all go off.

In the next Scene *Antipholis* of *Syracuse* makes Love to *Luciana*, Sister to *Adriana*, she upbraids him with his Falshood to his Wife; he swears he is not married to her Sister, and that he cannot be happy without her. *Luciana* threatens to acquaint his Wife with his Treachery, and leaves him.

His Slave, *Dromio*, then enter, and *Antipholis*, from the strange Accidents that had happened both to himself and his Slave, believing the Place inhabited by Witches, resolves to be gone immediately, and orders *Dromio* to go to the

Harbour, and bring him Intelligence if any Bark was to sail that Night, telling him he will walk in the Mart till his Return.

*Dromio* goes away to perform his Commission; and the same Moment the Jeweller, *Angelo*, enters with the Chain, and gives it to *Antipholis* of *Syracuse*, whom he takes for the other.

*Antipholis* denies that he had ever ordered such a Chain to be made, but the Jeweller insisting that he had, and telling him that he will call in the Evening at his House for the Money: *Antipholis* offers to pay him immediately, lest, as he says, he should never see the Chain or Money more, which the Jeweller refusing, and leaving him, *Antipholis* goes to the Mart to wait for *Dromio*, which ends the third Act.

In the fourth Act a Merchant, to whom the Goldsmith, *Angelo*, owes a Sum of Money, demands instant Payment, or threatens to arrest him by an Officer, whom he has with him. *Angelo* tells him *Antipholis* owed him just as much Money as he was indebted to him for a Gold Chain, which he had delivered to him a Moment ago, and desired him to go with him to his House to receive the Money for it.

*Antipholis of Ephesus*, and his Slave, *Dromio*, enter, as from the House of the Courtezan, where they had dined. *Antipholis* orders *Dromio* to go and buy a Rope's-end, that he may chastise his Wife, he says, for locking him out of Doors, and that in the mean Time he will go to the Goldsmith; but seeing him, he reproaches him with not bringing the Chain as he had promised.

*Angelo* desires him to pay the Money for the Chain to the Merchant there present, to whom he owes as much. *Antipholis* replies, that he has not so much Money about him, but bids the Jeweller take the Gentleman and Chain to his House, and his Wife would pay for it. *Angelo* says he gave him the Chain, and presses him to pay for it. *Antipholis* denies it. The Merchant, weary of this Altercation, arrests the Jeweller, and he arrests *Antipholis*.

*Dromio* of *Syracuse* then enters, and taking *Antipholis* of *Ephesus* for his Master, tells him that a Ship is ready to sail, and that he had carried their Baggage on board as he commanded him. *Antipholis* calls him a Madman, and asks him for the Rope's-end, which he had sent him to buy: *Dromio* tells him he sent him to the Bay to see if any Bark was ready to sail, not for a Rope.

*Antipholis*, in a Passion, threatens him with future Punishment, and then orders him to go to *Adriana*, tell her he was arrested in the Street, and give her the Key of his Desk, and bid her send the Purse of Ducats that was in it to him. *Dromio* remembers that *Adriana* is the Lady with whom they had dined, and accordingly he goes thither, tells her what had happened, and she dispatches him away with the Gold.

The Scene then changes to the Street, *Antipholis* of *Syracuse* enters alone, and a Moment after *Dromio* of *Syracuse* meets him, and gives him the Purse. *Antipholis*, full of Wonder, questions his Man about it, and he talking enigmatically of

Arrests and Durance, *Antipholis* thinks him distracted, and prays earnestly to be delivered out of that City.

The Courtezan then enters, and seeing the Gold Chain about *Antipholis's* Neck, whom she takes for *Antipholis* of *Ephesus*, who had dined with her, she requires him to perform his Promise, and give her the Chain instead of the Diamond Ring he had taken from her. *Antipholis* flies from her, and *Dromio* follows.

The Courtezan, from this strange Behaviour, concluding him mad, resolves to go to his House, and tell *Adriana* that he had forcibly taken her Ring from her, hoping to recover it again by this Means. She goes out, and *Antipholis* of *Ephesus* enters with the Jaylor, whom he had desired to accompany him to his own House for Money to release him. As they are going thither *Dromio* of *Ephesus* returns with the Rope he had been sent to buy; his Master asks him for the Money he went to fetch from *Adriana*. *Dromio* protests he had been sent not for Money, but for a Rope's-end. *Antipholis*, violently enraged, beats him, and whilst he is thus employed, his Wife, whom the Courtezan had alarmed with an Account of his being mad, enters with one *Pinch*, a Conjurer, whom she employed to cure her Husband of his Frenzy.

*Antipholis* growing furious at this Treatment, his Wife calls for People to bind him, the Jaylor opposes it, he being his Prisoner, but upon *Adriana's* promising to pay him, he suffers *Antipholis* to be carried off: And as *Adriana* is going out with the rest, *Antipholis* and *Dromio of Syracuse* enter with their Swords drawn, and they supposing him to be the *Antipholis* who they had just before sent away bound, crying out for Help, and *Antipholis* and *Dromio* again set out for the port.

In the fifth Act the Scene is a Street before a Priory, the Jeweller, and Merchant who arrested him appear, and while they are discoursing about *Antipholis's* denying that he received the Chain, *Antipholis* and *Dromio* of *Syracuse* enter. *Angela*, seeing him with the Chain about his Neck, reproaches him with having denied the Receipt of it, and refusing to pay for it. *Antipholis* protests he neither denied the one or the other; the Merchant hereupon taxes him with Falsehood. *Antipholis* draws his Sword, and as the Merchant and he are fighting, *Adriana* enters, cries out that he is mad, and orders some People she had brought with her to bind both him and *Dromio*, and carry them home. *Antipholis* and *Dromio* to avoid this, take Shelter in the Monastery, and immediately the Lady Abbess appears, and demands the Cause of the others thronging thither.

*Adriana* tells her that her Husband, who ran into her House, is mad, and that she wants to have him fetched from thence, and carried home. The Abbess, after cunningly questioning her concerning her Behaviour to her Husband, and taking Advantage of her Answers, to prove that she had occasioned his Disorders, declares that she will not let him depart, but undertake the Cure herself.

The Duke that Moment, who is attending the Execution of old *Ægeon*, enters, and *Adriana*, throwing herself at his Feet, demands Justice against the Abbess, whom she accuses of keeping her Husband from her, and recounts all the mad

Actions he had been guilty of that Day. The Duke sends to bid the Lady Abbess come out and answer to this Accusation, and in the mean Time a Servant of *Adriana's* enters, and tells her that his Master and *Dromio*, who had been left bound at home, had broken loose, and committed the most terrible Outrages on the Doctor and Servants at home. *Adriana*, who had seen him, as she thought, go into the Priory a few Minutes before, insists upon it that this Report is false, when immediately *Antipholis* and *Dromio* of *Ephesus* enter.

*Antipholis* complains to the Duke of his Wife's having locked him out of Doors; she declares that he had dined with her that Day; *Antipholis* goes on to relate all that had happened to him. The Jeweller, the Merchant, the Courtezan, his Wife, and her Sister, having been all deceived by the Resemblance of the two *Antipholis's*, charge the one they are speaking to with all that had passed between them and the other; this occasions a great deal of Confusion and Perplexity. Old *Ægeon* on seeing *Antipholis* of *Ephesus*, and taking him for his Son *Antipholis*, whom he had parted from seven Years before in the Port of *Syracuse*, tells the Duke that he has now found a Friend who will pay his Fine, and save his Life, and accordingly goes up to him, and naming him, asks him if he does not know his Father.

*Antipholis* protests he never saw him before; the old Man reminds him that it is seven Years since they parted at *Syracuse*, and deplores his own Misery in having been so soon forgotten by his own Son. *Antipholis* tells him he never saw his Father in his Life, nor was ever in *Syracuse*, which the Duke confirmed.

In the midst of this new Perplexity the Abbess enters with *Antipholis* and *Dromio* of *Syracuse*, all stand amazed at the exact Likeness of the two Gentlemen, and their Slaves; the Abbess spying *Ægeon*, owns herself to be *Emilia*, his Wife, the Mother of those two *Antipholis's*, and informs him that she and the *Antipholis*, with the Twin *Dromio*, were taken out of the Sea by Men of *Epidamnum*, but that some Fishermen of *Corinth* took away her Son and *Dromio*, and left her with the *Epidamniens*, that what became of them afterwards she never knew, but that herself arrived to the Fortune of being Abbess of that Priory.

The two *Antipholis's* being now discovered, all the Mistakes which arose from their Resemblance are cleared up, *Ægeon* has his Life given him by the Duke, and they all go into the Priory to discourse more at large upon their several Fortunes.

The Unity of Time is exactly observed in the *Comedy of Errors*; the Incidents of this Play take up the Space of one Day like those of the *Menaechmi*; but the Action which in the last is single, and the most simple that can possibly be, is by *Shakespear* multiplied into several, some of which are far from being either probable or necessary. He has taken all the Characters in the *Menaechmi*, except *Peniculut* the Parasite, and the old Man, Father-in-law to *Menaechmus* of *Epidamnum*, and has added several others; every one of the Incidents he has likewise made Use of, but varied and added Circumstances so freely, that his Play seems to be rather an Imitation, than, as *Langbain* calls it, a Translation or Paraphrase of the *Menaechmi*.

The Addition of the two *Dromio's* increases the Business of the Play, but renders the Object still more improbable, which is sufficiently so in the *Menachmi*, where but half the Degree of Credulity is necessary to make it be relished.

The Mistakes which arise from the Resemblance of the Twins, are conducted with much less Art by *Shakespear* than *Plautus*.

In the *Latin* Poet all appears the Effects of Chance, in *Shakespear* of Design; the Persons in his Drama are hardly ever introduced with Propriety; they appear on the Stage, and go off again, evidently for no other Purpose than to give Occasion for the Blunders which ensue.

Thus *Antipholis* of *Syracuse* being resolved to leave *Ephesus*, sends *Dromio* to the Port to see if any Vessel is ready to sail, and bids him come to him to the Mart, where he will wait his Return, accordingly they separate, and it may now be reasonably supposed that *Antipholis* is gone thither, but instead of that we find him a Scene or two afterwards standing in the same Place, where he is met either by the Wife, the Friends, or the Servants of the other *Antipholis*; and after having with great Difficulty disengaged himself from abundance of perplexing Adventures, again he declares he is going to the Mart, and goes off for that Purpose, and again he is found in the same Place to give Rise to new ones.

In this Manner the whole Business of the *Comedy of Errors* is conducted. Those Errors do not as in the Play, which *Shakespear* borrowed from, arise out of a natural and probable Succession of Incidents, but every Thing is put out of its Course to introduce them, and each Error is produced by an Absurdity.

---

## 1773—Samuel Johnson and George Steevens. "Annotations Upon the *Comedy of Errors*," from *Annotations by Sam. Johnson & Geo. Steevens, and the Various Commentators upon the Comedy of Errors*"

Samuel Johnson (1709–84), often referred to simply as Dr. Johnson, was one of England's greatest literary figures: a poet, essayist, biographer, lexicographer, and often considered the finest critic of English literature. A prolific writer, his works include *The Vanity of Human Wishes* (1749), *Rasselas* (1759), *Lives of the Poets* (1779–81), and a journal, *The Rambler* (published from 1750 to 1752).

George Steevens (1736–1800) was a Shakespearean editor and commentator. An accomplished scholar working in collaboration with Samuel Johnson, together they produced a 10-volume edition of *The Plays of William Shakespeare*. Along with Edward Malone, Steevens is the editor of *Historical Account of the Rise and Progress of the English Stage, and of the Economy and Usages of the Ancient Theatres in England* (1800) and *Twenty of the Plays of Shakespeare, Being the Whole Number Printed in Quarto During His Life-Time* (1766).

---

# Act I.

*Page 4. Scene Ephesus.*] In the old copy, these brothers are occasionally styled Antipholus *Erotes*, or *Errotis*; and Antipholus *Sereptus*; meaning, perhaps, *erraticus* and *surreptus*. One of these twins *wandered* in search of his brother, who had been *forced* from Aemilia by fishermen of Corinth. The following acrostick is the argument to the Menaechmi of Plautus: Delph. Edit. p. 654.

> Mercator Siculus, cui erant gemini filii,
> Ei, surrepto altero, mors obtigit.
> Nomen surreptitii illi indit qui domi est
> Avus paternus, facit Mensechmum Sosiclem.
> Et is germanum, postquam adolevit, quaeritat
> Circum omnes oras. Post Epidamnum devenit:
> Hic fuerat auctus ille surreptitius.
> Meneechmum civem credunt omnes advenam :
> Eumque appellant, meretrix, uxor, et socer.
> Ii se cognoscunt fratres postremo invicem.

The translator, W. W. calls the brothers, Mensechmus *Sosicles*, and Mensechmus *the traveller*. Whencesoever Shakspeare adopted *erraticus* and *surreptus*, (which either he or his editors have mis-spelt,) these distinctions were soon dropped, and throughout the rest of the entries the twins are styled of Syracuse or Ephesus.

See this translation of the *Menaechmi*, among *six old Plays on which Shakspere founded*, &c. published by S. Leacroft, Charing-Cross.

At Stationers-Hall, Nov. 15, 1613: "A booke called *Two Twinnes*," was entered by Geo. Norton. Such a play indeed, by W. Rider, was published in 4to. 1655. And Langbaine suspefts it to be much older than the date annexed: otherwise the *Twins* might have been regarded as Shakspere's *Comedy of Errors*, under another title. STEEVENS.

*Page 5. Comedy of Errors.]* I suspect this and all other plays where much rhyme is used, and especially long hobbling verses, to have been among Shakspere's more early productions. BLACKSTONE.

A play with this title was exhibited at Gray's-Inn, in December 1594 ; but it was probably a translation from Plautus.—"After such sports, a *Comedy of Errors (like* to Plautus his *Menechmus)* was played by the players: so that night was begun, and continued to the end in nothing but confusion and errors. Whereupon it was ever afterwards called *The Night of Errors.*" *Gesta Grayorum,* 1688. The Registers of Gray's-Inn have been examined, for the purpose of ascertaining whether the play above mentioned was our author's;—but they afforded no information on the subject. MALONE.

*Line 34. Was wrought by nature, not by vile offence.*] All his hearers understood that the punishment he was about to undergo was in consequence of no private crime, but of the publick enmity between two states, to one of which he belonged: but it was a general superstition amongst the ancients, that every great and sudden misfortune was the vengeance of heaven pursuing men for their secret offences. Hence the sentiment put into the mouth of the speaker was proper. By my past life (says he), which I am going to relate, the world may understand, that my present death is according to the ordinary course of Providence [*wrought by nature*] and not the effects of divine vengeance overtaking me for my crimes [*not by vile offence.*] WARBURTON.

> 132. *Roaming* clean *through the bounds of Asia.*] In the northern parts of England this word is still used instead of *quite, fully, perfectly, completely.* So, in *Julius Caesar:*
> "*Clean* from the purpose of the things themselves." STEEVENS.
> 157. *wend,*] i, e. go. See catch-word Alphabet.
> 222. *I shall be* post *indeed,*
> *For she will score your fault upon my pate.*]

Perhaps before writing was a general accomplishment, a kind of rough reckoning concerning wares issued out of a shop, was kept by chalk on a *post,* till it could be entered on the books of a trader. So, *Kitely,* the merchant, making his jealous inquiries concerning the familiarities used to his wife, *Cob* answers:

> "if I saw any body to be kiss'd, unless they would have kiss'd the *post* in the middle of the warehouse," &c. STEEVENS.
> 224. *Methinks your maw, like mine, should be your* clock.] The only authentick ancient copy of this play reads *"your cook."* Mr. Pope, I believe, made the change. MALONE.
> 237. *that merry* sconce *of yours,"*] *Sconce* is *head.* So in *Hamlet,* act v. "why does he suffer this rude knave now to knock him about the *sconce?*" STEEVENS.
> 234. *o'er-raught*—] That is *over-reached.* JOHNSON.
> So in *Hamlet:*
> "certain players
> We *o'er-raught* on the way." STEEVENS.
> 255. *They say, this town is full of cozenage* ;] This was the character the ancients gave of it. WARBURTON.

257. Dark-working *sorcerers, that change the mind*, Soul-killing *witches, that deform the body*;] Perhaps haps the epithets have been misplaced, and the lines should be read thus:
*Soul-killing sorcerers, that change the mind,*
Dark-working *witches, that deform the body*;]
By *soul-killing* I understand destroying the rational faculties by such means as make men fancy themselves beasts. JOHNSON.
Witches or sorcerers themselves, as well as those who employed them, were supposed to forfeit their souls by making use of a forbidden agency. In that sense they may be said to destroy the souls of others as well as their own. STEEVENS.
260.—*liberties of sin* :] Sir T. Hanmer reads, *libertines*; which, as the author has been enumerating not acts but persons, seems right. JOHNSON.

## ACT II.

*Line* 14. ADR. *There's none but asses will be bridled so.*
Luc. *Why head-strong liberty is* lash'd *with woe.*"]
Should it not rather be *leash'd, i. e.* coupled, like a head-strong hound?

The high opinion I must necessarily entertain of the learned Lady's judgment, who furnished this observation, has taught me to be diffident of my own, which I am now to offer.
The meaning of this passage may be, that those who refuse the *bridle* must bear the *lash*; and that woe is the punishment of head-strong liberty. It may be observed, however, that the seamen still use *lash* in the same sense as *least*; as does Greene in his *Mamillia*, 1593: " Thou didst counsel me to beware of love, and I was before in the *lash*." Again, in George Whetstone's *Castle of Delight*, 1576: "Yet both in *lashe* at length this Cressid leaves." *Lace* was the old English word for a *cord*, from which verbs have been derived very differently modelled by the chances of pronunciation. So, in *Promos and Cassandra*, 1578:
"To thee, Cassandra, which dost hold my freedom in a *lace*."
When the mariner, however, *lashes* his guns, the sportsman *leashes* his dogs, the female *laces* her clothes, they all perform one act of fastening with a *lace* or *cord*. Of the same original is the word *windlass*, or more properly *windlace*, an engine, by which a *lace* or *cord* is wound upon a barrel.

To *lace* likewise signified to bestow correction with a cord, or rope's end. So in the Second Part of *Decker's Honest Whore*, 1630:
"the lazy lowne
"Gets here hard hands, or *lac'd* correction."
Again, in *The Two angry Women of Abingdon*, 1599:

"So, now my back has room to reach; I do not love to be *laced* in, when I go to *lace* a rascal." STEEVENS.

30. *start some other* where?] I cannot but think, that our author wrote: *start some other* hare?

So, in *Much Ado about Nothing*, Cupid is said to he *a good hare-finder*. JOHNSON.

I suspect that *where* has here the power of a *noun*. So, in *Lear:*
"Thou losest *here* a better *where* to find."

Again, in Tho. Drant's translation of Horace's Satires, 1567:
"they ranged in eatche *where*,
"No spousailes knowne," &c.

The sense is, *How, if your husband fly off in pursuit of some other woman?* The expression is used again, sc. 3. "his eye doth homage *otherwhere*." STEEVENS.

32. *though she pause;*] To *pause* is to rest, to be in quiet. JOHNSON.

41.—*fool'd-begg'd*—] She seems to mean, by *fool'd-begg'd patience*, that *patience* which is so near to *idiotical simplicity*, that your next relation would take advantage from it to represent you as a *fool*, and *beg* the guardianship of your fortune. JOHNSON.

54. *that I could scarce* understand *them.*] i. e. that I could scarce *stand under* them. This quibble, poor as it is, seems to have been the favourite of Shakspere, It has been already introduced in the *Two Gentlemen of Verona*, "my staff *understands* me." STEEVENS.

83. *Am I so round with you, as you with me.*] He plays upon the word *round*, which signified *spherical* applied to himself, and *unrestrained, or free in speech or action*, spoken of his mistress. So the king, in *Hamlet*, bids the queen be *round* with her son. JOHNSON.

86. *case me in leather,*] Still alluding to a football, the bladder of which is always covered with leather. STEEVENS.

99. *Of my* defeatures.] By *defeatures* is here meant *alteration of features.* At the end of this play the same word is used with a somewhat different signification. STEEVENS.

99. *My decayed fair*] Shakspere uses the adjective *gilt*, as a substantive, for *what is gilt*, and in this instance *fair* for *fairness*. In the *Midsummer Night's Dream*, the old quartos read:
"Demetrius loves your *fair.*" STEEVENS.

*Fair* is frequently used *substantively* by the writers of Shakspere's time. So Marston in one of his satires:
"As the greene meads, whose native outward *faire*
"Breathes sweet perfumes into the neighbour air." FARMER.

101. *too unruly deer*, ] The ambiguity of *deer* and *dear* is borrowed, poor
as it is, by Waller, in his poem on life *Ladies Girdle:*
"This was my heav'n's extremest sphere,
"The pale that held my lovely *deer.*" JOHNSON.
Shakspere has played upon this word in the same manner in his *Venus
and Adonis:*
"Fondling, saith she, since I have hemm'd thee here,
"Within the circuit of this ivory *pale,*
"I'll be the park, and thou shall be my *deer,*
"Feed where thou wilt on mountain or on dale." The lines of Waller
seem to have been immediately copied from these. MALONE.

102. *poor I am but his stale,*] I believe my learned coadjutor mistakes the use
of the word *stale* on this occasion. "*Stale* to catch these thieves;" *Stale* here seems
to imply the same as *stalking-horse; pretence.* I am, says Adriana, but his *pretended
wife*, the mask under which he covers his amours. So, in *K. John* and *Matilda*, by
Robert Davenport, 1655, the queen says to Matilda:

"I am made your *stale,*
"The king, the king your strumpet," &c.

Again in the old translation of the *Menaechmi* of Plautus, 1595, from whence
Shakspere borrowed the expression:

"He makes me a *stale* and a laughing-stock." STEEVENS.
110. *I see, the jewel, best enamelled,*
*Will lose his beauty; and* the *gold 'bides still,* ] I would read:
*and* though *gold 'bides still, &c.*

and the rest, with Dr. Warburton. STEEVENS.

146. *And make a common of my serious hours.*] *i. e.* intrude on them when
you please. The allusion is to those tracts of ground destined to *common*
use, which are thence called *commons.* STEEVENS.
155. *and* insconce *it too,*] A *sconce* was a petty fortification.

So in *Orlando Furioso*, 1599:

"Let us to our *sconce,* and you my lord of Mexico." Again:
"Ay, sirs, *ensconce* you how you can." Again:
"And here *ensconce* myself despight of thee."

178. *Lest it make you. choleriek, &c.*] *So* in the *Taming of the Shrew:*
'I tell thee Kate, 'twas burnt and dry'd away,
"And I expressly am forbid to touch It,
"For it engenders *choler*, planteth anger," &c. STEEVENS.
200 . *Not a man of those, but he hath the wit to lose his hair.]* That is, *Those who have more hair than wit*, are easily entrapped by loose women, and suffer the consequences of lewdness; one of which, in the first appearance of the disease in Europe, was the loss of hair. JOHNSON.
So in the *Roaring Girl*, 1611:
"His *hair sheds off*, and yet he speaks not so much in the nose as he did before." STEEVENS.
210. *falsing.*] This word is now obsolete. Spenser and Chaucer Often use the verb to *foist*. STEEVENS.
231. *That never words were musick to thine ear.*] Imitated by Pope:
"My musick then you could for ever hear,
"*And all my words were musick to your ear.*"
*Epistle from Sapho to Phaon.* MALONE.
242. *may'st thou* fall] To *fall* is here a verb active. STEEVENS.
See catch-word Alphabet.
257. *I am possessed with an adulterate* blot;
*My blood is mingled with the* CRIME *of lust* :]

Both the integrity of the metaphor, and the word *blot*, in the preceding line, shew that we should read:

    *with the* GRIME *of lust:*
*i. e.* the *stain*, smut. So again in this play—*A man may go over shoes in the* GRIME *of it.* WARBURTON.
261. *Being* strumpeted] Shakspere is not singular in his use of this verb.
So in Heywood's *Iron Age*, 1632:
"By this adultress basely *strumpeted.*" Again:
"I have *strumpeted* no Agamemnon's queen." STEEVENS.
263. *I live* dis-stain'd, *thou undishonour'd.*] To *dis-tain* (from the French word, *destaindre*) signifies, to *stain, defile, pollute*. But the context requires a sense quite opposite. We must either read, *unstain'd*; or, by adding an *hyphen*, and giving the preposition *a privative* force, read *dis-stain'd*; and then it will mean, *unstain'd, undefil'd.* THEOBALD.
I would read :
*I live distained*, thou dishonoured.
That is, As long as thou continuest to dishonour thyself, I also live distained. REVISAL.

288. *you are from me* exempt,] *Exempt*, separated, parted. The sense is, *If I am doomed to suffer the wrong of separation, yet injure not with contempt me who am already injured.* JOHNSON.

291. *Thou art an elm, my husband, I a vine*;]
"Lenta qui velut assitas
"Vitis implicat arbores,
"Implicabitur in tuum
"Complexum." *Catull.*
So Milton, *Par. Lost.* B. v:
"They led the vine
"To wed her elm. She spous'd, about him twines
"Her marriageable arms." MALONE.

295. idle *moss.*] *i. e* moss that produces no fruit, but being unfertile is useless. So in *Othello:*
antres vast and desarts *idle.* STEEVENS.

303. *the* favour'd *fallacy.*] Thus the modern editors. The old copy reads:
*the* free'd *fallacy.*
Which perhaps was only, by mistake, for
*the* offer'd *fallacy.*
This conjecture is from an anonymous correspondent. STEEVENS.

307. *We talk with goblins,* owls, *and elvish sprights;* ] It was an old popular superstition, that the screechowl sucked out the breath and blood of infants in the cradle. On this account, the Italians called witches, who were supposed to be in like manner mischievously bent against children, *strega* from *strix*, the *screech-owl*. This superstition they had derived from their pagan ancestors, as appears from this passage of Ovid,
*Sunt avidae volucres, non quae Phinica mensis*
*Guttura fraudabant,* sed genus inde trahunt.
*Grande caput; stantes oculi; rostra apta rapina ;*
*Canities pcnnis, unguibus hamus inest.*
*Nocte molant,* PUEROSQUE PETUNT *nutricis egentes,*
*Et vitiant* CUNIS *corpora rapta suis.*
*Carpere dicuntur luflantia viscera rostris,*
*Et plenum* poto sanguine *guttur habent.*
*Est illis* strigibus *nomen :* Lib. vi. Fast.
WARBURTON.

*Ghastly owls* accompany *elvish ghosts*, in *Spenser's* Shepherd's *Calendar* for *June.* So in *Sherringham's* Discerptatio de Anglorum Gentis Origine, p. 333. "Lares, Lemures, *Stryges*, Lamias, *Manes* (Gastae dicti) et similes monstrorum Greges, Elvarum Chorea dicebatur." Much the same is said in *Olaus Magnus de Gentibus Septentrionalibus*, p. 112, 113. TOLLET.

*Owls* are also mentioned in *Cornu-Copice, or Pasquil's Night-Cap, or Antidote for the Headach*, 1623. p. 38:
"Dreading no dangers of the darkesome night,
"No *oules*, hobgoblins, ghosts, nor waterspright."
Again, in the *London Prodigal*, a comedy, 1605:
"Soul, I think I am sure cross'd or *witch'd* with an *owl*" MALONE.
The epithet *elvish* is not in the *first* folio, but is found in the *second*.
STEEVENS.
326. *And shrive you* ] That is, I will *call you to confession*, and make you tell your tricks. JOHNSON.
So in *Hamlet*: "not *shriving* time allow'd." STEEVENS.

## ACT III.

*Line* 4. *Carkanet*,] Seems to have been a necklace or rather chain, perhaps hanging down double from the neck. So Lovelace in his poem:

"*The empress spreads her* carcanets." JOHNSON.
"*Quarquan*, ornement d'or qu'on mil an col des damoiselles." *Le Grand Dict. de Nicot.*
A *Carkanet* seems to have been a necklace set with stones, or strung with pearls. Thus in *Partheneia Sacra*, &c. 1633: "Seeke not vermilion or ceruse in the face, bracelets of oriental pearls on the wrist, rubic *carkanets* on the neck, and a most exquisite fan of feathers in the hand."
STEEVENS.
16. *Marry, so it doth appear*
*By the wrongs I suffer, and the blows I bear* ] He first says, that his *wrongs* and *blows* prove him an *ass*; but immediately, with a correction of his former sentiment, such as may be hourly observed in conversation, he observes that, if he had been an *ass*, he should, when he was *kicked*, have *kicked* again. JOHNSON.
34. *Mome,* ] a dull, stupid blockhead, a stock, a post. This owes its original to the French word *Momon*, which signifies the gaming at dice in masquerade; the custom and rule of which is, that a strict silence is to be observed: whatever sum one stakes, another covers, but not a word is to be spoken: from hence also comes our word *mum!* for silence.
HAWKINS.
So in Heywood's *Rape of Lucrece*, 1630:
"Important are th' affairs we have in hand;
"Hence with that *Mome!*"
"—*Brutus*, forbear the presence." STEEVENS.
38. *patch!* ] *i. e.* fool. See catch-word Alphabet. STEEVENS.
44. I owe?] *i. e.* I *own*. STEEVENS.

58. I trow.] The old copy reads, *I hope.* STEEVENS.

74. *we shall part with neither.*] In our old language, *to part* signified *to have part.* See Chaucer, Cant. Tales, ver. 9504:

"That no wight with his blisse *parten* shall." The French use *partir* in the same sense. TYRWHITT.

79. *bought and sold.*] This is a proverbial phrase. "To be *bought and sold* in a company."

See Ray's Collection, p. 179. edit. 1737. STEEVENS.

89. *we'll pluck a crow together.*] We find the same quibble on a like occasion in one of the comedies of Plautus.

The children of distinction among the Greeks and Romans had usually birds of different kinds given them for their amusement. This custom Tyndarus in the *Captivu* mentions, and says, that for his part he had *tantum upupam.*

*Upupa* signifies both a *lapwing* and a *mattock,* or some instrument of the same kind, employed to dig stones from the quarries. STEEVENS.

96. Once this—*your long experience of her wisdom.*] *Once this,* may mean, *Once for all;* let me recommend *this* to your consideration. STEEVENS.

100. *the doors are* made *against you.*] To *make* the door, is the expression used to this day in some counties of England, instead of, *to bar the door.* STEEVENS.

108. *Supposed by the common rout*] *Supposed is founded on supposition,* made by conjecture. JOHNSON.

The second folio has *once;* which rather improves the sense, and is not inconsistent with the metre. TYRWHITT.

115. *And, in despight of* mirth,—] Though mirth hath withdrawn herself from me, and seems determined to avoid me, yet in despight of her, and whether she will or not, I am resolved to be merry. REVISAL.

131.—*that you have quite forgot*] In former copies:
*And nay it be, that you have quite forgot*
*An husband's office? Shall Antipholis,*
*Ev'n in the spring of love, thy love-springs rot?*
*Shall love* in buildings *grow so ruinate?*

This passage has hitherto labour'd under a double corruption. What conceit could our editors have of *love in buildings* growing ruinate? Our poet meant no more than this: Shall thy love-springs rot, even in the spring of love and shall thy love grow ruinous, even while 'tis but building up? The next corruption, is by an accident at press, as I take it; this scene for fifty-two lines successively is strictly in alternate rhimes; and this measure is never broken, but in the *second* and *fourth* lines of these two couplets. 'Tis certain, I think, a monosyllable dropt from the tail of the second verse: and I have ventured to supply it by, I hope, a probable conjecture. THEOBALD.

> *Love-springs* are young plants of love. Thus in the *Faithful Shepherdess* of
> Beaumont and Fletcher:
> "The nightingale among the thick-leav'd *springs*
> "That sits alone in sorrow." STEEVENS.

*Love-springs* I believe, are not the *young* plants *of love*, but the SHOOTS. Love is here considered by Luciana, as a root or stock in the heart of Antipholis, the first (or what is called the maiden) growth of which having been lopped off by marriage, a renovation of shoots springs forth. This sense of the metaphor is confirmed by the following passage from Evelyn:—"There are some who would have no stakes cut from the trees, save here and there one, so as to leave half the head naked, and the other standing; but the overhanging bows will kill what is under them, and ruin the tree; so pernicious is this halftopping : let this be a total amputation for a *new and lusty* SPRING." See Mr. Tollet's note on *Coriolanus*, act v. line 134.

The *thick-leaved* SPRINGS, in the passage from the *Faithful Shepherdess*, are the luxuriant young growth of the *coppice*, which are even the nightingale's favourite haunt. HENLEY.

*Shall* Love *in building grow so* ruinate?] So in our author's 119th Sonnet:

"And *ruin'd love*, when it is *built* anew.—"

In support of Theobald's emendation, a passage in our author's tenth Sonnet may be produced:

"thou art so possess'd with murderous *hate*,
"That 'gainst thyself thou stick'st not to conspire,
"Seeking that beauteous roof to *ruinate*,
     "Which to repair should be thy chief desire."
Again, in the *Rape of Lucrece:*
"To *ruinate* proud *buildings* with thy hours." MALONE.

151. *Alas, poor women! make us* not *believe*, &c.] From the whole tenour of the context it is evident, that this negative (*not*), got place in the first copies instead of *but*. And these two monosyllables have by mistake reciprocally dispossess'd one another in many other passages of our author's works. THEOBALD.

152. *Being compact of credit*, means, *being made altogether of credulity*. So in Heywood's *Iron Age*, Part II. 1633:

"she's *compact*
"Merely of blood" STEEVENS.

157. *vain,*] is *light of tongue, not veracious.* JOHNSON.

175. *sweet* mermaid,] *Mermaid* is only another name for *syren.* So in
the Index to P. Holland's translation of Pliny's *Nat. Hist.* "Mermaids in
Homer were witches, and their songs enchauntements." STEEVENS.

179.—*as a* bed *I'll take thee,*] The old copy reads—*as a* bud.
Mr. Edwards suspects a mistake of one letter in the passage, and would
read:
And as a bed I'll take *them,* and there lye.
Perhaps, however, both the ancient readings may be right:
As a *bud* I'll take *thee, &c.*
*i. e.* I, like an insect, will take thy bosom for a rose, or some other flower,
and,
"phoenix like, beneath thine eye
"Involv'd in fragrance, burn and die."
It is common for Shakspere to shift hastily from one image to another.
Mr. Edward's conjecture may, however, receive support from the
following passage in the *Two Gentlemen of Verona,* act i. sc 2:
"my bosom as a *bed*
"Shall lodge thee." STEEVENS.
The second folio has *bed.* TYRWHITT.

182. *if* she *sink!*] I know not to whom the pronoun *she* can be referred.
I have made no scruple to remove a letter from it. The author of the
REVISAL has the same observation. STEEVENS.

The author of the REMARKS, however, thinks there can be little doubt but
that the pronoun *she* must be referred to Love, that is Venus; and Mr. Reed, in
confirmation of this interpretation, cites the following lines from the old ballad
of *The Spanish Lady:*

"I will spend my days in prayer,
"*Love* and all HER laws defy."
184. *Not mad, but* mated,] *i. e.* confounded. So in *Macbeth:*
"*My mind she has* mated, *and amaz'd my sight*" STEEVENS.
187. *Gaze* where] The old copy reads, *when,* STEEVENS.
196. *My sole earth's heaven, and my heaven's claim.*] When he calls the
girls his *only heaven on the earth,* he utters the common cant of lovers.
When he calls her *his heaven's claim,* I cannot understand him. Perhaps
he means that which he asks of heaven. JOHNSON.
198. *for I mean thee:*] Thus the modern editors. The folio reads,
*for I am thee.*

Perhaps we should read:

*for I* aim *thee.*

He has just told her, that she was his *sweet hope's* aim.

So in *Orlando Furioso*, 1594:

"like Cassius,

"Sits sadly dumping, *aiming* Caesar's death."

Again, in Drayton's Legend of *Robert Duke of Normandy*:

"I make my changes *aim* one certain end." Steevens.

243. S. Ant. *What's her name?*

S. Dro. *Nell, sir; but her name is three quarters; that is, an ell and three quarters, &c.]*

This passage has hitherto lain as perplexed and unintelligible, as it is now easy and truly humourous. If a *conundrum* be restored, in setting it right, who can help it if I owe the correction to the sagacity of the ingenious Dr. Thirlby. Theobald.

This poor conundrum is borrowed by Massinger in *The Old Law*, 1653:

"*Cook.* That *Nell* was Hellen of Greece.

"*Clown.* As long as she tarried with her husband she was *Ellen*, but after she came to Troy she was *Nell* of Troy.

"*Cook.* Why did she grow shorter when she came to Troy?

"*Clown.* She grew longer, if you mark the story, when she grew to be an ell," &c. Malone.

257. S. Ant. *Where France?*

S. Dro. *In her forehead arm'd and reverted, making war against her* hair.]

Our author here sports with an allusion, in which he takes too much delight, and means that his mistress had the French disease. The ideas are rather too offensive to be dilated. By a forehead *armed*, he means covered with incrusted eruptions: by *reverted*, he means having the hair turning backward. Johnson.

271. *to be* ballasted] Thus the modern editors. The old copy reads only *ballast*, which may be right. Thus in *Hamlet:*

"to have the engineer

"*Hoits* with his own petar." i. e. *hoisted*. Steevens.

275.—*assured* to her;] *i. e.* affianced to her. Thus in *K. John:*

"For so I did when I was first *assur'd*." Steevens.

280. *And, I think, if my breast had not been made of* faith, *&c.* ] Alluding to the superstition of the common people, that nothing could resist a witch's power of transforming men into animals, but a great share *of faith:* however the Oxford editor thinks *a breast made of flint*, better security, and has therefore put it in. Warburton.

305. *at the Porpentine:*] It is remarkable, that throughout the old editions
of Shakspere's plays, the word *Porpentine* is used instead of *Porcupine*.
Perhaps it was so pronounced at that time.

I have since observed the same spelling in the plays of other ancient
authors. Mr. Tollet finds it likewise in p. 66. of Ascham's Works, by
Bennet, and in Stowe's Chronicle, in the years 1117. 1135. Steevens.

## ACT IV.

*Line* 4. *WANT* gilders] A *gilder* is a coin valued from one shilling and six-pence,
to two shillings.

Steevens.

8. *Is* growing *to me* ] *i.e.* accruing to me. Steevens.

95. *thou* peevish *sheep,*] *Peevish* is *silly.* So in *Cymbeline:*
"Desire my man's abode where I did leave him:
"He's strange and *peevish.*" Steevens.
See catch-word Alphabet.

112. *Where* Dowsabel—] This name occurs in one of Drayton's Pastorals:
"He had, as antique stories tell,
"A daughter cleaped *Dowsabel,*" &c. Steevens.

121. *meteors tilting in his face?*] Alluding to these meteors in the sky, which
have the appearance of lines of armies meeting in the shock. Warburton.

The allusion is more clearly explained by the following comparison in the
second book of *Paradise Lost:*

"As when to warn proud cities, war appears
"Wag'd in the troubled sky, and armies rush
"To battle in the clouds, before each van
"Prick forth the aery knights, and couch their spears
"Till thickest legions close; with feats of arms,
"From either end of heaven the welkin burns." Steevens.

136. *sere,*] That is, *dry,* withered. Johnson.

139. *Stigmatical in making,*——] That is, *marked* or *stigmatized* by nature
with deformity, as a token of his vicious disposition. Johnson.
So, in *The Wander of a Kingdom,* 1636:
"If you spy any man that hath a look,
"*Stigmatically* drawn, like to a fury's," &c. Steevens.

144. *Far from her nest the* lapwing, *&c.*] This expression seems to be proverbial.
I have met with it in many of the old comic writers. Greene, in his Second Part
of *Coney-Catching,* 1592, says: "But again to our priggers, who, as before I said,

*cry with the lapwing farthest from the nest*, and from their place of residence where
their most abode is." And several others.

See this passage yet more amply explained in a note on *Measure for Measure*,
act i. line 374. STEEVENS.

151. *an* everlasting *garment*] *Everlasting* was in the time of Shakspere, as well
as at present, the name of a kind of durable stuff. The quibble intended here, is
likewise met with in Beaumont and Fletcher's *Woman Hater:*

"I'll quit this transitory

"Trade, and get me an *everlasting* robe,

"Sear up my conscience, and turn *serjeant.*" STEEVENS.

153. A *fiend*, a fairy, pitiless and rough;] Dromio here bringing word in haste
that his master is arrested, describes the bailiff by names proper to raise horror
and detestation of such a creature, such as, a *devil*, a *fiend*, a *wolf*, &c. But how
does *fairy* come up to these terrible ideas? we should read, *a fiend, a fury &c.*
THEOBALD.

There were fairies like *hobgobblins*, pitiless and rough, and described as
malevolent and mischievous. JOHNSON.

155. *A back friend, a shoulder-clapper, &c. of alleys, creeks, and* narrow lands;] It
should be written, I think, *narrow lanes*, as he has the same expression, *Richard
II.* act v. scene 6.

"Even such they say as stand in narrow lanes." GREY.

*Narrow-LANDS* is certainly the true reading, as not only the rhime points
out, but the sense; for as a *creek* is a narrow-water, forming an inlet from the
main body into the neighbouring shore, so a narrow land is an outlet or tongue
of the shore that runs into the water.—Besides, *narrow* LANES and ALLEYS are
synonymous. HENLEY.

A shoulder-clapper is a bailiff:

"——fear none but these same shoulder-clappers." Decker's Satiromastix.
STEEVENS.

157. *A hound that runs counter, and yet draws dry-foot well;*] To run counter
is to run backward, by mistaking the course of the animal pursued; to draw
dry-foot is, I believe, to pursue by the track or prick of the foot; to run counter
and draw dry-foot well, are, therefore, inconsistent. The jest consists in the
ambiguity of the word *counter*, which means the *wrong way in the chase*, and a
*prison* in London. The officer that arrested him was a Serjeant of the *counter.*
For the congruity of this jest, with the scene of action, let our author answer.
JOHNSON.

Ben Jonson has the same expression; *Every Man in his Humour*, act ii. sc. 4.

"Well, the truth is, my old master intends to follow my young, *dry-foot* over
Moorfields to London this morning," &c.

To draw *dry-foot*, is when the dog pursues the game by the scent of the foot;
for which the blood-hound is fam'd. GREY.

158. *poor souls to hell.* ] *Hell* was the cant term for on obscure dungeon in any of our prisons. It is mentioned in the *Counter-Rat*, a poem, 1658:

"In Wood-Street's-Hole, or Poultry's *Hell*."

There was likewise a place of this name under the Exchequer-Chamber, where the king's debtors were confined till they had paid the uttermost farthing. STEEVENS.

160. *on the case.*] An action upon the case, is a general action given for the redress of a wrong done any man without force, and not especially provided for by law. GREY.

167. *was he arrested on a* band?] Thus the old copy, and I believe rightly; though the modern editors read *bond*. A bond, *i. e.* an obligatory writing to pay a sum of money, was anciently spelt *band*. A *band* is likewise a *neckcloth*. On this circumstance I believe the humour of the passage turns.

So, in *Histriomastix*, 1610:

"tye fast your lands

"In statute staple, or these merchants' *bands*." STEEVENS.

179. *If* time *be in debt,*] The old edition reads—If *I* be in debt. STEEVENS.

197.—*what have you got the picture old Adam new apparell'd?*] A short word or two must have slipt out here, by some accident in copying, or at press; otherwise I have no conception of the meaning of the passage. The case is this: Dromio's master had been arrested, and sent his servant home for money to redeem him: he, running back with the money, meets the twin Antipholis, whom he mistakes for his master, and seeing him clear of the officer before the money was come, he cries, in a surprise;

*What, have you got* rid *of the pidure of old Adam new apparell'd?*

For so I have ventured to supply, by conjecture. But why is the officer called old Adam new apparell'd? The allusion is to Adam in his state of innocence going naked; and immediately after the fall, being cloath'd in a frock of skins. Thus he was new apparell'd: and, in like manner, the Serjeants of the counter were formerly clad in buff, or calves-skin, as the author humorously a little lower calls it. THEOBALD.

The explanation is very good, but the text does not require to be amended. JOHNSON.

These jests on Adam's dress are common among our old writers. So in *King Edward* III. 1599: "The register of all varieties

"Since *leathern Adam* to this younger hour." STEEVENS.

210. *he that sets up his rest to do more exploits with his mace, than a* MORRIS-pike.] *Sets up his rest*, is a phrase taken from military exercise. When gun-powder was first invented, its force was very weak compared to that in present use. This necessarily acquired firearms to be of an extraordinary length. As the artists improved the strength of their powder, the soldiers proportionably shortened their arms and artillery; so that the cannon which Froissart tells us was once

fifty feet long, was contracted to less than ten. This proportion likewise held in their muskets; so that till the middle of the last century, the musketeers always supported their pieces when they gave fire, with a *rest* stuck before them into the ground, which they called *setting up their rest*, and is here alluded to. There is another quibbling allusion too to the serjeant's office of arresting. WARBURTON.

This conjecture is very ingenious, yet the commentator talks unnecessarily of the *rat of a musket*, by which he makes the hero of the speech set up the *rest of* a *musket*, to *do exploits* with a *pike*. The *rest* of a *pike* was a common term, and signified, I believe, the manner in which it was fixed to receive the rush of the enemy. JOHNSON.

Dr. Johnson's explanation of the *rest* of a *pike* is given without any clear idea of his subject; for how can a thing, which is represented by him as having a positive and distinct existence, be at the same time a mode only of some other thing, which depends for its efficacy upon it?—But, exclusive of this confusion, *if a pike* EVER HAD a *rest*, its primary use must have been to support the staff in *charging* an enemy, unless the weapon were merely defensive; and if the pike were only a weapon of defence, as described by the doctor, it would ill suit the purpose to which Shakspere has applied it:—"he that *sets up his* REST to do more exploits with his *mace*, than a *morris-pike*."

The phrase, *he that sets up his* REST, in this instance, signifies only, I believe *he that* TRUSTS—*is confident in his expectation*. Thus, Bacon:—"Sea-fights have been final to the war, but this is, when princes *set up tkeir* REST upon the battle." Again, Clarendon—" they therefore resolved to *set up their* REST upon that stake, and to go through with it, or perish." This figure of speech is certainly derived from *the* REST which Dr. Warburton has described, as that was the only kind of rest which was ever SET UP. The REST for *the* SPEAR was of quite another nature. Dr. Johnson, however, seems to have supposed that the *spear* was the same weapon with the *pike*; but they were very different, and though the *spear*, in tilting, was used with a *rest*, neither the *pike*, nor *mace* (on which Shakspere here quibbles) ever was. HENLEY.

212. A *morris-pike*.] This is mentioned by the old writers as a formidable weapon. "*Morespikes* (says Langley in his translation of *Polydore Virgil*) were used first in the siege of Capua." And in *Reynard's Deliverance of certain Christians from the Turks*, "the English mariners laid about them with brown bills, halberts, and *morrice-pikes*." FARMER.

*Polydore Virgil* does not mention *morris-pikes* at the siege of Capua, though Langley's translation of him advances their antiquity so high. TOLLET.

So in Heywood's *King Edward* IV. 1626 : "Of the French were beaten down "*morris-pikes* and bowmen," &c.

Again, in Holinshed, p. 816:

"they entered the gallies again with *morris-pikes*, and fought," &c. STEEVENS.

*Morris-pikes*, or the pikes of the Moors, were excellent formerly ; and since, the Spanish pikes have been equally famous. See Hartlib's Legacy, p. 48. TOLLET.

243.—*if you do expect spoon-meat*, or *bespeak a long spoon.*] *Or*, which modern editors have thrown out of the text, signifies, *befure.* Of this use of the word many instances occur in ancient writers. So in *Arden of Feversham*, 1592:

"He shall be murdered or the guests come in." See a note on *King John*, act iv. scene 3. STEEVENS.

The author of the REMARKS thinks the passage *erroneously* pointed, and says, that *or* is a mistake for *and.*

*Cour.* We'll mend our dinner here.

*S. Dro*, Master, if you do, expect spoon-meat, *and* bespeak a long spoon.

320. *a* school-master *called Pinch,*] Thus the old copy: in many country villages the pedagogue is still a reputed conjurer.

So, in Ben Jonson's *Staple of News:*

"I would have ne'er a cunning schoole-master in England: mean a cunning man as a schoole-master; that is a *conjurour*," &c. STEEVENS.

322. *Mistress*, respice finem, *respect your end; or rather the prophecy, like the parrot, Beware the rope's end.*] These words seem to allude to a famous pamphlet of that time, wrote by Buchannan against the lord of Liddington; which ends with these words, *Respice finem, respice funem.* But to what purpose, unless our author could shew that he could quibble as well in English, as the other in Latin, I confess I know not. As for *prophesying like the parrot*, this alludes to people's teaching that bird unlucky words; with which, when any passenger was offended, it was the standing joke of the wise owner to say, *Take heed, sir, my parrot prophesies.* To this Butler hints, where, speaking of Ralpho's skill in augury, he says:

"*Could tell what subtlest parrots mean*,
"*That speak and think contrary clean;*
"*What member 'tis of whom they talk*,
"*When they cry* rope, *and* walk, knave, walk!" WARBURTON.

So in Decker's *Satiromastix:*

"But come, *respice funem.*" STEEVENS.

356. *Certes,*] i. e. *certainly.* STEEVENS.

*Kitchen-vestal,*] Her charge being like that of the vestal virgins, to keep the fire burning. JOHNSON.

396.—*thou* peevish *officer?*] This is the second time that in the course of this play, *peevish* has been used for *foolish.* STEEVENS.

406. unhappy *strumpet!*] *Unhappy* is here used in one of the senses of *unlucky;* i. e. *mischievous.* STEEVENS.

## *ACT V.*

*Line* 64. *THE* copy] *i. e.* the theme. We still talk of setting *copies* for boys. STEEVENS.

81. *But moody and dull melancholy*, &c.] So in *King Henry* VI. Part I. "But rather *moody* mad." MALONE.

82. *Kinsman to grim and comfortless despair*,] Shakspere could never make melancholy a *male* in this line, and a *female* in the next. This was the foolish insertion of the first editors. I have therefore put it into hooks, as spurious. WARBURTON.

The defective metre of the second line, is a plain proof that some dissyllable hath been dropped there. I think it therefore probable our poet may have written:

*Sweet recreation barred, what doth ensue,*
*But moodie* [moping] *and dull melancholy,*
*Kinsman to grim and comfortless despair?*
*And, at their heels, a huge infectious troop.* REVISAL.
*Kinsman* means no more than *near relation.* Many words are used by Shakspere with much greater latitude. REMARKS.

83. *And, at her heels, a huge infectious troop.*] I have no doubt that the emendation proposed by Mr. Heath [*"their heels"*] is right. In the English manuscripts of our author's time the pronouns were generally expressed by abbreviations. In this very play we have already met *their* for *her*, which has been rightly amended:

"Among my wife and *their* confederates." Act iv. scene i. MALONE.
107.—*a* formal *man again:*] See catch-word Alphabet. STEEVENS.
123. *The place of* death, *and sorry execution,*] The first and second folio read—"the place of *depth.*" Mr. Rowe made the change. MALONE.
sorry *execution,*] So in *Macbeth:*
*"Of sorriest* fancies your companions making."
*Sorry,* had anciently a stronger meaning than at present. STEEVENS.
Thus, Macbeth looking on his bloody hands after the murder of Duncan:
"This is a *sorry sight!"* HENLEY.
139. *Whom I made lord of me, and all I had,*
*At your* important *letters,* ] *Important* seems to be for *importunate.* JOHNSON.
So in one of Shakspere's Historical plays:
"great France
"My mourning and *important* tears hath pitied.
Again, in George Whetstone's *Castle of Delight,* 1576:

"yet won by *importance* accepted his courtesie."
Shakspere, who gives to all nations the customs of his own, seems, from this passage, to allude to a *court of wards* in Ephesus.

The *court of wards* was always considered as a grievous oppression. It is glanced at as early as in the old morality of *Hyche Scorner:*
"these ryche men ben unkinde:
"Wydowes do curse lordes and gentyllmen.
"For *they contrayne them to marry with theyr men*,
"Ye, wheder they wyll or no." Steevens.

148.—*to take* order] *i.e.* to *take measure*. So, in *Othello*, act v.
"Honest Iago hath *ta'en order* for it." Steevens.

152. *And, with his mad attendant* AND *himself,*] We should read: Mad *himself*. Warburton.

We might read,
*And* here *his mad attendant and himself*. Steevens.

172. *Beaten the maids* a-row] *i. e.* Successively, one after another. So in Chaucer's *Wife of Bath*, Tale v. 6836, late edit.
"A thousand times *a-row* he can hire kisse." Steevens.

173. *Whose beard they have sing'd off with brands of fire;*] Such a ludicrous circumstance is not unworthy of the farce in which we find it introduced; but is rather out of place in an epick poem, amidst all the horrors and carnage of a battle:

"*Obvius ambustum torrem Corynaeus ab ara*
"*Corripit, et venienti Ebuso plagamque ferenti,*
"*Occupat os fiammis. Olli ingens barba reluxit,*
      "*Nidoremque ambusta dedit.*"
Virg. Aeneid. lib. xii. 298. Steevens.

Shakspere was a great reader of Plutarch, where he might have seen this method of shaving in the life of Dion. p. 167, 410. . . . S.W.

177. *His man with scissors nicks him like a fool:*] The force of this allusion I am unable to explain. Perhaps it was once the custom to cut the hair of ideots or jesters close to their heads. There is a proverbial simile—"Like *crop* the conjurer;" which might have been applied to either of these characters. Steevens.

There is a penalty of ten shillings in one of king Alfred's ecclesiastical laws, if one opprobriously *shave* a common man like a *fool*. Tollet.

207. *with harlots* ] Antipholis did not suspect his wife of having entertained courtezans, but of having been confederate with cheats, to impose on him and abuse him, therefore he says to her, act i. sc. 4:

are these your customers, &c.

By this description he points out *Pinch* and his followers.

*Harlot* was a term of reproach applied to cheats among men, as well
as to wantons among women. Thus, in the *Fox*, Corbacchio says to
Volpone:
"Out *harlot* I"
Again, in *The Winter's Tale:*
"for the *harlot* king
"Is quite beyond mine arm"

The learned editor of Chaucer's *Canterbury Tales*, 4 vol. 8vo. 1775, observes,
that in *The Romaunt of the Rost*, v. 6068, *King of Harlots* is Chaucer's Translation
of *Roy des ribaulx*. Chaucer uses the word more than once:

"A sturdy *harlot* went hem ay behind,
"That was hir hosts man," &c.
*Sompnoures Tale*, v. 7336.

Again, in the *Dyers' Play*, among the Chester Collection in the Museum,
Antichrist says to the male characters on the stage:

"Out on ye *harlots*, whence come ye?" STEEVENS.
216. *I am advis'd* ] *i.e.* I am not going to speak precipitately or rashly, but
on reflection and consideration. STEEVENS.
284. *mated,*] *i. e.* wild, foolish, from the Italian *matto*.
"I think you are all *fools* or madmen."
301. *deformed*] for *deforming*. STEEVENS.
302. *strange defeatures*] *Defeature* is the privative *of feature*. The meaning
is, time hath cancelled my features. JOHNSON.

*Defeatures* are *undoings, miscarriages, misfortunes*; from *defaire*, Fr. So, in
Daniel's *Complaint of Rosamond*, 1599:

"The day before the night of my *defeature*,
(*i. e.* undoing)
"He greets me with a casket richly wrought."
The sense is, I am *deformed, undone*, by misery. Misfortune has left its
impression on my face.
STEEVENS.

I rather think *defeatures* mean here, as in another place in this play, *alteration of feature, or deformity*. So in our author's *Venus and Adonis*, 1593:

"To cross the curious workmanship of Nature,
"To mingle beauty with infirmities,
"And pure perfection with *impure defeature.*"

If we understand by *defeatures*, in this place, *miscarriages*, or *misfortunes*, then we suppose Pigeon to say, "that careful hours, i. e. *misfortunes*, have written *misfortunes* in his face." MALONE.

*Defeatures* are certainly neither more nor less, than *features*; as *demerits* are neither more nor less than *merits*. Time, says Aegeon, hath placed *new and strange features* in my face; *i. e.* given it quite a different appearance; no wonder therefore thou dost not know me. REMARKS.

314. *this* grained *face*] i.e. furrow'd, like the *grain of wood*. So in *Coriolanus:*
"my *grained ash.*" STEEVENS.

321. *All these* OLD *witnesses (I cannot err)* I believe should be read: *All those* OLD *witnesses cannot err.*

*i. e.* all these continue to testify that I cannot err, and tell me, &c. WARBURTON.

The old reading is the true one, as well as the most poetical. The words, *cannot err*, should be thrown into a parenthesis. By *old witnesses*, I believe he means *experienced, accustomed ones*, which are therefore less likely to err. So in the *Tempest:*
"If these be *true eyes* that I wear in my head," &c. STEEVENS.

353. *Besides her urging of her wreck at sea,*] This is one of Shakspere's oversights. The abbess has not so much as hinted at the shipwreck. Perhaps, indeed, this and the next speech should change places. STEEVENS

That however would scarcely remove the difficulty: the *next* speech is Aegeon's: both it and the following one should precede the duke's; or there is possibly a line lost. REMARKS.

405. *Twenty-five years* ] In former editions:
Thirty-three *years*.

'Tis impossible the poet should be so forgetful, as to design this number here: and therefore I have ventured to alter it to *twenty-five*, upon a proof, that, I think, amounts to demonstration. The number, I presume, was at first wrote in figures, and perhaps, blindly; and thence the mistake might arise. Aegeon, in the first scene of the first act, is precise as to the time his son left him, in quest of his brother:

*My youngest boy, and yet my eldest care,*
*At eighteen years became inquisitive*
*After his brother, &c.*

And how long it was from the son's thus parting from his father, to their meeting again at Ephesus, where Aegeon, mistakingly, recognizes the twin-brother, for him, we as precisely learn from another passage in the fifth act:

*Aege. But* seven *years since, in Syracusa bay,*
*Thou knowest we parted;*
So that these two numbers, put together, settle the date of their birth beyond dispute. THEOBALD.

407. *My heavy burden* not *delivered:*] The old copy reads—*"are* delivered."
I believe, the author wrote:
My heavy burdens *are not* deliver'd.
Printers sometimes omit words, but never insert a new word not in the manuscript, except where they mistake one word for another.—The compositor's eye might have passed over the word *not*; but *are* could scarcely have been printed by mistake instead of it. MALONE.
411. *After to long grief, such nativity!*] She has just said, that to her, her sons were not *born* till now. STEEVENS.

# THE COMEDY OF ERRORS
# IN THE NINETEENTH CENTURY
### ❧

Nineteenth-century criticism of *The Comedy of Errors* marks a sharp distinction from earlier commentary on the play in that it ushers in the beginnings of an increasing awareness of the ways in which Shakespeare revised and enhanced his sources in Plautus as well as a heightened consciousness in regard to the depth of characterization achieved in the play. Though appreciation for *The Comedy of Errors* is never universal and is widely varied in focus and approach, the new century represents an era of increasing critical interest in and acclaim for Shakespeare's consummate artistry in exceeding the boundary lines of conventional farce and presenting profound insights into the distinct human qualities of his characters. In his recognition of the imaginative possibilities introduced by Shakespeare's addition of a second set of twins, as well as the complexity of the misapprehensions that introduce an element of drama into an otherwise dizzying series of comic events, Schlegel's commentary inaugurates a new era in the critical reception of *The Comedy of Errors*. By midcentury, there is a marked increase in attention to Shakespeare's representation of complex psychological issues, including that of an early medical practitioner, A. O. Kellogg, who was impressed with Shakespeare's insight into the mental instability and illness and was equally passionate in his belief that the poet was advanced beyond the times in his understanding of this affliction.

In addition to the abiding interest in Shakespeare's reworking of Plautus, critics have shown an increasing focus on certain individual characters and the significance of their narratives within the play, such as the love story surrounding Antipholus of Syracuse and Luciana and the pathos of Egeon's continuing desperation. Further analyses of the depth and complexity of character development to be found in Shakespeare when compared with Plautus reveal an increasing awareness of and renewed appreciation for the artistic and psychological achievements to be found in *The Comedy of Errors*. Likewise, the question of genre still remains a major focal point for later nineteenth-century critics, as compelling and irresolvable as ever. Though some critics, such as Denton Snider, begin by insisting on interpreting *The Comedy of Errors* as pure farce, a work devoid of characterization, they are nevertheless compelled to acknowledge that elements of pathos and tragedy are present in the play and cannot be readily invalidated and, as in Snider's case, are thus forced to alter their original thesis. By the late nineteenth century, Bernhard ten Brink's praise of Shakespeare's achievement is nothing short of effusive in his evaluation of the new genre wrought from a skillful intertwining of comic and tragic elements. Ten Brink ultimately finds a spiritual message, founded on an unmistakable medieval influence, inherent in *The Comedy of Errors*. In making this symbolic identification, ten Brink thus introduces a new critical approach to the play that will receive considerable attention in the twentieth century in regard to the role of religion.

August Wilhelm von Schlegel's early nineteenth-century commentary praises *The Comedy of Errors* as an innovative and imaginative reworking of Plautus's *Menaechmi* and defends Shakespeare's addition of a second set of twins as entirely understandable once the fundamental premise of an absurd plot is accepted. Furthermore, Schlegel appears to be responding to various critical accusations that the play is concerned with crude and lowbrow incidents as well as slapstick gestures and unappealing language by stating that the work nevertheless succeeds in captivating its audience. Schlegel further points out that Shakespeare has done everything possible to elevate his subject matter through his inclusion of complex situations of love and jealousy accompanied by a gravity of subject matter in the separation of parents and children. Working within the confines of the genre, Schlegel maintains that Shakespeare has far exceeded Plautus's comedy of mistaken identity.

In his commentary on *The Comedy of Errors*, Nathan Drake finds the play enormously entertaining, filled with surprises in its surfeit of increasingly comical errors and unexpected twists and turns of plot. Drake likewise believes that Shakespeare has improved on Plautus in elaborating on the ancient fable of mistaken identity and extended the farcical theme as far as possible, although Drake does not state specifically what he perceives to be the limits of that genre.

Opposed to Schlegel and Drake is William Hazlitt's view of *The Comedy of Errors*. Hazlitt finds no improvement in Shakespeare's reinterpretation of Plautus's *Menaechmi* and instead accuses the bard of having been essentially lazy. Moreover, Hazlitt finds little evidence of Shakespeare's genius and expresses great difficulty in distinguishing characters that are caught within a web of confusing, duplicate identities. Hazlitt further finds the issue of stage presentation especially problematic for the audience from a visual standpoint since the twins' dress and appearance is identical. In sum, he does not believe that Shakespeare's genius resides in reworking classical plays but, rather, in his own unique imaginative creations. Nevertheless, Hazlitt admires the passage in which the abbess is able to obtain an admission of culpability from Adriana in causing her husband's mental instability and cites this as an example of Shakespeare's powers of invention.

Samuel Taylor Coleridge praises Shakesepeare for his exemplary treatment of the genre of farce in *The Comedy of Errors*, a category of comedic writing that he believes is in a class by itself, premised on its own unique conditions allowing for a multitude of absurdities. Coleridge elevates farce into a predetermined philosophical category, the requirements of which he maintains that Shakespeare has faithfully adhered to in this play.

A. O. Kellogg's essay expresses great appreciation for Shakespeare's insight into the causes of insanity with the sincere hope that the playwright will finally receive the recognition he deserves for his understanding of mental illness and the different factors that produce the condition. As a mid-nineteenth-century medical practitioner, Kellogg is impressed with Shakespeare's "clinical" knowledge of the attendant causes of and potential cures for mental affliction. Writing in defense of Shakespeare's psychoanalytical abilities, Kellogg reminds us that the playwright was well ahead of his times, noting that around the year 1600, insanity was widely believed to be a sign that one was possessed by the devil, a conviction shared by both the medical practitioners of the time as well as the general populace, and that some sort of exorcism was called for. Contrary to this prevailing notion of insanity, Kellogg praises Shakespeare for understanding mental illness as a disease that could be cured by medical intervention. Kellogg offers five different assertions on insanity based on his reading of several Shakespearean plays, and it is the last one outlined, that insanity can be precipitated from excessive grief, anxiety, and melancholy, that relates to *The Comedy of Errors*. Highlighting the abbess's admonishment to Adriana, Kellogg argues that Shakespeare is attributing Antipholus of Ephesus's derangement and insomnia to the jealous naggings of his wife. Kellogg concludes that Shakespeare gained his exceptional knowledge of human behavior from his keen powers of observation, drawing his characters from real life rather than staging them as figments of his imagination.

Richard Grant White, vis-à-vis William Warner, questions whether Shakespeare is directly imitating Plautus or only familiar with the *Menaechmi*. Ultimately, he comes out on the side of Shakespeare. Grant admires the structure of *The Comedy of Errors* for its evidence of theatrical experience, since he believes Shakespeare wrote the first and last scenes during a prolonged interval preceding its publication. Furthermore, Grant appreciates Shakespeare's addition of twin attendants and his imaginative introduction of such characters as Luciana, who instructs her sister, Adriana, in regard to the husband's role as lord of his household and all other living things. He further maintains that, in creating Luciana, Shakespeare provided himself with the opportunity to expand on Antipholus of Syracuse's characterization, namely the fashioning of a love story.

Denton Snider begins his analysis of *The Comedy of Errors* by categorizing it as a pure comedy, which he defines as one based on circumstances, working solely through the vehicle of natural resemblance, and, accordingly, almost devoid of "human purpose." As a result of the characters' inability to act of their own accord, Snider contends that they simply act out a predetermined set of absurd conditions in which they easily go astray. Given the lack of character development here as opposed to high dramas in which human action is the result of feelings, thoughts and motives, Snider believes the individuals in *The Comedy of Errors* are victims of chance and therefore utterly superficial, mere puppets devoid of any control over their lives. Nevertheless, for all the frivolity and superficiality with which Snider faults *The Comedy of Errors*, he admits that the inaugural event of Egeon's desperate situation approaches the level of tragedy and, at the same time, provides a moral center that propels the action forward. Essentially, Snider sees the tragic element as creating an arena in which the ensuing errors can be staged. It is significant that from this point forward in his argument, Snider continually refers to *The Comedy of Errors* as a drama, thus recasting his former complaint by discovering an elevating dramatic theme and a real human motivation within the play.

Snider then proceeds to analyze the action as unfolding in three distinct parts—Egeon's narrative of a father who has first been separated from a wife and two children due to a shipwreck and then bereft of his remaining son and servant when they embark on a journey in search of their missing siblings and fail to return. He identifies the second part as the interval during which errors and confusion arise out of an inability to distinguish between the two Antipholuses and Dromios, resulting in such an extreme level confusion that even social institutions appear unstable. The third part is distinguished by the social disruption that ensues when Antipholus of Ephesus, a well-respected member of society and friend of the duke, confronts his twin brother and the resulting bedlam that affects the entire community. Ultimately, Snider maintains that the genres of comedy and drama coexist in *The Comedy of Errors*, the drama providing the ethical vehicle through which all comedic irrationality is dispelled and true human emotions are made manifest. Accordingly, he argues that it is because the play contains an element of tragedy that the ultimate reconciliation of family can take place.

Andrew Lang's review for *Harper's Magazine* begins with a lengthy synopsis of Plautus's *Menaechmi*, a play that he compares, rather thoroughly, with *The Comedy of Errors*. While at first it appears that Lang is dismissive of Shakespeare's efforts in reworking a classical fable—finding *The Comedy of Errors* to be largely imitative, lacking in the humor that he finds in Plautus, and nonetheless composed of a very convoluted plot that defies description—he ultimately finds much to appreciate. Lang praises Shakespeare for his sensitive treatment of women in *The Comedy of Errors*, an issue absent from Plautus's *Menaechmi*, thus introducing a line of inquiry that will become a major critical debate in the latter part of the twentieth century. As Lang points out, Plautus's Menaechmus treats his wife with contempt, giving away her prized possessions to a courtesan named Erotion in order to "tame" her, while Shakespeare's treatment of a jealous wife is far more sensitive and poetic. As a first indication of a softening of the theme of a "jealous wife as shrew," Lang sees the addition of Luciana as an important instance of tempering Adriana's theatrics with a benign sister who gently lectures her on the wife's status in the household. Furthermore, Lang finds the characterization of Adriana herself to be commendable, for while she pleads with her husband (who happens to be the wrong Antipholus), she is filled with a passion that is transformed into poetry through Shakespeare's incomparable artistry. Finally, unlike the wife who is ultimately sold at auction by her husband, Menaechmus, Adriana is reconciled with her husband and, according to Lang, has learned Shakespeare's intended lesson well, namely that goodness and forgiveness are enough for all men to be happy.

Bernhard ten Brink writes in praise of Shakespeare's imaginative powers and unique artistic ability to produce comedies that break the traditional boundary lines of genre through a skillful intertwining of comic and tragic elements. Ten Brink sees Shakespeare's artistry as far exceeding that of both his classical predecessors and a popular and esteemed French comic playwright, Molière (Jean-Baptiste Poquelin, 1622–73), with whom Shakespeare is compared. Using Molière as a paradigm of modern comedy, the bulk of ten Brink's essay consists of a general assessment of Shakespeare's superior abilities as a writer of comedies as well as an examination of the variety of sources from which he drew. With respect to the comparison with Molière, ten Brink makes it clear that Shakespeare has far surpassed him, the critical difference between them being that while Molière's conception of the genre is based on strongly marked characters with some exceptional idiosyncrasy or situations that are highlighted by some peculiar circumstance, Shakespeare's comedies are complex works in which multiple plots are intertwined and focused on some principal action rather than comic figures or situations. Ten Brink is so impressed with Shakespeare's artistry that he suggests Shakespeare may have been suffering from a surfeit of imagination as evidenced by the preponderance of psychological motivations and situations and the surplus of witticisms in *The Comedy of Errors*. Ultimately, ten Brink identifies a spiritual message in Shakespeare's comedies, seeing a link with the medieval romance and recognizing that comedy is most effective when blended with some threat of evil or agitation that must be overcome. Furthermore, ten Brink argues that the inclusion of this romantic element provides the audience with a sense of immunity from harm for, as they witness the characters overcoming evil, they recognize a transcendent message. With respect to *The Comedy of Errors*, ten Brink focuses on Shakespeare's enhancement of the theme of chance in multiple instances, taking Plautus's tale of madness to increased comic heights. Ten Brink maintains that Shakespeare, in so doing, injects an important element of mystery that exerts an unconscious power over the audience, most notably the love episode that bears a spiritual message that is transmitted when the audience understands that a divine providence ultimately controls the outcome of all the errors, confusion, and potentially tragic implications that precipitated the initial crisis.

## 1809—August Wilhelm von Schlegel. "The Comedy of Errors," from *Lectures on Dramatic Art and Literature*

An important figure in German romanticism, August Wilhelm von Schlegel (1767–1845) was a poet, translator, and critic. In 1796, he went to the University of Jena, where, in 1798, he was appointed extraordinary professor and began his translation of Shakespeare, one of the finest in German.

*The Comedy of Errors* is the subject of the *Menaechmi* of Plautus, entirely recast and enriched with new developments: of all the works of Shakspeare this is the only example of imitation of, or borrowing from, the ancients. To the two twin brothers of the same name are added two slaves, also twins, impossible to be distinguished from each other, and of the same name. The improbability becomes by this means doubled: but when once we have lent ourselves to the first, which certainly borders on the incredible, we shall not perhaps be disposed to cavil at the second; and if the spectator is to be entertained by mere *perplexities* they cannot be too much varied. In such pieces we must, to give to the senses at least an appearance of truth, always pre-suppose that the parts by which the misunderstandings are occasioned are played with masks, and this the poet no doubt observed. I cannot acquiesce in the censure that the discovery is too long deferred: so long as novelty and interest are possessed by the perplexing incidents, there is no need to be in dread of wearisomeness. And this is really the case here: matters are carried so far that one of the two brothers is first arrested for debt, then confined as a lunatic, and the other is forced to take refuge in a sanctuary to save his life. In a subject of this description it is impossible to steer clear of all sorts of low circumstances, abusive language, and blows; Shakspeare has however endeavoured to ennoble it in every possible way. A couple of scenes, dedicated to jealousy and love, interrupt the course of perplexities which are solely occasioned by the illusion of the external senses. A greater solemnity is given to the discovery from the Prince presiding, and from the re-union of the long separated parents of the twins who are still alive. The exposition, by which the spectators are previously instructed while the characters themselves are still involved in ignorance, and which Plautus artlessly conveys in a prologue, is here masterly introduced in an affecting narrative by the father. In short, this is perhaps the best of all written or possible *Menaechmi*; and if the piece be inferior in worth to other pieces of Shakspeare, it is merely because nothing more could be made of the materials.

# 1817—Nathan Drake. From *Shakespeare and His Times*

Nathan Drake (1766–1836) was English essayist and physician. In 1780, he was apprenticed to a doctor in York, then, in 1786, proceeded to Edinburgh University, where he took his degree as M.D. in 1789. In 1790, he became a general practitioner at Sudbury, Suffolk, and, in 1792, relocated to Hadleigh, where he died in 1836. Drake's writings include several volumes of literary essays and some papers contributed to medical periodicals, but his most important work was *Shakespeare and His Times,* published in 1817.

As to the comic action which constitutes the chief bulk of this piece, if it be true that to excite laughter, awaken attention, and fix curiosity, be essential to its dramatic excellence, the "Comedy of Errors" cannot be pronounced an unsuccessful effort; both reader and spectator are hurried on to the close, through a series of thick-coming incidents, and under the pleasurable influence of novelty, expectation, and surprise; and the dialogue . . . is uniformly vivacious, pointed, and even effervescing. Shakspeare is visible, in fact, throughout the entire play, as well in the broad exuberance of its mirth, as in the cast of its more chastised parts, a combination of which may be found in the punishment and character of Pinch the pedagogue and conjurer, who is sketched in the strongest and most marked style of our author. If we consider, therefore, the construction of the fable, the narrowness of its basis, and that its powers of entertainment are almost exclusively confined to a continued deception of the external senses, we must confess that Shakspeare has not only improved on the Plautian model, but, making allowance for a somewhat too coarse vein of humour, has given to his production all the interest and variety that the nature and the limits of his subject would permit.

# 1817—William Hazlitt. "The Comedy of Errors," from *Characters of Shakespear's Plays*

William Hazlitt (1778–1830) was an English essayist and one of the finest Shakespearean critics of the nineteenth century. He is the author of *Lectures on the English Poets* (1818), *A View of the English Stage* (1818), and *The Spirit of the Age* (1825).

This comedy is taken very much from the Menaechmi of Plautus, and is not an improvement on it. Shakespear appears to have bestowed no great pains on it, and there are but a few passages which bear the decided stamp of his genius. He seems to have relied on his author, and on the interest arising out of the intricacy of the plot. The curiosity excited is certainly very considerable, though not of the most pleasing kind. We are teased as with a riddle, which notwithstanding we try to solve. In reading the play, from the sameness of the names of the two Antipholises and the two Dromios, as well from their being constantly taken for each other by those who see them, it is difficult, without a painful effort of attention, to keep the characters distinct in the mind. And again, on the stage either the complete similarity of their persons and dress must produce the same perplexity whenever they first enter, or the identity of appearance which the story supposes, will be destroyed. We still, however, having a clue to the difficulty, can tell which is which, merely from the practical contradictions which arise, as soon as the different parties begin to speak; and we are indemnified for the perplexity and blunders into which we are thrown by seeing others thrown into greater and almost inextricable ones. This play (among other considerations) leads us not to feel much regret that Shakespear was not what is called a classical scholar. We do not think his *forte* would ever have lain in imitating or improving on what others invented, so much as in inventing for himself, and perfecting what he invented,—not perhaps by the omission of faults, but by the addition of the highest excellencies. His own genius was strong enough to bear him up, and he soared longest and best on unborrowed plumes. The only passage of a very Shakespearian cast in this comedy is the one in which the Abbess, with admirable characteristic artifice, makes Adriana confess her own misconduct in driving her husband mad.

"*Abbess.* How long hath this possession held the man?
*Adriana.* This week he hath been heavy, sour, sad,
And much, much different from the man he was;
But, till this afternoon, his passion
Ne'er brake into extremity of rage.
*Abbess.* Hath he not lost much wealth by wreck at sea?
Bury'd some dear friend? Hath not else his eye
Stray'd his affection in unlawful love?
A sin prevailing much in youthful men,
Who give their eyes the liberty of gazing.
Which of these sorrows is he subject to?
*Adriana.* To none of these, except it be the last:
Namely, some love, that drew him oft from home.
*Abbess.* You should for that have reprehended him.
*Adriana.* Why, so I did.
*Abbess.* But not rough enough.
*Adriana.* As roughly as my modesty would let me.

*Abbess.* Haply, in private.
*Adriana.* And in assemblies too.
*Abbess.* Aye, but not enough.
*Adriana.* It was the copy of our conference:
In bed, he slept not for my urging it;
At board, he fed not for my urging it;
Alone it was the subject of my theme?
In company, I often glanc'd at it;
Still did I tell him it was vile and bad.
*Abbess.* And therefore came it that the man was mad:
The venom'd clamours of a jealous woman
Poison more deadly than a mad dog's tooth.
It seems, his sleeps were hindered by thy railing:
And therefore comes it that his head is light.
Thou say'st his meat was sauc'd with thy upbraidings:
Unquiet meals make ill digestions,
Therefore the raging fire of fever bred:
And what's a fever but a fit of madness?
Thou say'st his sports were hinder'd by thy brawls:
Sweet recreation barr'd, what doth ensue,
But moody and dull melancholy,
Kinsman to grim and comfortless despair;
And, at her heels, a huge infectious troop
Of pale distemperatures, and foes to life?
In food, in sport, and life-preserving rest
To be disturb'd, would mad or man or beast:
The consequence is then, thy jealous fits
Have scar'd thy husband from the use of wits.
*Luciana.* She never reprehended him but mildly,
When he demeaned himself rough, rude, and wildly.—
Why bear you these rebukes, and answer not?
*Adriana.* She did betray me to my own reproof."

Pinch the conjuror is also an excrescence not to be found in Plautus. He is indeed a very formidable anachronism.

"They brought one Pinch, a hungry lean-fac'd villain,
A meer anatomy, a mountebank,
A thread-bare juggler and a fortune-teller,
A needy, hollow-ey'd, sharp-looking wretch,
A living dead man."

This is exactly like some of the Puritanical portraits to be met with in Hogarth.

―――――――

## 1818—Samuel Taylor Coleridge. "Comedy of Errors," from *Shakspeare, with Introductory Remarks on Poetry, the Drama, and the Stage*

Samuel Taylor Coleridge (1772-1834) was a preeminent poet, essayist, philosopher, and literary critic. Along with his friend, William Wordsworth, Coleridge was one of the founders of the romantic movement in England and one of the Lake Poets. He is the author of *Biographia Literaria* (1817) and *Lectures and Notes on Shakespeare and Other English Poets* (delivered in 1818 and first published in 1883).

The myriad-minded man, our, and all men's, Shakspeare, has in this piece presented us with a legitimate farce in exactest consonance with the philosophical principles and character of farce, as distinguished from comedy and from entertainments. A proper farce is mainly distinguished from comedy by the license allowed, and even required, in the fable, in order to produce strange and laughable situations. The story need not be probable, it is enough that it is possible. A comedy would scarcely allow even the two Antipholises; because, although there have been instances of almost indistinguishable likeness in two persons, yet these are mere individual accidents, *casus ludentis natural*, and the *verum* will not excuse the *in-verisimile*. But farce dares add the two Dromios, and is justified in so doing by the laws of its end and constitution. In a word, farces commence in a postulate, which must be granted.

―――――――

## 1844—A. O. Kellogg. Commentary from "Insanity–Illustrated by Histories of Distinguished Men, and by the Writings of Poets and Novelists"

A. O. Kellogg was a doctor at the Poughkeepsie Asylum in New York. He wrote, at the government's request for an assessment of his patient's competency, a paper titled "An Analysis of the Mental Condition of Charles J. Guiteau."

In truth, Shakspeare himself is as great a mystery as any case of insanity,—as singular an instance of variation from the ordinary standard of mental manifestation.

The more we read Shakspeare, the more we are astonished; not so much at his wonderful imagination, but at the immensity and correctness of his knowledge.

And on no one subject in our opinion, has he shown more of his remarkable ability and accuracy than on insanity. He has not, like many other writers, alluded to a few cases and thrown out a few hints on the subject, but his dramatic works abound with remarks upon this disease. There is scarcely a form of mental disorder he has not alluded to, and pointed out the causes and method of treatment.

It appears to us Shakspeare has not had sufficient credit for his knowledge on this subject—probably because those who have commented upon his works, had not themselves much knowledge of insanity, and were not aware of the extent and variety of that which he has exhibited.

In treating of this subject we propose to show that his knowledge of insanity was not only great and varied, but that his views respecting it—its causes and treatment, were far, very far in advance of the age in which he lived.

Let us call to mind that Shakspeare flourished about two hundred and fifty years since, or about the year 1600—and at a time when insanity was generally regarded as caused by the agency of the Devil. This was not merely popular opinion, but the opinion of some distinguished medical writers. For its cure, sometimes Saints were invoked, and sometimes whipping was resorted to. In fact whipping was the most general remedial measure in the time of Shakspeare. He was aware of this, as he himself alludes to the fact in his play of *As you Like It*. "Love," says Rosalind, "is merely a madness; and I tell you, deserves as well a dark house and a *whip*, as madmen do."

An examination of his writings will show that he believed the following facts, all of which were in advance of the general opinions of his age, and are now deemed correct.

1. That a well-formed brain, a good shaped head, is essential to a good mind.

2. That insanity is a disease of the brain.

3. That there is a general and partial insanity.

4. That it is a disease which can be cured by medical means.

5. That the causes are various, the most common of which he has particularly noticed.

These assertions we shall endeavor to prove.

*First.* That a well-formed brain is essential to a good mind, he often mentions. He particularly notices the excellence of a high forehead. Thus, Cleopatra, anxious to know the personal appearance of her rival Octavia, asks the messenger, "Bearest thou her face in mind, is't long or round?" to which he replies, "Round even to faultness, and her forehead as low as she would wish it." This so pleased Cleopatra that she replied, "There is gold for thee," and rewarded him for his gratifying intelligence.

So in the Two Gentlemen of Verona, Julia contemplating the picture of her rival Silvia, says, "Her *foreheads' low*, what should it be that he respects in her?"

Again; Caliban, in the Tempest, fears they "may all be turned to Barnacles, or to apes with foreheads villainous low!"

*Second.* Shakspeare considered insanity to be a disease of the brain.

In Macbeth, the struggle between sanity and insanity is well illustrated, particularly in the dagger scene. At first Macbeth doubts and asks:—

Is this a dagger, which I see before me,
The handle towards my hand? Come, let me clutch thee.

Not succeeding, he doubts his eye-sight and exclaims,

Art thou but
*A dagger of the mind: a false creation,*
*Proceeding from the heat oppressed brain*!

Yet looking again, he sees it in form so "palpable," that he for an instant believes in its existence,—but finally reason triumphs and he exclaims,

There's no such thing;
It is the bloody business, which informs
Thus to mine eyes.

The whole passage is beautiful and instructive, and finely exhibits the struggle between reason and delusion.

Macbeth also believed Lady Macbeth to be affected by mental disorder, and asks the Doctor if he can not

Minister to a mind diseased;
Pluck from the memory a rooted sorrow;
Raze out the written troubles of the *brain*?

Showing that he considered her disorder seated in that organ.

Othello when perplexed in the extreme was thought to be insane. Hence Lodovico asks, "Are his wits safe? Is he not light of *brain*?"

Disordered mind is sometimes called by Shakspeare *Brain Sickness*, the result of a hot, boiled or dried brain—terms which are pathologically correct. King

Henry exclaims, "What madness rules in brain-sick men!" So Prince Henry says of King John,

> His pure brain
> Doth by the idle comments that it makes
> Foretell the ending of mortality—

In Titus Andronicus, Tamerlane says,

> This fits his lunacy—feeds his brain-sick fits.

Laertes, on seeing Ophelia deranged, exclaims,

> Oh heat dry up my *brains*
> Thy madness shall be paid with weight.

Falstaff, when outwitted by the merry ladies of Windsor, asks—"Have I laid my brain in the sun and dried it, that it wants matter to prevent so gross o'erreaching as this?" And Jacques, in As you Like It, speaking of a fool, says,

> In his brain—
> Which is as dry as the remainder biscuit
> After a voyage,—he hath strange places cramm'd
> With observation, the which he vents
> In mangled forms.

But we have referred to instances enough to show that Shakspeare considered the brain the organ of the mind, and insanity to arise from disease of this organ.

*Thirdly*. Shakspeare knew and has accurately described several varieties of insanity. In some of the cases the insanity is very slight, in others the most violent.

The case of Macbeth is one in which the actual insanity is very slight and momentary. Perhaps it should not be called one of insanity at all, but merely hallucination of sight.

Neither is Lady Macbeth represented as insane. She was a somnambulist and walked and talked in her sleep, but when awake was not insane.

Many narratives strikingly similar are on record, when fear—remorse of conscience—and sleeplessness have produced like troubles of the brain and individuals have seen signs and heard voices which they believed from heaven and have refrained from crime and been lead to a reformation of life—or to the divulgence of crimes which they had long concealed. Shakspeare, therefore, in delineating the characters of Macbeth and lady Macbeth, drew from nature—not imagination.

The insanity of Hamlet is very finely portrayed, though by many it is thought that Shakspeare meant to represent his insanity as altogether feigned. But this we are confident is erroneous. The mental disorder of Hamlet is most exquisitely drawn and no doubt from observation. Shakspeare knew much more about insanity than many of his commentators—and therefore they have mistaken and obscured his meaning. Shakspeare well knew that insane persons often advance sentiments that evince not only a sound but an acute and vigorous understanding—but Mr. Boswell and other of his critics did not, and therefore argue that as Hamlet conversed rationally at times, he was not insane at all.

In the life of Hamlet as represented by Shakspeare we have a full history of a case of insanity, of a peculiar kind. It was not a case of mania—nor of general insanity, but a case of melancholy madness—in which the reason was only occasionally overpowered—while the feelings were much disordered by disease.

Shakspeare carefully prepares him for this disease—he predisposes him to it, if we may so say, and Hamlet exhibits premonitory symptoms of the malady before he saw the ghost of his father—to which his insanity has by some been ascribed. Before this he was melancholy, and talked of committing suicide. "All the uses of the world, had already," as he says, become to him, "weary, stale, flat and unprofitable." Then he sees and converses with the ghost of his father which increases his disorder. As described by Polonius he became more sad, sleepless, light of head, and then raving. At first he can hardly be deemed insane—merely melancholy, and in most that he does and says exhibits but little mental disorder, which is made thus gradually to increase upon him. In all this, nature was followed. Had his insanity come on suddenly or with violence, it would not have been the natural course of this form of the disease.

Finally, after the mock play, the disease is fully developed. True, he at one time intimates that he is feigning insanity, and at another denies that he is deranged. Now all this is very often observed in Lunatic Asylums. Not a month occurs but we have patients say to us, they are feigning insanity by such and such acts, while others more frequently exclaim, like Hamlet, "It is not madness, bring me to the test," and are as ingenious as the most sane persons would be in explaining their conduct in a manner to disprove insanity.

The case of Ophelia in the same play is also exquisitely drawn, though it is not like that of Hamlet among the rare varieties; but being of a kind more frequently seen, it has attracted more attention. A common notion of insanity is, that those laboring under it, are always violent and raving or else talking incoherently or nonsensically. Yet every person who has seen much of this disease knows, as Shakspeare did, that not unfrequently the insane, for the most part, conduct with propriety, and converse rationally on a great variety of subjects.

But in King Lear, Shakspeare has developed his views respecting insanity, more fully than in any other of his plays.

Lear's is a genuine case of insanity, from the beginning to the end; such as we often see in aged persons. On reading it we can not divest ourselves of the idea, that it is a real case of insanity, correctly reported. Still, we apprehend the play or *case* is generally misunderstood. The general belief is, that the insanity of Lear originated *solely* from the ill-treatment of his daughters, while in truth he was insane before that, from the beginning of the play, when he gave his kingdom away, and banished as it were Cordelia and Kent, and abused his servants. The ill-usage of his daughters only aggravated the disease and drove him to raving madness.

Had it been otherwise, the case as one of insanity would have been inconsistent and very unusual. Shakspeare, and Walter Scott, prepare those whom they represent as insane, by education and other circumstances, for the disease—they predispose them to insanity, and thus its outbreak is not unnatural.

In the case of Lear, the insanity is so evident before he received any abuse from his daughters that, professionally speaking, a feeling of regret arises that he was not so considered and so treated. He was unquestionably very troublesome, and by his "new pranks," as his daughter calls them, and rash and variable conduct, caused his children much trouble and introduced much disorder into their households; keeping, as Goneril says,—

> A hundred knights and squires;
> Men so disorder'd, so debauch'd, and bold,
> That this our court infected by their manners,
> Shows like a riotous inn: epicurism and lust
> Make it more like a tavern or a brothel,
> Than a grac'd palace.

In fact, a little feeling of commiseration for his daughters, at first arises in our minds from these circumstances, though to be sure they form no excuse for their subsequent bad conduct.

Let it be remembered they exhibited no marked disposition to ill-treat or neglect him until after the conduct of himself and his knights had become outrageous. Then they at first reproved him, or rather asked him to change his course in a mild manner. Thus Goneril says to him, "I would you would make use of that good wisdom whereof I know you are fraught; and put away these dispositions, which of *late* transform you from what you rightly are;" showing that previously he had been different. This, however, caused an *unnatural* and violent burst of rage, but did not *originate* his insanity, for he had already exhibited symptoms of it, and it would naturally have progressed even if he had not been thus addressed.

Lear is not after this represented as constantly deranged. Like most persons affected by this kind of insanity, he at times converses rationally.

In the storm scene, he becomes violently enraged, exhibiting what may daily be seen in a mad-house, a paroxysm of rage and violence. It is not until he has seen and conversed with Edgar, the "Philosopher and learned Theban," as he called him, that he became a real maniac. After this, aided by a proper course of treatment, to which we shall again allude, he falls asleep, and sleep, as in all similar cases, partially restores him. But the violence of his disease and his sufferings were too great for his feeble system, and he dies, and dies deranged. The whole case is instructive, not as an interesting story merely, but as a faithful history of a case of *senile insanity*, or the insanity of old age. Slighter degrees of it are not unfrequent in aged people, who, after having given their property to their children, are made unhappy and partially insane because they can not still control it.

Edgar, who is represented in the same play as insane, merely pretends to be so, and for safety assumes the garb, character, and conduct of a class of beggars— known as Tom O'Bedlams. They were persons who had been insane and shut up in a Lunatic Hospital in London, called Bedlam, and from which they were discharged after they became partially restored and harmless. They were licensed to go out as beggars and conducted much as Edgar represents. They often chanted and sang wild ditties and songs, some of which have been preserved.

D'Israeli, in his *Curiosities of Literature*, has inserted a *Tom-a-Bedlam song*, which he discovered in a scarce collection of "Wit and Drollery," published in 1661. The last stanza is as follows, and which he says, "contains the seeds of exquisite romance, worth many an admired poem."

With a heart of furious fancies,
Whereof I am commander;
  With a burning spear,
  And a horse of air,
To the wilderness I wander;
With the knight of ghosts and shadows,
  I summoned am to Tourney:
    Ten leagues beyond
    The wide world's end;
Methinks it is no journey.

Scott represents Madge Wildfire as having been in Bedlam, and makes her sing the following stanza of the same song;

In the bonnie cells of Bedlam
  Ere I was one-and-twenty,
I had hempen bracelets strong

And merry whips, ding-dong,
  And prayer and fasting plenty.

*Fourthly*. Shakspeare believed insanity could be cured by medical treatment. This has been denied, and he is often quoted as authority against medicine and physicians, and principally because he makes Macbeth exclaim, "Throw physic to the dogs—I'll none of it."

But this, Macbeth was led to say in consequence of the reply of the Doctor to a previous question—that he could do nothing to relieve Lady Macbeth, and that "the patient must minister to herself." Professionally speaking, the reply was a very incorrect one—but it was necessary for the plot that Lady Macbeth should not be cured, or else a more correct reply, and better prescription would have been given. That Shakspeare knew of a better course of treatment is evident from the fact that he makes the physician of King Lear adopt it.

Let it be recollected also that this exclamation of Macbeth against physic was made when arming for battle, and when his mind was intently engaged in making arrangement to meet his enemies. Viewed in this light, this careless remark is rational and proper, but surely can not be adduced as evidence that Shakspeare held to such an opinion. On the contrary, that remedial measures are beneficial, and that insanity can be cured by medical means, he has repeatedly stated.

Thus, in King Lear, Cordelia asks in reference to her father, "What can man's wisdom do, in the restoring of his reason?" The physician promptly, and truly answers:

There are means, Madam;
Our foster-nurse of nature is repose,
The which he lacks, that to provoke in him,
Are many simples operative, whose power
Will close the eye of anguish.

So the Abbess, in the Comedy of Errors, proposes to restore Antipholus to his wits,

With wholesome syrups and drugs.

The efficacy of music to calm the disordered mind, Shakspeare also alludes to, and calls it the "best comforter to an unsettled fancy."

The danger of a relapse, and the best means of guarding against it, are stated in the advice given to Cordelia by the physician. He says:

Be comforted, good Madam, the great rage
You see is cured in him, and yet it is danger

To make him even o'er the time he has lost;
Desire him to go in, trouble him no more
Till further settling.

Now we confess, almost with shame, that although near two centuries and a
half have passed since Shakspeare thus wrote; we have very little to add to his
method of treating the insane, as thus pointed out. To produce sleep and to
quiet the mind by medical and moral treatment, to avoid all unkindness, and
when patients begin to convalesce, to guard, as he directs, against everything
likely to disturb their minds, and to cause a relapse—is now considered the best
and nearly the only essential treatment.

*Lastly.* Shakspeare knew that the causes of insanity were various, and has
particularly mentioned some of the most common. He has most frequently alluded
to the influence of grief, anxiety, and melancholy, as the most common causes.

Thus, in Taming of the Shrew, he says

Too much sadness hath congeal'd your blood,
And melancholy is the nurse of frenzy.

In Timon of Athens, he says

His wits are drowned and lost in his calamities.

These, truly, are the most common causes, but he speaks of others. In Troilus
and Cressida, he supposes madness may be caused "by too much blood, and too
little brain," and we regard this as not an unfrequent predisposing cause, though
it is one not often mentioned.

In Macbeth, he alludes to the fact, that some narcotics cause insanity; thus
Macbeth says:

Have we eaten of the insane root
That takes the reason prisoner.

Meaning probably, hen-bane, which has this effect when eaten.

In the Comedy of Errors, he happily alludes to several of the causes of insanity.

In accounting for the insanity of Antipholus, the Abbess after ascertaining
that he had neither lost *wealth or friends*, learns that his wife was jealous of him,
and was constantly reprehending him, and adds,

Therefore came it, that the man was mad:
The venom clamors of a jealous woman
Poison more deadly than a mad dog's tooth.

It seems his sleeps were hinder'd by thy railing:
And therefore comes it that his head is light.
Thou sayest his meat was sauced with thy upbraidings:
Unquiet meals make ill-digestions,
Therefore the raging fire of fever bred;
And what's a fever but a fit of madness?
Thou say'st his sports were hinder'd by thy brawls;
Sweet recreation barred, what doth ensue,
But moody and dull melancholy,
(Kinsman to grim and comfortless despair;)
And, at her heels, a huge, infectious troop
Of pale distemperatures, and foes to life?
In food, in sport, and life-preserving rest
To be disturb'd would mad or man or beast;
The consequence is, then, thy jealous fits
Have scar'd thy husband from the use of wits.

It will be seen, by a careful perusal of the quotation we have made, that he mentions many of the causes of this disease, and those, of which no one who was not an accurate observer, or a thorough student of the disease would ever have thought.

The loss of sleep he mentions first, and according to our observation, this, of all the immediate causes of insanity, is by far the most common. We are apt to say that it is this or that circumstance that caused the insanity; but it is very rare for any anxiety whatever to cause mental aberration unless the sleep is much disturbed; and when this is disturbed to a great degree, and for a long time, as a general rule, insanity or death takes place.

Shakspeare's test of insanity is often mentioned, and sometimes referred to in Courts of Justice. It occurs in Hamlet—when he sees the ghost of his father; his mother, the queen, says to him,

This is the very coinage of your brain
This bodiless creation ecstacy.

To which he replies,

Ecstacy!
My pulse, as yours, does temperately keep time
And makes as healthful music; It is not madness
That I have uttered. Bring me to the test,
And I the matter will reword; which madness
Would gamble from.

Now we admit that this is a very correct test in many cases of insanity, and know of none better in order to determine whether there is a sufficient degree of mental soundness requisite to make a will. In all such cases the person suspected of insanity should be asked at different times to *reword*, or repeat what he had said or proposed. And if the memory does not *gamble* from the subject, the mind may be deemed sufficiently sound to dispose of property by will—provided there is no evidence adduced of disorder of the moral powers by disease, and to such an extent as to bias the intellect. The test is generally a good one, but as an universal one it is not, as in many varieties of mental aberration there is no defect of memory.

But it was very proper for Hamlet, although deranged, to allude to it. There is scarcely a day but we are thus addressed by patients. That the pulse is regular and the memory good is often adduced by patients as evidence of their not being insane, as their friends regard them. And it is not given as an opinion of Shakspeare, but is Hamlet's own comment on his case, which, as we have said, is similar to that which we almost daily hear from those decidedly deranged at this Asylum.

In conclusion;—where did Shakspeare obtain his minute and accurate knowledge of insanity, of its causes, varieties, and treatment? Something he may have learned from books; but far more, we believe, from his own observation. He must have seen individuals affected with the various forms of insanity he has described; heard their histories and marked their conduct and conversation, or he could not have been so minutely correct.

The insane he has described are not imaginary characters, but may now be found in every large Asylum. In this extensive establishment are all the insane characters described by Shakspeare. Here may be seen Jacques, "wrapt in a most humorous sadness." At times sociable and merry, but more frequently sad and melancholy; but not like others, as he has, like his prototype, a "melancholy of his own." Here, too, is Macbeth, much of the time conversing rationally, and manifesting a most noble nature, and at other times clutching imaginary daggers, or screaming, terrified by the ghosts of the departed.

Here, also, is Hamlet; the well-bred gentleman and scholar, once the "glass of fashion and the mold of form; the observed of all observers;" whose conversation is now often instructive and interesting, but who, at other times is overwhelmed with imaginary troubles, that cause him to exclaim more frantically than Hamlet, and to our terror, "oh, that the Everlasting had not fixed his canon against self-slaughter."

Here, also, is King Lear, in a paroxysm of wrath, at some trivial occurrence, but much of the time venting all his rage upon his relations and friends, for abuse of him; and then occasionally in good humor, and conversing with much apparent satisfaction with some demented or half-idiotic patient, whom he considers a "Philosopher and most learned Theban."

Here, also, is the gentle Ophelia; past cure, past hope, with her pure mind in fragments, playing on the piano and singing the songs of Moore and other modern poets, instead, like the Ophelia of Shakspeare, those of the poets of that time.

Shakspeare must have seen Lear, and Hamlet, and Ophelia; no reading would have enabled him to have given such complete and minute histories of them, as cases of insanity. With him, however, as we have already said, a little observation no doubt, would suffice. One visit to the Bedlam Hospital, would teach him much; for, what on other minds would have made no impression, or been immediately forgotten, was by Shakspeare treasured up, even as to the most minute particulars, and when he wished, every look, word, or action of the patient, and every idea he heard advanced by the attendants, he was able to recall.

As already mentioned, this wonderful power of memory and accuracy of observation is possessed to a greater or less extent by all men of genius, and therefore, the writings of such, should not be neglected by those who study man, whether sane or insane. Human nature, as respects the passions and emotions, is ever the same, and correct descriptions of mental phenomena, though of ancient date, are still worthy of our attention.

## 1865—Richard Grant White. From the introduction to *The Comedy of Errors* in *The Works of William Shakespeare*

Richard Grant White (1821–85) was an American writer and Shakespearean scholar. He is the author of *England Without and Within* (1887), *National Hymns: How They Are Written and How They Are Not Written: A Lyric and National Study for the Times* (1861), and *Essay on the Authorship of the Three Parts of Henry VI* (1859).

There is no doubt that *The Comedy of Errors* is an imitation of the *Mencechmi* of Plautus; but the question whether the imitation was direct or indirect has not been decided. We know, from the Record of the Revels at Court, that a play called *The History of Error* was in existence in the year 1576–7; for among the entries for that year is the following:—"The Historie of Error, shewn at Hampton Court on New yeres daie at night, enacted by the children of Pawles."

Malone, who first directed attention to this memorandum, also pointed out a passage in the *Gesta Grayorum*—a contemporary record of the festivities at Gray's Inn, published in 1688—which shows that "a Comedy of Errors, like to Plautus his Menechmus, was played by the players" during the Christmas Revels at that venerable Inn of Court in December, 1594. In 1595 there was published in London a free translation of the *Menazchmi*.[1] Finally, Meres gives us evidence that Shakespeare's *Comedy of Errors* was written at least as early as 1597. These are all the facts on record from which we can determine the origin of this comedy or the date of its production; but as the old *History of Error* is entirely lost, and as we do not know whether the play at Gray's Inn was Shakespeare's Comedy or the older History, we are unable to decide from these data whether Shakespeare's play existed in any form before the publication of the translation from Plautus.

Of internal evidence upon this subject there is very little, and that not of much weight. *Dromio's* reply to *Antipholus,* Act III. Sc. 2, that he found France in the forehead of the globe-like dame who asserted uxorial rights over him, "armed and reverted,[2] making war against her heir," is, however, so plainly a punning allusion to the war of the League, which was closed by Henry IV.'s apostasy in 1593, that there can hardly be a doubt as to the existence of the passage before that date. For although it is true that 'heire' might be a misprint or loose spelling of 'haire,' to which it is changed in the folio of 1632, the allusion yet exists in as full force, in the otherwise senseless words "armed and reverted, making war," and the pun remains with a different spelling. The likeness between the phraseology of the translated *Mencechmi* and *The Comedy of Errors* is very slight indeed; and all other similarity is due, of course, to the original. *Adriana* says, Act II. Sc. 1, "poor I am but his stale," and the Wife in the translated *Mencechmi* says, "He makes me a stale and a laughing stock": W. W. translates,

> nunc ibo in tabernam: vasa et argentum tibi Referam,
> "Ile go strait to the Inne, and deliver up my accounts, and all your stuffe,"

and *Antipholus* of Syracuse says, "Come to the Centaur; fetch our stuff from thence;" and although 'stuff' and 'stale' were generally used in Shakespeare's time as they are here used, in these speeches they have somewhat the air of reminiscences.

That the author of *The Comedy of Errors* knew the story of the *Mencechmi*, needs, of course, no setting forth; but that he had studied it closely, either in the original or in a translation, is evident from similarity in minor points between the plays. In both the resident brother is married; in both the wife is shrewish; in both she has brought her husband a large dowry; in both the Courtesan appears; and in both the resident brother seeks refuge at her table from the jealous clamors of his wife; the incident of the chain is common to both, and is used by each dramatist, though with a difference, for the same purpose; in both the wandering brother gives his purse to his servant to be carried to the inn; in both the wife, on account of the behavior of his double, finally supposes her husband to be lunatic, and in the one case sends and in the other brings a leech to take him in charge, who in both encounters the husband himself. It is also noteworthy that in the first stage directions of the original, one *Antipholus* is called *"Errotis"* and the other *"Sereptus,"*—misprints, doubtless, for *'Erraticus'* and *'Surreptus'*—meaning 'wandering' and 'stolen.' Now, in *The Comedy of Errors* the resident brother is not stolen, but in the *Mencechmi* he is, and is designated as *Surreptus;* and the traveller, who is not called *Erraticus* in Plautus' Dramatis Persons, but *Sosicles,* is, however, called 'the Traveller' in W. W.'s translation. This translation, although not published until 1595, had then been made and handed about for some time, as we know by the address of "The Printer to the Readers" which introduces it. In this he says, or, without doubt, the author for him,—"The writer hereof (loving Readers) having diverse of this Poettes Comedies Englished, for the use and delight of his private friends, who in Plautus owne words are not able to understand them: I have prevailed so far with him as to let this one go farther abroad," &c.

In the absence of evidence which amounts to proof, we may yet form an opinion; and my own, based upon a consideration of the facts just stated and of the play itself, is, that Shakespeare, at the very beginning of his dramatic career, wishing to supply his theatre with an amusing comedy to take the place of a rude imitation of the *Mencechmi,* already somewhat known to the public, read that play in the original as thoroughly as his "small Latin" (small in the estimation of so complete a scholar as Jonson) enabled him to read it; that he also read W. W.'s translation in manuscript; and that then, using for the more comic parts the doggerel verse in which the elder play was written, for the passages of sentiment the alternate rhymes of which *Venus and Adonis* and *Romeo and Juliet* show his early preference and his mastery, and for the serious Scenes the blank verse which he was the first to bring to perfection, and which appears in great though not yet matured beauty in *The Two Gentlemen of Verona,* he wrote *The Comedy of Errors:* that, in the extravagant Scenes, he deliberately imitated, *populo ut placeret,* the versification of the old play, and perhaps adopted some of it with improvement; that this was done about 1589–90; and that the play thus produced may have been somewhat rewritten by him in its first and last Scenes in the long period during which it remained unprinted in the possession of the theatre.

It is to be observed that although the poetical value of *The Two Gentlemen of Verona* is much greater than that of *The Comedy of Errors,* the dramatic arrangement of the latter is much more skilful, and indicates longer theatrical experience on the part of the author.

The difference between the comedy of the Latin and that of the English dramatist is very wide, both in the way of addition and alteration; the most important addition being that of another pair of twins as attendants upon those who figure in the Latin play. The introduction of these tends greatly to complicate the confusion out of which the fun of this extravaganza arises. Whether the thought was original with Shakespeare or was taken from the old play, we have no means of ascertaining; but in the use made of the bondsmen we recognize the younger hand of him in whose maturer works his perception of the ridiculous and enjoyment of the broadest humor are no less apparent than his delight in all that is grand and beautiful in Man and Nature. Yet the very passages in which the *Dromios* are most prominent are those which seem most unmistakably the production of an inferior and more ancient writer. How difficult is it to believe that the rhyming part of Act III. Sc. 1, for instance, was written, at any time or for any purpose, by the author of the fine blank verse which precedes and follows it! It is more than possible that the two slaves were added in the older play to doubly supply the clown or buffoon, without which, on our ancient stage, a comedy was not a comedy. In the substitution of *Luciana,* the sister of *Adriana,* for the Father of the Latin comedy, we very surely have an indication of Shakespeare's dramatic skill; the expostulations which he puts into the mouth of the young woman are far more convincing and to the purpose than the reproaches which Plautus makes the old man deal out to both husband and wife. The introduction of *Luciana* also enabled the author to establish, in the relations between her and *Antipholus* of Syracuse, a new interest entirely wanting to the Latin play. The Parasite, who figures so largely in the *Mencechmi,* as in all Latin comedies, is omitted, as a character altogether foreign to the taste of an English audience, and needless to the production of that confusion which is the only motive of Shakespeare's play; in which, too, the action is more intricate than in its model, the movement more rapid, and the spirit much more lively, light, and humorous.

Concerning the place and the period of the action of this play, it seems that Shakespeare did not trouble himself to form a very accurate idea. The Ephesus *of The Comedy of Errors* is much like the Bohemia of *The Winter's Tale*—a remote, unknown place, yet with a familiar and imposing name, and therefore well suited to the purposes of one who as poet and dramatist cared much for men and little for things, and to whose perception the accidental was entirely eclipsed by the essential. Anachronisms are scattered through it with a profusion which could only be the result of entire indifference—in fact, of an absolute want of thought upon the subject. The existence of an abbey in Ephesus, however, is not to be considered as among them. For Christianity was established there about the middle of the fourth century; and Ephesus remained a Greek and Christian city till about A. D. 1313. The action of the play may, perhaps, be referred to about the middle of this period.

## NOTES

1. "A pleasant and fine Conceited Comoedie, taken out of the most excellent wittie Poet Plautus: Chosen purposely from out the rest, as least harmefull, and yet most delightfull. Written in English by W. W.—London. Printed by Tho. Creede, and are to be sold by William Barley, at his shop on Grations srreete, 1595." This W. W. is supposed by Anthony Wood, in his *Athence Oxonienses,* to have been William Warner, the author of *Albion's England,* a sort of chronicle in verse, first published at London in 1586. 4to.

2. A misprint, left uncorrected here.

‑‑‑≈∾∿∥∞‑‑‑          ‑‑‑≈∾∿∥∞‑‑‑          ‑‑‑≈∾∿∥∞‑‑‑

## 1877—Denton J. Snider. "The Comedy of Errors," from *System of Shakespeare's Dramas*

Denton Jacques Snider (1841-1925) was a writer, educator, literary critic, accomplished classicist, and one of the original members of the St. Louis Philosophical Society. He is the author of *Homer in Chios: An Epopee* (1891), *Modern European Philosophy: The History of Modern Philosophy Psychologically Treated* (1904), and *Lincoln in the White House: A Dramatic Epos of the Civil War* (ca. 1913).

This play should be placed first in the list of Shakespeare's Pure Comedies, not only on account of the period of its origin, but also on the score of logical development. It is simply a comedy of Situation, whose sole instrumentality is Natural Resemblance, for not even Disguise is employed. It, therefore, exhibits an action of the most external kind; human purpose is almost wholly removed from its sphere. Man is thus represented as controlled by chance; his will is reduced to the narrowest limits possible. All the individuals—even the clowns—are fully in earnest in the pursuit of their ends, though these ends are an utter deception. The characters are always doing something quite different from what they seem to be doing; there is an appearance continually dancing before their senses, whereby they are led into the most ridiculous acts. Comic Situation, into which the individual is thrust from without, through no volition of his own, is the rule of this drama; life is a complete, sensuous delusion. Nowhere else has the Poet indulged in such a play of wholly external influences.

It is easy to see that there can be but little development of character in a work of this kind. Character rests upon the internal nature of the person; his disposition must be shown in his actions, and his actions must, therefore, be made the means of its portraiture. For the Drama takes the human deed as the vehicle of expressing the feelings, motives, purposes, thoughts—in fine, the entire spiritual nature—of man. Such is the Drama in its highest form. Freedom cannot be wholly obliterated. But, if the individual is made the victim of chance—of unforseen external power—his character has little to do with his destiny. He is determined, not from within, but from without; his enforced actions thus become a very slight indication of his nature. Still, no doubt there is some manifestation of character, even under such circumstances, though it is very superficial and inadequate. In the present drama, therefore, characterization stands decidedly in the background. We are to think only of the ridiculous situations in which the people who appear in it are placed.

The characterization, incomplete as it is, should, however, be noticed, and contrasted with the riper procedure of the Poet. It moves in certain stiff, traditional types, which hardly rise to a living, concrete individuality—that is, the persons are more like puppets than complete men and women—an abstraction rather than a reality. Let us take notice of the most definite figures here. The two Dromios are the ever-recurring clowns, with their merry pranks; Pinch is the old picture of the narrow-minded pedant, which is repeated by Shakespeare several times without essential variation. Adriana is the jealous shrew, whose scolding propensity the Poet will develop fully in a succeeding drama. All these forms are borrowed from older and foreign comedies. Their bareness is manifest; one or two peculiarities make up the sum of their characterization; the complete exhibition of all the qualities of a subjective nature, such as we find in other creations of the Poet, is wholly wanting. The individual, when thus made purely the sport of external influences, cannot show any of the deeper elements of character.

There are three movements to the drama, though the first and the last are very short—the one having more the nature of an introduction, the other of a hasty close. We are, in the beginning, told of the disruption of the family of Ægeon; this is the serious—indeed, almost tragic—background of the action; it furnishes the ethical element in which the play moves. The second part shows the "errors" which are rendered possible by this separation of the members of the Family. Here are found the comic situations, as well as the greater portion of the drama. The mistakes of the two pairs of twins, through Natural Resemblance, spring from their previous separation. The third part is the mutual recognition of parents and children, and the restoration of all the members of the disrupted Family. This reunion, in its turn, results from the mistakes which produce so much confusion.

The first movement is the narrative of Ægeon, who is the father, and, therefore, the head, of the Family. The two pairs of twins, and their personal resemblance, are noted; but an accident—a shipwreck—has separated Ægeon from his wife, from one of his sons, and one of the servants. Many years have elapsed; the twins have grown up to manhood; their relations, however, are unknown to themselves, to their parents, and to the world. Should they happen to meet, then the mistakes would follow. The family of Ægeon is thus cut in two just in the middle. Now comes the second separation—the father permits the remaining son and servant to travel in search of the lost brother. But they, too, disappear—do not return to the parent. We also learn, later in the play, that a corresponding misfortune happens to the mother in respect to the other children. Thus the Family seems utterly disrupted and destroyed, but just this unhappy condition of things is the basis for a return to unity. The present family is endowed with certain peculiarities which will rescue it—which will force the world to untie the knot of difficulties which arise. These peculiar elements are the double pair of twins, the personal resemblance of the twin sons and of the twin servants, and the identity of their respective names. Here we see the chief means for a discovery of the lost members, and their restoration to the Family. The ground now being cleared, and all the pre-suppositions being explained, the main action of the play begins.

The second movement shows the mistakes which arise from a double Natural Resemblance, and the consequences of taking one person for another in society. These consequences are carried to such a degree of bewilderment that quite all the relations of life become confused and uncertain, and everything fixed seems to be unsettled; even institutions are turned into the sport of accident. The one thread moves about the Ephesian Antipholus as the central figure; he is a substantial and well-known citizen—an old and intimate friend of the ruler; in times past he has been a brave soldier in defense of the country. He is married also, and thus belongs to the domestic relation; still further, he is engaged in business, and, hence, is brought into familiar contact with the other members of the community. It will be seen that he is an important personage of society, to which he stands in manifold relations. He is known by everybody, and is recognized as having a certain established position and character. In general, he is the substantial man who is connected by an indefinite number of ties with the world around him. Now, into this network, a total stranger is introduced, who resembles him, and is everywhere taken for him. This is the Syracusan Antipholus, who is totally unknown to all these relations, still he is thrown into them; neither he nor society is aware of the change. Personal resemblance is the cause of the mistakes, and the sameness of names prevents the deception from being discovered. The remarkable result is that, by the displacement of one individual, the whole community is thrown into disorder.

To introduce more complications, the same circumstances are repeated in the two servants. The foreign Dromio is put into the relations of the Ephesian Dromio; there thus arises a continual crossing of purposes, which can almost be reduced to a mathematical diagram, so completely external is the procedure.

The first of these relations, therefore, which is seriously disturbed is that of master and servant. The double similarity becomes the source of the most ridiculous confusion. The one Dromio is sent out upon an errand, and meets the wrong master; it is evident that their presuppositions are entirely different—that their talk will lie in two wholly separate worlds. The result is that at first each supposes the other to be jesting; but afterwards the matter becomes serious, and the servant gets a flogging. Now, when the rightful servant appears, he is no longer in his former relation to his master, on account of the intervention of the former servant. So they pass and repass, with increasing entanglement; one party sends a Dromio, who comes to the wrong master with an incomprehensible message. All soon see that something is out of joint, yet what it is they cannot tell; some external influence is clearly interfering, which is the more terrible because unknown. The foreign master and servant become frightened; they very naturally conclude that it is the land of spirits and goblins; they will leave it at the earliest opportunity. But here, again, trouble arises; cause and effect no longer hold; their means for departure are defeated at every move. Dromio is sent to find a ship to sail away in, and brings back a remittance of money. Thus they are tossed about—the helpless victims of chance. It is no wonder that they believe themselves to be dreaming, to be transformed into beasts, to have come to a supernatural realm, for all natural mediation has ceased.

Next the difficulty is carried into the Family. The wife sends the servant to bring her husband home to dinner; again the wrong man is found; it is the Syracusan Antipholus, who has no wife, and who denies the relation on the spot. His answer is brought back to her; the result is a violent fit of jealousy. Then the woman appears in person—berates the stranger for his infidelity; the ethical feeling of the wife thus becomes comic, for its object is an appearance—a delusion. But he has to go home with her to dinner; the integrity of the Family seems in jeopardy; we tremble lest the mistake may lead to an ethical violation. But a happy turn is made—the young Syracusan is attracted to the unmarried sister, and turns away from the married woman. Now all is again right and proper. This sister, too, is victimized, for she thinks she is receiving the attentions of her brother-in-law—a fact which, no doubt, makes her hesitate longer than she otherwise would. Then comes the true husband to his own house; he finds himself locked out, and appearances look very suspicious; in his spleen he goes off and indulges in a naughty revenge. In all these cases the manifold relations of the Family are endangered by a mere appearance; the individuals are victims of a mistake; one person is substituted for another in the wrong place. The result is that the ethical ties of marriage, for a time, become the playthings of accident. The same phase is reflected in low life in the affair of Dromio and the kitchen queen.

Other complications follow, which it is not necessary to give in detail; the result is, the wife and the community consider the husband to be mad, and Pinch is called upon to cast out the devil. This is the extreme point; man now seems to be irrational—seems to have lost entirely the ability of understanding his relation in the world. Yet it is an appearance merely; Antipholus is still sane, though he is now bound like a maniac. The truth is, society itself has become irrational in its delusion; Mistaken Identity has brought it to the verge of dissolution. But the Family is quite disrupted, for the husband, who is here in chains, must charge, and, indeed, does charge, the wife with the worst species of infidelity. Such is the outcome of the domestic thread of the play. The comic element is that the whole difficulty is a phantom springing from a deception of the senses; the spectator knows where the trouble lies, and is aware that there is no real conflict; he can laugh to his heart's content at a collision which must vanish at once when the cause of the delusion is discovered.

The third principle which is involved in this entanglement is business—the commercial relations of the community. Of Angelo, the goldsmith, a chain has been ordered, which he, however, delivers to the wrong Antipholus, and afterwards demands payment of the other Antipholus. The matter is at first treated as a jest, then it grows serious, and at last an officer is called in to enforce the demand. Here Authority is drawn into the meshes, and is victimized by appearance. Moreover, the goldsmith wants to pay his debts with the money; his good name and commercial credit are involved. Public order is disturbed; an encounter takes place on the street, when the Syracusan pair flee to an abbey—to the protection of a religious house, whereby the abbess, a representative of the Church, becomes entangled in the fantastic sport of chance. Let us notice the situation. The community has now unconsciously eliminated both disturbing elements; the two pairs cannot live in the same society if their resemblance continues to remain unknown. Yet they have done no wrong. But the difficulty cannot rest here; the abbess has defied the Family in the wife, and the Law in the officer; the conflict can only be settled by an appeal to the supreme authority of the land.

This is the State, whose highest representative—the Duke—now comes along very conveniently, bringing Ægeon to execution for a violation of law. All parties rush forward to see the ruler with their grievances; the testimony is heard, but the strange thing is that each side produces several witnesses and proves the truth of its statement; the evidence of the senses becomes a mass of confusion and contradiction. The ruler is himself drawn into the delusion; he concludes that they all have drunk of Circe's cup. To solve the difficulty is beyond his power; the matter is incapable of any adjustment. The supreme institution—the State—which has come to secure justice to man, is whirled into the wild play of chance, and cannot perform its function. The drama can go no further; the solution must soon come, or human institutions will show themselves less firm and substantial than an empty appearance. So much for the second movement.

The third essential element of the action is now to be unfolded, namely, the discovery of the difficulty, and the restoration of the separated members of the Family. For the mystery will be pursued until its origin is found; the human mind is rational, and cannot believe that the world is irrational; it must investigate any unusual disturbance of causation. Ægeon, the father, is present with the Duke, as before states; he recognizes his son, whom, however, he takes to be the Syracusan Antipholus; but Resemblance still has sway, for it is the Ephesian Antipholus. Then the Syracusan Antipholus appears; at once the source of the deception is brought home to the senses themselves when the brothers are seen side by side. Moreover, there is now a mutual recognition between the one son and the father; they have been separated only a few years. The mother is found to be the abbess; Ægeon is pardoned; all the members of the Family are again united. The other apparent conflicts of the wife, Adriana, of the Business, of the

State, are fully explained; the delusion vanishes like a dream; ethical harmony once more prevails; the world is no longer a deceptive mirage of which man is the helpless victim.

The solution of a comedy which rests upon Natural Resemblance is thus made manifest. The resembling individuals are brought together—in fact, they are forced together by the disturbance which they produce. The cause is then clear; the serious purposes, the angry conflicts, are traced to a mistake—to a false conclusion resulting from a sensuous appearance. Such is the one instrumentality of the present play—Natural Resemblance—whose combinations are quite exhausted in its manifold situations. This narrowness makes it somewhat bald and abstract; its externality, too, can never engage human interest very deeply. Still, the simple means is wonderfully employed; it temporarily reduces to its sway the highest institutions, and confounds all the relations of life; to the individual the world seems enchanted, while to the world the individual seems crazy—that is, both sides have lost their true relation toward each other; both sides appear to have become irrational. We become reconciled, however, with this unfree and chaotic representation of human action when we see its profound ethical purpose, namely, the restoration of the disrupted Family.

Let us, even at the risk of being charged with undue subtilization, try to reach down to the foundation of the dramatic instrumentality here employed. Mistaken Identity, as used in this and other comedies, shows how the individual is through society, and society through the individual. We see that, if one unit be displaced and another taken for it, the whole fabric will fall into disorder. All must be reflected in each, and each in all. If one person is put in the place of another person without their knowing the fact and without society's knowing it—that is, without the reflection of all in the one, and of the one in all—the world becomes a craze, and man seems to be irrational. The individual must have society, in which he finds his true relations—he can exist as a reasonable being only in society; on the other hand, society requites the favor and recognizes him as this individual, and none other, in all his manifold relations, and thus gives him a true objective personality. Mistaken Identity steps between society and the individual, and, for a time, destroys their connection. Each side, having its existence through the other, will, by such separation, rapidly pass into confusion and dissolution. But the difficulty rests upon Mistaken Identity, not upon Lost Identity; the trouble, therefore, is not permanent, but the mistake is discovered, and the old relations are all restored.

The interpretation should bring out prominently the ethical elements, which always constitute the living principle of the Drama. These ethical elements are not intended to be confined to mere subjective morality—to the demands of individual conscience. Their purport is far broader; the Ethical World signifies essentially the world of institutions. In the present drama the Family is the sphere in which the action takes place, though other institutions play in; the movement is from the separation of its members to their restoration; between these two extremes lies the entire work.

The disruption of the closest domestic ties is of tragic import, and constitutes the serious element of the drama under consideration. The background is dark and threatening, whose most somber shade is found in the fate of Ægeon, who is even being led out to execution. The parent, in search of his children, has fallen into conflict with the Law. Here we behold a genuine tragic collision, with its two justifiable sides. But of course the comic element is paramount, and strengthened by the contrast with the serious thread. Its force lies in deception— in the reduction of the individual and society to a huge delusion—in making institutions the sport of a mere appearance.

Thus both the Tragic and the Comic are present, side by side, though not completely transfused. Another point must not be overlooked—the entire comic effect rests upon the fact that the audience fully understands the source of the mistakes and complications; the characters, too, are, for the most part, in deep earnest, and do not sport with themselves; thus there is felt to be a chasm between the laughing spectator and the sober-faced actor. Such is, however, the nature of all Comedy of Situation—the audience must be placed above the deception of the characters.

Nor should the reader expect too much of interpretation; no analysis of an artistic work can take the place of the work itself. An explanation of wit is not, and ought not to be, witty, else it is no true explanation; criticism of poetry, too, is not poetical, but it must be quite free itself from the poetical form. A statement of the chemical ingredients of water will not take the place of water itself to a thirsty man; just as little can the sensuous charm and exhilaration of Art be supplied by an abstract account of its content. The feelings often revolt against an analytic interpretation, because people expect too much; they are dissatisfied at the absence of what seems the very essence of the production, namely, the sensuous form. But explanation implies always a change of this form, which is, therefore, just the side which disappears. Poetical natures strongly protest against the substitution of an interpretation for the poem. They are right; no such substitution ought for a moment to be entertained by the critic.

But to ascertain the rationale of an artistic product is not only reasonable, but indispensable. A great drama is a phenomenon quite as wonderful as any which Nature furnishes; let its law be investigated and stated as soon as possible. In fact, Art can be elevated and sustained only by the retroactive power of the critical judgment. The difference between a barbarous and a cultivated taste is acknowledged; whence does it arise? Only from the application of truer canons of Art. But these canons are originally derived from the understanding, though by descent into the feelings and become instinctive in their influence upon the taste of the individual. Simple emotion is blind; it should be directed and filled with intelligence. Feel deeply about that which is rational; reason ought always to furnish the content. The difference between the savage and the civilized man lies, not so much in the feelings themselves, as in the objects about which each person feels. Do not, therefore, read an interpretation of a work of Art with the expectation of finding therein the imaginative or emotional element of that work—disappointment will surely follow.

---

## 1891—Andrew Lang. *"The Comedy of Errors,"* from *The Comedies of Shakespeare*

Andrew Lang (1844–1912) was a Scottish literary critic and classical scholar in addition to writing extensively on mythology, folklore, and religion. He is the author of *Old Friends: Essays in Epistolary Parody* (1890), *Homer and the Epic* (1893), *Myth, Ritual and Religion* (1899), and *History of English Literature: From "Beowulf" to Swinburne* (1912).

If the plays of Shakespeare, like the characters of holy men in the Catholic Church, Roman and Apostolic, had a critic, an *Advocatus Diaboli*, it is thus that he might attack the *Comedy of Errors*. It is somewhat thus that M. Darmesteter does write in a recent popular work on Shakespeare in French: "Of all Shakespeare's plays, the *Comedy of Errors* is, save in the qualities of sympathy and mercy, the least Shakespearian. Perhaps only one quotation from it, 'The pleasing punishment that women bear,' has found a way among our household words. The richness of poetry which Shakespeare lavishes even in such a farce as the *Merry Wives of Windsor* is but rarely present here, in spite of Mr. Halliwell's opinion; and, in place of humor, we have often puns of more than mortal dulness, and the practical joke of thumping slaves with sticks. An ingenious Frenchman has written a treatise on the rôle of the *bâton* in comedy. Nowhere in Shakespeare does the stick play so large a part as in the *Comedy of Errors*. We scarcely recognize the author, except in the grave blank-verse of the opening scenes, in his one study of woman's jealousy, the character of Adriana, and in his kind and happy solution of the comic problem. Parts that seemed made for the play of his humor—the characters of the Courtesan and of Pinch, the 'mad-doctor,' school-master, and conjurer—are almost slurred over, and in these Shakespeare falls very far below his master and original, Plautus. The behavior, again, of Antipholus when charged with being insane has little or none of the pleasant farce which Molière gives us in *Monsieur de Pourceaugnac*, and Plautus in the determination of Menaechmus to be mad if he must. The Dromios are not to be called diverting when compared with the rival Sosii of Plautus, or of Molière in the *Amphitryon*, with their Coleridgian distinctions between their double selves—the self out-of-doors and the self indoors." Thus the hostile critic might speak, and not without truth; but, to follow his argument, we must try to remember the plot of the play.

Now the attempt to describe the plot of the *Comedy of Errors* reminds one of M. Sarcey's labor to analyze *Les Surprises de Divorce*. You clasp your aching brow as you study M. Sarcey, M. Lemaître says, and in place of being comic, the story, when analyzed by him, has the "austerity of a fair page of algebra." But before coming to analysis of the play, and to comparison with its Roman originals, let us glance at the necessary antiquarianisms of the subject, at the date of the piece, and at Shakespeare's mean's of studying his Roman original.

The *Comedy of Errors* was never published in quarto as the "book of the play," or no hint of such a publication has reached us. This perhaps may be a proof that it was not very popular, was not deemed worth printing or pirating. It first appears in the folio (1623). Prynne, the scourge of the stage, says: "Some Playbooks are grown Quarto into Folio, which yet bear so good a price and sale that I cannot but with grief relate it. Shackspeer's Plaies are printed in the best Crowne-paper, far better than most Bibles." On this excellent paper, then, the *Comedy of Errors* was first printed—after Shakespeare's death, of course— but the date when the play was written remains uncertain. As Meres mentions it in his *Palladis Tamia* of 1598, it must, of course, have been earlier than that year, and 1593, 1592, and 1591 have been selected as the most probable dates. One is naturally anxious to put the piece as far back as possible, and it is a pleasant hypothesis of Elze's that Shakespeare may have taken the play with him to town when he left Stratford for London in 1605. Elze remarks that as Green in 1592 called Shakespeare "the only Shakescene in a countrie," he must have been sufficiently popular and noted by that time. Had he not been successful beyond others, Green would not, of course, have envied and assailed him. Now three or four years at least, one may guess, must have been spent in attaining such eminence as provokes literary envy, hatred, and malice. The rudimentary, tentative, and imitative manner of the *Comedy of Errors* is so manifest that we may provisionally look on it as one of Shakespeare's very first essays, and some even put it back among the eighties. But we cannot feel certain that Mr. Richard Simpson is right when he attributes it to the end of 1585. Mr. Thornbury has conjectured that Shakespeare's mind was directed to the humors of twins when he became the parent of twins in January of that year. Much more probably, Shakespeare was merely following, like Molière, on the track of Plautus. His "little Latin" may have been enough to master the *Menaechmi* and the *Amphitryon* of the Roman; or, as we shall see, he may have used a translation. His next step would be to "combine his information," to furnish the twin Menaechmi of one play with twin valets answering to the two Sosii of the other. The number of more or less comic combinations thus added was arithmetically incalculable, and much of the mirth of the *Comedy of Errors* lies in the development of those purely practical jests. Whatever the date of the piece, and however Shakespeare got at his knowledge of Plautus. there can be no doubt that Plautus was the source from which he drew.

The "errors" of the comedy, the mistakes that arise from the existence of persons who are "doubles," must have been among the very earliest things that occurred to the primitive jester when he had to tell a story. The "doubles" may be obtained in various ways, and the development of their adventures may be tragic or comic. To minds believing in magic, the notion of assuming the shape and personality of another was always familiar. Eustathius has preserved a Greek legend according to which Paris won Helen by magic art, having assumed the guise and voice of her husband, Menelaus. It has been argued, from Penelope's reluctance to recognize her returned husband, Odysseus, that Homer was acquainted with this tradition. The story of Jupiter and Amphitryon, how the god assumed the shape of the mortal and deceived his wife, is ancient, and was turned by Plautus to a comic use. He added the idea of making Mercury put on the form of Amphitryon's servant, Sosius, and bully that unlucky slave out of the belief in his own identity. These "shape-shiftings," comic to the fancy of the South, became real and tragic in the imagination of the North, as when Signy changes forms with the witch-wife, and visits her brother Sigmund in this disguise, or when Sigurd lies by Brynhild in the outward form of Gunnar, in the *Volsunga Saga*. Tragic, too, is the exchange in the *Roman de Merlin*, when Uther Pendragon, in the form of Ulfin, her husband, wins the love of Ygerne, and so becomes the father of King Arthur. But confusions of identity lend themselves more easily to comedy. The magical or miraculous element is discarded, and the persons are "doubles" merely because they are twins, and are naturally like each other. This is the *donnée* of the *Menaechmi*, the play of Plautus from which Shakespeare borrows most directly. How much he took, and how much he gave, can only be estimated after studying a brief sketch of the *Menaechmi*.

A merchant of Syracuse (to abridge the prologue of the Latin play) had twin sons, so like that the mother who bore them could not tell one from the other. When the boys were seven years old, the father took one of them, Menaechmus, on board ship, with much merchandise, to Tarentum, and left the other twin at home with the mother. There were games at Tarentum when they arrived, and the father lost his boy in the crowd. A merchant of Epidamnus picked the child up, and carried him home thither. The father died, news of these events reached Syracuse, and the grandfather of the remaining twin called the child by the name of the lost brother, Menaechmus. The merchant of Epidamnus, being childless, adopted *his* Menaechmus, endowed him with all his wealth, saw him married, and died. The Syracusan twin, in the Roman comedy, visits Epidamnus in search of his brother, and all the comic perplexities arise, as each is taken for the other brother.

The play of Plautus, after the usual prologue, begins with a scene in which the Epidamnian Menaechmus, speaking to himself in the presence of his parasite

Peniculus, rehearses a discourse to his jealous wife: "Whenever I go out you ask me where I am going, what business calls me. . . . I have married a spy, not a wife; I have spoiled you by kindness, and presents of slaves, wool, purple, gold. Now I'll try the other tack—I'll seek a lady friend; I'll dine out." And he sends his parasite to a lady named Erotion with presents which he has taken from his wife's wardrobe and jewel-case. It is plain that the wife of Menaechmus has too good reason to be jealous of her rival, Erotion. "How I detest my wife when I see *you!*" he cries to Erotion, when she comes on the stage. "Spoils of hers for you, my rose," he says, offering his gifts. She gives her cook orders to provide dinner for herself, Menaechmus, and the parasite, who "eats for ten." In the second act comes Menaechmus of Syracuse, landed from his ship in Epidamnus, with his slave Messenio, who gives him a very bad account of manners and morals in Epidamnus. Erotion's cook now enters, and in the Syracusan Menaechmus recognizes and addresses the Menaechmus of Epidamnus, asking "where his parasite is." Menaechmus, who, of course, never saw the man before, tells him he must be mad, and bids him buy a pig to sacrifice for his cure. Orestes, in the *Eumenides*, says that he had been purified of his matricidal guilt in the blood of swine; the same expiatory sacrifice was sovran for insanity. The cook maintains that Menaechmus is the lunatic. Erotion bustles about her *partie fine*, and she too recognizes and invites the wrong Menaechmus. "She is drunk or mad," says that hero; but she tells him his name, his father's name, his native country, and everything else which she has learned from Menaechmus of Epidamnus. In real life, of course, the Syracusan Menaechmus would have said, "Why, you take me for my brother," and there the comedy would have ended. But Menaechmus of Syracuse, finding a pretty and hospitable lady, makes up his mind to dine with her, and see the adventure out. *Minore nusquam bene fui dispendio*, he remarks. Peniculus, the parasite of the other Menaechmus, meets him, and charges him with giving his wife's robes and jewels to Erotion. More confusion! Then Erotion's maid bids him take the bracelet which the Epidamnian Menaechmus had given her (his wife's bracelet) to the jeweller's to be repaired. Still more surprises for the Syracusan Menaechmus. He leaves these suspicious quarters, when the wife of Epidamnian Menaechmus enters, upbraiding her husband with stealing her property and carrying it to Erotion. The Epidamnian Menaechmus enters: he has been detained by affairs. He has a scene with his angry wife, and goes to Erotion, who attacks him about the bracelet (which she has now given to *his* twin-brother), and Erotion is as angry as his wedded wife. The wife next assails the wrong Menaechmus. She will be a widow for him, and he replies that she may be "till kingdom come"—*usque dum regnum obtinebit Jupiter*. Her father enters, is appealed to by her, and tells her, as he has often done before, that she must not play the spy on her husband, nor watch his comings and goings. Her husband is a good husband, treats her generously; his amusements are no affair of hers. These were Roman ideas. "But he has given her property to another." "That's bad, if it is true." The old man asks Menaechmus of Syracuse if he has really done this. He denies it by the head of Jupiter, and both men accuse each other of lunacy. Menaechmus even enters into the humor of the scene by affecting to be mad; he invokes Bacchus—*Evoe, evoe, Bromie!*—and begins to rave. At last the old man brings a physician to his supposed son-in-law, and there is an amusing scene in which the mad-doctor interrogates his patient. "Do you sleep well? Do you drink white wine or claret?" In the end the twins meet, explain themselves, and go home together, the Epidamnian Menaechmus arranging for an auction of his goods and the sale of his jealous wife, "if any one will buy her."

This is a curt analysis of the Roman comedy, and if it be obscure as "a fair page of algebra," the *résumé* is lucid in comparison with a *résumé* of Shakespeare's piece, where there is a double self of twins. Now in what way did Shakespeare obtain his knowledge of Plautus and the germ of his farce? Was there an older English play on the matter which he may have recast and accommodated? Mr. Halliwell points out that as early as 1576–7 *The History of Errors* (miswritten "of Terrors") was shown at Hampton Court on New-Year's Day. The "Children of Paul's" acted it, and the pieces played by these school-boys were usually taken from classical sources. Shakespeare may at least have glanced through this old *History of Errors*. As to the original source, Plautus, if Shakespeare *did* attend Stratford Grammar-school (which we cannot demonstrate—Nash talks of his "country learning"), and if that school was conducted like others of its kind, he may well have studied Plautus in the sixth form. Mr. Baynes has proved as much in his essays on the school learning of Shakespeare. He undeniably had "a little Latin"; and what seemed little in Ben Jonson's learned eyes would be amply enough for Shakespeare's purpose. But it is a curious and perhaps noteworthy coincidence that while the *Comedy of Errors* was certainly acted at Grey's Inn in December, 1594, an English prose version of its Latin original, the *Menaechmi*, was published perhaps *before* that date. This old and lively paraphrase bears, it is true, the year 1595, but booksellers have a way of anticipating time, that their books may be longer new. Thus Shakespeare may have seen the translation, in proof at least, or even in MS., before he wrote his own comedy. The translation is entitled

> Menaechmi
> A Pleasant and fine conceited Comedie taken out of the most wittie Poet, Plautus. Chosen purposely out of the rest, as least harmful, and yet most delightful. Written in English by W(illiam) W(arner). T. Creede. London, 1595. 4.

The British Museum has a copy of this very rare quarto, and Mr. Halliwell has reprinted it in his large Shakespeare. The translator tells us in his preface that he "had diverse of the pretty comedies Englished for the use and delight of his private friends, who, in Plautus's own words, are not able to understand them." No doubt the translations were handed about in manuscript, as was the manner of that and later times, and it is perfectly possible that Shakespeare may thus have gained his knowledge of the *Menaechmi*. Recent paradoxical writers about Shakespeare deny him any scholarship. For my own part, I believe he could spell out Plautus in the original; but even if he could not, it has been shown that a translation was not out of his reach. The Elizabethan age was much richer in translations than the sciolists who stir up controversy about Shakespeare and Bacon, suppose. The style of the version by William Warner is like that of B. R's contemporary *Herodotus*, almost too colloquial and idiomatic. "Brahling foole and mad-brained scold as ye are," is Menaechmus's address to his wife, "I mean to dine this day with a sweet friend of mine." Again, "Would every mail could *tame his shrew* as well as I doe mine!" he remarks, after he has taken the poor wife's goods and given them to his "sweet friend." The dinner he orders at Erotion's house has a noble and Shakespearian anachronism: "Some oysters, a marybone pie or two, some artichokes and *potato-rootes*." Shakespeare himself introduces America into his *Comedy of Errors*, but he can hardly be said to have inferred the ancient knowledge of America from W. W.'s "potato-rootes."

From the *Menaechmi*, then, or from W. W.'s translation, or from an older English piece, Shakespeare took the germ of the *Comedy of Errors*; but he has gallantly added as much as he borrowed, has introduced new errors without end, and has reconciled all quarrels in a tender affection and sympathy. Here the opponent of the *Advocatus Diaboli* finds the strength of his case. You do not know how good, how Shakespearian the *Comedy of Errors* is till you have compared it with the Roman treatment of the same situation by Plautus. First. Shakespeare moves the scene from Epidamnus to Ephesus, and queer it is to read of an "Abbess" in the sacred city of Artemis. Then he makes the father of his first pair of twins, the Antipholi, still alive; he comes from Syracuse to Ephesus in his long search for his lost boys. But Syracuse and Ephesus are on ill commercial terms; protection is so strict that if a citizen of one town appears in the markets of the other, he must pay a heavy fine or lose his life. The old father, Aegeon, is in evil plight, and as he has neither the money nor the friend to lend it, he must die. But first he tells the Duke of Ephesus his lamentable story. At Epidamnus his wife had borne him twin boys, and "a poor mean woman" in the self-same inn also bore twins (the Dromios). These Aegeon bought; but he, his wife, and the two brace of twins were all shipwrecked. In drifting on the sea, they were severed. The mother, with one Dromio and one Antipholus, was taken up by one ship; the father, with his Antipholus and his Dromio, by another. When *his* twin came to eighteen years of age he started (with his Dromio) after the other brother, and never came back. Aegeon has set out to find as many of them as he can, and has come at last to Ephesus, where he suffered, as we have seen, from the rancorous system of protection and the war of tariffs. The Duke of Ephesus is very sorry, and reprieves him for a day, during which his younger and later lost son turns up in Ephesus, with *his* Dromio, pretending to be from Epidamnus to evade the protection laws, as before. And now the trouble begins, each Antipholus and each Dromio being taken for the other, and themselves taking either for each. I have no head for mathematics, "the low cunning of algebra" has never been mine, and I recoil from the attempt to disentangle the innumerable complications. The reader would be as puzzled as the writer by an attempt at close analysis. It is like the poem in which a lover who dwells in four-dimensioned space attempts to describe to his lady a dreadful dream in which he beheld a world in three-dimensioned space—our own.

> "Ah, in that dream-distorted clime,
>   These fatal wilds I wandered through,
> The boundaries of space and time
>   Had got most frightfully askew.
> 'What is askew?' my love, you cry.
>   I cannot answer, can't portray;
> The sense of everything awry
>   No language can convey."

In the *Comedy of Errors*, with two sets of "doubles," and with these doubles not able to discriminate between their parallels in either group, with two Antipholi and two Dromios, similar, but dissimilarly situated, everything is, indeed, awry. Do not urge me to be more definite; it is not kind; it may quite shatter a brain which otherwise might last for years, and be moderately serviceable at light work. Even in looking at Mr. Abbey's drawings I feel a kind of hysterical emotion, a feverish frantic ambition to discern t'other from which, just as one is occasionally mad enough to cope with *Bradshaw's Railway Guide*, with the money article in the newspapers, with Lycophron's *Cassandra*, with the family system of the Australian blacks. Nobody should ask to be told the plot of the *Comedy of Errors*. In the play when acted it is not particularly perplexing to a person with fair mathematical ability; but a summary of it, as Sir Walter Scott's child friend, Pet Marjory, said of Nine times Nine, "is devilish." Let it be granted that either Antipholus equals either Menaechmus, and that the Dromios may, therefore, cancel each other for the present. We shall then study the relations of the Ephesian Antipholus to his wife, to his "sweet friend," and his mad doctor, as compared with the similar relations of Plautus's Epidamnian Menaechmus to *his* wife, to Erotion, and to *his* mad-doctor. In these combinations, if we set aside the appearance of old Aegeon, the father, lies such ethical interest as the *Comedy of Errors* can yield; nor, after all, is that slight; and, after all, it is not unworthy of Shakespeare.

The Menaechmus of Plautus treats his wife not only like a profligate, but like a person hopelessly *mal élève*. He gives away her trinkets and dresses to his "dear mouse," as the Elizabethan translator calls Erotion. But Plautus, I think, intends us to understand that Menaechmus has been goaded to this excess by the irritating and perhaps originally causeless jealousy of his wife. Having been long accused, he determines to *deserve* his wife's lectures, as the other Menaechmus feigns to go mad because mad he is everywhere styled. If this idea be correct, Menaechmus is merely bent on "taming his shrew," as the old translator says, quoting the title of the *Taming of the Shrew* in its earlier form, published in 1594 (the translation is of 1595). Now great latitude was permitted of old to the husband with a shrewish wife, as ducking-stools prove. Still Menaechmus, in Plautus, goes too far even for the patience of the wife's father. The old father, in Plautus, exactly holds Dr. Johnson's theory, and a startling theory it sounds to us: "Wise married women don't trouble themselves about infidelity in their husbands." Johnson was not only a religious but a good man; yet Boswell—no pattern—was staggered by the Doctor's ethics. Boswell says, with equal truth and sense, that "a husband's infidelity must hurt a delicate attachment, in which a mutual constancy is implied with such refined sentiments as Massinger has exhibited in his play of *The Picture*." He quotes, indeed, a counter-statement of the great Doctor's; yet, years later, Johnson repeated his original observation. The truth is that Boswell was, comparatively, a Liberal, while the Doctor's Toryism on this point dated from pagan antiquity; from the morals of Plautus and of that republican Rome when a wife was *in manu mariti*: her husband's chattel.

When we turn to Shakespeare's treatment of this question, we first observe that the jealousy of womankind is all but absent from his dramas. Here he shows his inevitable artistic tact. A man's jealousy is tragic, like that of Othello or Leontius, or it is comic, like that of Ford in the *Merry Wives*. It is an affair of *Don Garcie de Navarre*, on one hand, or of George Dandin on the other. But the jealousy of a woman in modern society may be neither dignified and terrible enough for tragedy, nor grotesque and humorous enough for comedy; it is bitter, shrill, ugly, a deathless torment, a poison and perversion of nature; too mean for tragedy, too hateful for comedy. In the old comedy, the Restoration comedy, the luckless husband is a standing though cruel joke. The luckless wife no man nor woman laughs at. Yet she does not fit with tragedy unless she be an empress or a queen, say an Amestris or an Eleanor, who can give her passion a tragic scope, and indulge it with a full cup of revenge. This may, at least, be offered as an explanation; or perhaps others may say that of all passions feminine jealousy is most remote from the sympathy of men, and that it is the men who write the plays.

Shakespeare, unlike Plautus, has tempered the spectacle of Adriana's green-eyed and watchful rage by placing a sweeter-tempered sister, Luciana, beside her. "A man is master of his liberty," says this good-humored wench, when the married Antipholus does not come home in time for dinner, and when, as Dromio cries (to the wrong brother):

"The capon burns, the pig falls from the spit,
The clock hath strucken twelve upon the bell;
My mistress made it one upon my cheek:
She is so hot, because the meat is cold."

The shrew, he adds, "will score your fault upon my pate"; and he has "some of my mistress's marks upon my shoulders." For Adriana is not only jealous, she is a termagant. Adriana will not listen to Luciana's

"Self-harming jealousy!—fie! beat it hence."

Adriana replies:

"Unfeeling fools can with such wrongs dispense.
          * * * * * *
Since that my beauty cannot please his eye,
I'll weep what's left away, and weeping die."

Then, pleading as it were to her husband with the wrong Antipholus, she breaks into poetry and passion, for even in this play passion cannot come in Shakespeare's mind without moving him to poetry, nor can even a shrewish jealousy fail to rouse his sympathy with mortal pain:

"How comes it now, my husband, O! how comes it,
That thou art then estranged from thyself?
Thyself I call it, being strange to me,
That, undividable, incorporate,
Am better than thy dear self's better part.
Ah, do not tear away thyself from me;
For know, my love, as easy may'st thou fall
A drop of water in the breaking gulph,
And take unmingled thence that drop again,
Without addition or diminishing,
As take from me thyself, and not me too.
          * * * * * *
Come, I will fasten on this sleeve of thine;
Thou art an elm, my husband, I a vine."

So she bids her husband (that is, *not* her husband, but the wrong Antipholus) dine with her, and Dromio drives the real Antipholus from his own door. The wretched married Antipholus, in Shakespeare, then, does not seek

> "a wench of excellent discourse;
> Pretty and witty; wild, and yet too, gentle,"

that he may dine with her, till he is turned away from his very door, while his wife entertains a stranger. Thus Shakespeare provides his Antipholus with such an excuse as Plautus never granted to his Menaechmus. Elizabethan England was not Rome, after all, and Shakespeare's morality is better than Dr. Johnson's. Meanwhile Luciana pleads for her jealous sister very prettily with the wrong Antipholus, who is a little minded to fall in love with her. The chain, the trinket in Shakespeare's play, has been purchased by the married Antipholus as a present for his wife, not stolen from her by him as a gift to another woman, as in Plautus. Thus, throughout, Shakespeare is gentle and kindly where Plautus is all but ruffianly. The prize of what poetry exists in the play goes to the Englishman; the Roman has the advantage in comic passages. When Antipholus is arrested, in the confusions, Adriana promptly sends him his ducats—an odd coin to keep in a Greek Ephesus of old. Yet the married Antipholus has been drawn so far (no doubt in his natural wrath at being locked out of his own house) as to promise the chain to the "wench of excellent discourse," and to receive a ring from her. Adriana has found a mad-doctor for her husband, a conjurer, who tries to exorcise a devil out of him, as in Plautus the madness is to be cured by an expiatory sacrifice of a pig. Finally Adriana desires to have the madman bound, as in old practice, when whipping was the cure of lunacy. And she might, by her own confession, have driven any husband mad by her jealousy.

> "In bed, he slept not for my urging it;
> At board, he fed not for my urging it;
> Alone, it was the subject of my theme;
> In company, I often glanced it:
> Still did I tell him it was vile and bad."

"And thereof," says the Abbess, who proves to be Aegeon's wife, and the mother of the twin Antipholi—

> "And thereof came it that the man was mad:
>       * * * * * *
> In food, in sport, and life-preserving rest
> To be disturb'd, would mad or man or beast.

The consequence is, then, thy jealous fits
Have scar'd thy husband from the use of wits."

But here that excellent good girl, Luciana, stands up for her sister against her
sister's self:

"She never reprehended him but mildly."

Then the Duke of Ephesus comes on the scene. Every one makes his complaint,
the married Antipholus particularly denouncing the mad-doctor, a forerunner
of Romeo's apothecary:

"a hungry, lean-faced villain;. . . .
A needy, hollow-eyed, sharp-looking wretch."

So all meet. Evening brings all home: Aegeon, now pardoned, his wife—the
Abbess—both their children, and both Dromios. Adriana is *not* sold by auction in Shakespeare as Menaechmus would have sold his wife; we may believe
that the bachelor Antipholus married the sweet Luciana, and that Adriana
learned a lesson for life in Shakespeare's *École des Femmes*. We may believe it,
for Shakespeare has goodness and forgiveness enough for them all, for all men.
Here, as in that darkling comedy, *Measure for Measure*, mercy is the burden of
his poem; mercy is the last word even of his buffooneries, no less than of that
match between love and life and death, where even Claudio and Angelo are
finally forgiven.

Nor need the lesson be wasted on the commentator, the indolent reviewer.
He may have come prepared to ban the *Comedy of Errors* almost utterly, and for
this once to join the modern chorus of those who carp at our earlier literature,
at our fathers and our betters of the dead generations. But, lo! he finds himself
blessing instead of cursing, and discovering in Shakespeare's prentice-work (as
the *Comedy of Errors* must be reckoned) still the same Shakespeare, the same
gentle heart, and that wisdom which watches men

"With larger, other eyes than ours,
To make allowance for us all."

The full force of Shakespeare's merit, however, will not strike the reader who
has not compared Shakespeare with his original, with Plautus. In Plautus
the jealous woman is a mere shrew; the husband is callous and a profligate.
Shakespeare pities even the pain of a groundless jealousy; he touches its bitter
passion with poetry; he gives it an excuse and an amiable contrast in Luciana.
Even were his comic humors weaker in this piece—and it is undeniably

weak—his advance in kindness, courtesy, in tolerant knowledge of human nature, marks him, even in his prentice-work, as already Shakespeare.

## 1895—Bernhard ten Brink. "Shakespeare as a Comic Poet," from *Five Lectures on Shakespeare*

Bernhard ten Brink (1849–1924) was a German philologist. He is the author of the *History of English Literature* (1895–96) and *The Language and Meter of Chaucer* (1884).

The first collected edition of Shakespeare's plays, the folio of the year 1623, is divided into three parts, and contains, as well as was then possible, all the material. First come the *Comedies*, then the *Histories*, and lastly the *Tragedies*. Later editors and commentators have often preferred a different division: Comedies, Tragedies, and Dramas [*Schauspiele*—There is no exact English equivalent for *Schauspiel*, which denotes something between tragedy and comedy.] and the latter classification is familiar to us. Now what relation does this modern arrangement bear to the old one? Does what we term drama coincide with the historical or chronicle play? or, if this be not the case, what is the reason that in Shakespeare's time they found no necessity of placing the drama in a different category from comedy and tragedy? and how is it that we, on the other hand, no longer recognize the "history" as a subdivision of the drama? The last question is easily disposed of.

The history is primarily so called only on account of the nature of its subject matter. By the term *history* or *chronicle play* is understood a drama whose action is taken from English history. The history of a foreign people, for instance, the Roman, was not classed under that head; "Julius Caesar," "Coriolanus," "Antony and Cleopatra," are accounted as tragedies. Neither does old Scottish history, nor the accounts, so rich in fable, of the old British kings, furnish material for the histories: neither " Macbeth," nor, on the other hand, " Lear" or "Cymbeline," belongs to the chronicle plays. It is, then, English history alone, in its narrower signification, that is understood; in reality, only such periods of that history as were not too far removed from that time; periods, finally, about which they possessed abundant sources of information, and which were vividly brought before Shakespeare's contemporaries by various representations of a popular character.

Among no other nation at that time was the knowledge of their own past so generally diffused, so incorporated into their very blood, so actively effective, as among the English. And with one great period of this past the Elizabethan age was pre-eminently familiar. It is the period which separates the Anglo-Norman era from the era of the Tudors, the time in which modern England, as regards its speech, its manners, its constitution, was being evolved in ever more definite outlines: the thirteenth, fourteenth, and fifteenth centuries. The Elizabethan epic drew its subjects chiefly from this period; it likewise furnished the material of the historical dramas. Almost all of Shakespeare's historical pieces, too, play in this epoch, and notably in the fifteenth century; only in his "Henry VIII." does he finally venture to portray more recent times.

It is evident that, from the standpoint of the aesthetic critic, there is no justification for the existence of the historical play as a separate species of dramatic composition, much as it may signify from the standpoint of the English patriot and politician. But it is not a question merely of names, of the fitness of the term *history*, and the adoption of a third species to be classed alongside of *tragedy* and *comedy*. In reality, politics and patriotism,—not aesthetics alone,—filled a very important part in the historical dramas of that time, and plays of this kind cannot, for the most part, be judged from the point of view of strict dramatic theory. The necessity of paying altogether unusual regard to the underlying story, the refractory character of that story, the abundance of facts and figures, the multitude of inevitable premises—all this does not, in many ways, allow the poet that symmetrical working out and transparent combination of motives, that intensifying of characteristics, above all, that concentration of dramatic interest, which theory justly demands of the drama. The king who gives the name to a piece is often not its real hero; in many cases we seek for one in vain, or find, instead of one, two, three, or more, and finally grow conscious that our sympathies are enlisted less in the individuals than in the fate of the personages as a whole, that the unity of the work lies not in the powers of attraction of an individual depicted as the central figure, but in the idea which proceeds from the relations between historical facts.

Among productions of this kind, however, two distinctly different types may be distinguished: a freer and a stricter art form, more or less strongly marked according to the individuality of the poet and the nature of the material. In the freer form the poet seeks to replace the dramatic advantages which he must dispense with, especially concentration, by other qualities—by the charm produced by the well-ordered abundance of varied events and interesting personages; by the blending of historical *genre* pictures, humourous scenes, with affairs of state. Historical plays constructed on this type exhibit a certain resemblance to the epic. The other form betrays the endeavour, by its condensation of the matter, by the energetic treatment and close interlacing of the chief elements, to approach the strictly dramatic form,—tragedy, in fact,—as closely as possible. In both forms Shakespeare has created unparalleled models; the freer culminates in his "Henry IV." the stricter in his "Richard III." On the whole, however, he favours the freer form, to which the story, as a rule, more readily lends itself.

If we comprehend now why the national historical play constitutes in Shakespeare a class apart, it still remains to be explained why he does not recognize the drama [*Schauspiel*] in general as a separate species, as distinguished from tragedy and comedy. The reasons for this fact will be evident to us when we shall have become acquainted with Shakespeare as a tragic and as a comic poet.

When discussion turns upon the favourites of the comic Muse in modern times, everyone at once thinks of Molière; Shakespeare's name will not so directly occur even to connoisseurs and worshippers. What is the cause of this? May it perhaps be that they are right who assert that Shakespeare does not equal the French poet in comic power? But how can such an opinion be maintained in face of obvious facts? Allow me to recall those facts to your minds.

If we review the different qualities which constitute a comic poet, and ask whether Shakespeare possessed them, we shall find that he commanded them to as great or even to a greater degree than Molière. Has there ever been one who has so profoundly fathomed the human heart, with its passions, its frailties, its vices? a more subtle observer of every species of peculiarity, whether it spring from the inmost fibres of the heart, or appear merely on the surface? Where has there been in modern times a poet who conceived the ludicrous with such keenness and represented it with so sure a touch? In what dramatist do we find a greater wealth of genuinely comic figures—figures whose mere appearance suffices to put us into the most jovial humour, whose speech and action irresistibly provoke us to laughter? And as for wit and humour, who can deny that Shakespeare's wit, though it may contain far more that is antiquated than Molière's, who presupposed a more fastidious taste and a severer reasoning tendency—who can deny that Shakespeare's wealth is so great that, even after abstracting all lighter and cheaper matter, enough remains to make him dispute Molière's precedence? while Shakespeare's humour in its depths as well as its cheerful glow far surpasses that of the Frenchman. In the art, too, with which he prepares the way for significant situations of highly comic effect he is second to no dramatist. Just recall the scene in "Love's Labour's Lost" where the members of the academy of Navarre, who have all forsworn the love of woman and have all perjured themselves, are in turn unmasked each by another, till finally each one, to his mortification, but, at the same time, to his comfort, becomes conscious that he can cast no reproach at the others nor they at him. The scene is so capitally introduced, and so effectively carried out with such simple means, that it can complacently bear comparison with any similar scene in Molière—for instance, with the one which leads to the catastrophe in the "Misanthrope." In one point only does the English poet seem decidedly inferior to the French: in the firm handling of the dramatic action, in the unity of structure of the comic drama. If we consider, however, that Shakespeare displays in a most eminent degree in his tragedies precisely those qualities which we sometimes miss in his comedies, it appears to us most improbable that this is a proof of inability. Such an assumption becomes untenable, yes, absurd, when we reflect that Shakespeare's earliest comedies are far more regularly and firmly constructed, are, indeed, in many respects more effective as comedies, than those of his ripest period.

The highly complicated action in "The Comedy of Errors" is managed with such perfect knowledge of the technique of the stage, and with so sure a hand, that the suspense is increased with every scene and is only removed in the catastrophe. No French drama of intrigue is more effectively constructed than is this, the first effort of Shakespeare's pen. Perfectly true to art, also, is the development of the first four acts of " Love's Labour's Lost," while in the last a certain diminution of suspense is, of course, noticeable. In "The Taming of the Shrew," where he enters into the style of an older author, and confines himself essentially to the reconstruction of the main action, this main action stands out in such powerful relief, and is evolved with such true logical sequence, and with so irresistible an effect, from the characters of the participants, that this play still forms a powerful attraction of the dramatic repertory, though in some respects it was already antiquated in Shakespeare's time. Among the comedies of Shakespeare's maturest period, "The Merry Wives of Windsor" exhibits the most regular structure; but those very comedies which are richest in substance and in poetic beauty lack the strict unity of a comedy of Molière. In Molière's best works we have either a strongly marked character with some prominent peculiarity or passion, who forms the centre of the action, or this place is taken by some dominant custom, that is to say, some dominant abuse, of the time, to which a number of the personages of the drama pay homage. That character or custom controls the whole action, and nearly all the dramatic effects may in the last instance be traced back to it. In Shakespeare's most important comedies we see two or even three actions artfully interwoven, yet in such a manner that, upon a purely superficial view, the dramatic structure appears in many ways somewhat loose, and is held together chiefly by the poetic idea. But, above all, that which here constitutes the centre of interest is, as a rule, no comic action at all, whether it spring from the faults of a character or the tendencies of a time; the principal action, indeed, has generally an earnest, touching, or, it may be, romantic colouring; while the really comic characters and situations figure principally in the subordinate action.

Our reflections, finally, lead us to the following conclusions: If Shakespeare as a comic poet has not found that universal and unqualified acknowledgment which has been accorded to Molière, it is not on account of any deficiency in his powers as a comic writer, but rather because of his too great inner wealth, which leads him to bring into play too great an abundance of motives and situations, which causes him to scatter his wit in too prodigal a fashion and without discrimination; because of a certain joyous light-heartedness and primitive freshness which finds pleasure in the simplest jest, and does not painfully weigh the effect of a witticism; because of the important influence which, pre-eminently in his comedies, he allows his fancy to exert, while Molière works far more with his understanding; but, above all, because Shakespeare's designs were far less exclusively comic than the Frenchman's. This is connected with a difference between their conceptions of comedy, a point which requires a somewhat closer examination.

Molière's conception of the comic is more nearly allied to our own view of it, as well as to that of the ancients, than is Shakespeare's. The latter, indeed, is also related to the ancient conception, not directly, however, but only through its mediaeval development.

The subject-matter of the comic drama is the ludicrous, and this is penned by Aristotle, in his "Poetics," as a kind of defect, as something ugly or bad, which is not, however, associated with anything painful, and which does not prove pernicious. The philosopher, to illustrate this by an example, cites most happily the comic mask itself, which represented something ugly and distorted, without expressing pain.

But should we submit the best and most celebrated of Molière's comedies to this test, we should find to our astonishment that it is by no means applicable to them. Let us take an unrivalled masterpiece like "L'École des Femmes": Arnolph, the old egoist, who has reared a young girl in utter isolation to absolute inexperience and ignorance with the intention of marrying her, and who must now learn to his dismay that Love has found a way even to his prisoner, and that he proves a consummate teacher even to this being so totally undeveloped; Arnolph, who is kept constantly informed of the progress of this love, and yet is not in a position to check it, whose fine-spun plans end in his own ruin— Arnolph is certainly a capitally comic, a decidedly ridiculous figure. But does that which is faulty, ugly, in him not prove painful? Arnolph undergoes positive torture, and, much as he may deserve it, the sympathetic reader feels with him. And the misanthrope, that noble, but too frank and heedless, character, who, while believing he hates and despises the world, becomes entangled in the snares of a coquette, from which he finally releases himself at the expense of a deep heart-wound, and then buries himself in solitude—is not painful the fate of this man, of which Goethe says it produces an absolutely tragic effect? And the miser: the fiendish passion which possesses Harpagon, which has killed all that is divine in him, and destroyed every filial emotion in his children—who would regard this passion as not pernicious? And finally Tartuffe, the hypocrite, who undermines the happiness of a whole family, a family that has heaped benefits upon him—is the nature, the conduct, of this man not pernicious?

We see, then, how it is the greatest masterpieces of the comic Muse that transgress the limits of the comic, and if, nevertheless, all these works succeed in creating a comic effect, it is owing to the art of the poet, who knows how to manage it so that the spectator does not become too vividly conscious of the painful and hurtful side of the ridiculous material presented to him. It seems clear to us that the question whether a certain failing or a certain evil appears ludicrous, depends not only upon the kind and degree of the evil and the extent of its influence, but very essentially upon the standpoint of those who happen to be the spectators at the time.

Upon this rests the development which took place in the conception of the comic in the Middle Ages, and which, in spite of its apparent *naiveté*, conceals a great deal of depth. What can there be more childish and uncultured than the idea that a tragedy is a play in which the people become unhappy and die? a comedy, one that has a happy termination? And yet but little need be added to bridge the way to the profoundest conception. The tragic conflict is of such a nature that it must have a bad ending; the comic, of a kind that can end happily and consequently should. By reflecting upon this definition we might easily arrive at a complete theory of both classes of plays. Likewise, if we examine the naive definition in Dante's letter to Can Grande, or in the " Catholicon" of Giovanni Balbi of Genoa. According to them comedy is distinguished from tragedy in that a tragedy is great and calm at the beginning, but at the end grows horrible and ghastly; while a comedy allows the beginning of the action to be painful in order to lead it to a happy conclusion.

This view has been scoffed at a hundred times, yet only by superficial critics. Let us try to look into the matter a little more thoroughly. Is not the tragic fate the more tragic the greater the height of bliss from which the hero is hurled? and—to go deeper—is not the effect of the tragedy greatest in those cases where the error which finally causes the hero's ruin appears at first perfectly harmless, particularly if the fatal error he commits be linked with his inmost nature, his noblest qualities? *And* comedy—is it not then most effective when the evil which it brings before us is most agitating, and is, nevertheless, happily overcome in an easy, natural way? It is this that is really characteristic of the mediaeval conception of the comic. The harmlessness, the immunity from pain, of the ugly and the bad which are presented on the scene are based upon the fact that the evil is conquered in the course of the action. The development leads the participants in the action as well as the audience up to a higher plane, to a height whence they behold the vicious and the ugly far beneath them and penetrate their hollowness, whence the evil veritably appears like an abandoned standpoint, and in so far like something ridiculous. This conception, in its profoundest sense, is embodied in the grandest comedy of all time—in Dante's Divine Comedy. As Dante urges his painful upward way through hell and purgatory to paradise, and here through all the heavenly spheres to a vision of the uncreated, he learns to regard divine justice, which at first appears to him as the vengeance of the Almighty, upon a higher plane, as a manifestation of the All-wise intent upon the bettering of mankind, until finally he recognizes infinite love as its real essence—the love which moves sun and stars.

This, of course, is not a comedy in the ancient sense, and just as little in ours. A play animated by such an idea would much rather realize our ideal of the drama [*Schauspiel*]. But this apprehension of comedy is closely related to that of Shakespeare.

Shakespeare sees that in the world good and evil, the sublime and ridiculous, joy and sorrow, stand close together, jostle each other, nay, are entwined with each other. The most innocent thing may prove noxious, and that which is pernicious be changed to good. Upon laughter follows weeping; upon weeping, laughter; the very occurrence, indeed, which draws tears from one may provoke another to mirth; according to the standpoint of the observer will an action or a situation appear pathetic or laughable; and even one and the same person may weep tears of laughter or smile amid tears.

Acting upon this comprehensive perception of the world around him, Shakespeare creates the world of his dramas. This is why he likes to interweave comic figures and motives into his tragic action, and why, conversely, he generally gives a serious background to his comic actions, or allows a graver note to be heard through the noisy outbursts of uncontrolled merriment. This is why his characters, like those of real life, do not appear simple, but complex, a compound of good and evil, of strength and weakness. None of the types, so easily interpreted, of the ancient or even of the classic French stage are to be found among Shakespeare's great tragic figures; but his comic characters, also, are, as a rule, richer, endowed with more individual traits, than those that owe their origin to the genius of Molière.

If in all this we have a high degree of realism, we find in closest union with this realism the ideality which characterizes Shakespeare's art. And to the poet's ideal conception of the world there is added a decidedly optimistic quality—a quality which, appearing now in a weaker, now in a stronger, form, and for a while disappearing altogether, still, in the end, proves itself indestructible. Shakespeare believes in the beautiful and the good, he believes that they are realized in the souls of men ; he believes in the value of this world and of this life. He has preserved his faith, even though not without hard struggles, even though not unshaken, in the eventual triumph of the good in the development of the destinies of the world. This optimism is not absent from Shakespeare's historical dramas, or even his tragedies, but it appears above all in his comedies. They are, as it were, moments of relaxation in which he indulges his inward tendency to optimism and trustful faith. He deals largely with such human conflicts, such human errors, as are capable of the most disasters; the most fatal consequences, but which, through a happy chain of events, are led to a favourable issue. One cannot always see in this fortunate turn of affairs a logical sequence of the actions of the characters concerned; the heroes in Shakespeare's comedies are often rendered happy beyond their deserts, let us say, without their own efforts—and where does this not occur upon the stage, where does it not occur in the world? This, then, were chance; but can the poet content himself with bare chance? Where the poet cannot see, he can at least dimly feel. Let us observe what terms he makes with chance in one of his earliest comedies, "The Comedy of Errors."

Shakespeare took the underlying motive of this play from the "Menaechmi" of Plautus.

The dramatic interest of the Roman comedy is centred, as is well known, in the consequences ensuing from the perfect resemblance in face and form and the identity of name of the heroes, twin brothers, who, by a strange destiny, are parted from each other at a tender age; one seeks the other half the world over, and, arrived at last at the place where his brother lives, without the remotest suspicion of it, he is mistaken for his brother by the latter's fellow-citizens and closest relations, even by his own slave. From this result apparent contradictions of the most delightful kind, strange complications, from which the brother residing in the place where the action occurs suffers most particularly, until through the personal meeting of the twins the confusion is suddenly cleared up. The improbable in the premises of the story could not be discarded without destroying the story itself.

And Shakespeare made no attempt to do so. On the contrary, since he accepts a world in which chance rules as the necessary groundwork of his play, he endeavours, with his own peculiar consistency, to extend the realm of chance; he gives it opportunity to assert itself not only in one but in many instances. To the one pair of twins he opposes another, in whom the fate of the first is repeated; to the two masters, so closely similar as to be mistaken for each other, two servants equally similar. Each Antipholus,—he has thus rechristened the Menaechmi,— has a Dromio for a follower. The story, mad as it was, becomes still madder; the complication grows comic to the highest degree. But the spectator becomes familiar meanwhile with the workings of chance, conceives, unconsciously, a certain respect for this mysterious power which displays such methods. The idea of putting the two pairs of twins in opposition was evoked in Shakespeare's mind, as was pointed out a few years ago, by another comedy of Plautus, the "Amphitruo," from which he borrowed, notably, a very effective scene.

This is not yet all. The repulsive moral relations disclosed to us by Plautus' Menaechmi were modified by Shakespeare with a delicate touch, in part entirely transformed, while, at the same time, he introduced a new element, a love episode, still somewhat shyly treated, but with a charming lyric colouring. But even this did not satisfy the poet. Before his soul floated a vision of the world more richly and profoundly conceived than that produced by this blending of two fables of Plautus. By weaving into the action the figures and fortunes of the parents of the two brothers Antipholus, old Aegeon and Aemelia, he gained for his play, so full of strange adventures, a setting which is romantic, fairylike, yet charged with deep meaning. It gives us at the opening of the play a glimpse of a fateful past and a threatening future, while, at the same time, it explains the plot of the comedy directly connected with it; but to the close of the drama, mingling itself with the main plot, it imparts a higher spiritual meaning. While the lighter and graver misconceptions, the entanglements, the grievances, of the different personages resolve themselves into the most delightful harmony; while the grief of longing is stilled, hopes long abandoned realized, and blessings showered upon one to whom but a moment before the grave seemed the only desirable goal—a feeling takes possession of us which makes us apprehend beyond the mysterious play of what we termed chance, the ruling of a higher power.

# THE COMEDY OF ERRORS
# IN THE TWENTIETH CENTURY
## ❧

Though twentieth-century critics continue to investigate many of the issues raised in the prior century, their analyses present an increasingly broader and more refined consideration of those critical matters. Interpretive questions centering on *The Comedy of Errors* during the next 100 years include a discussion of the play's generic features, a critical inquiry that generally admits of an intertwining of farcical and romantic elements. As a result of this abiding interest in Shakespeare's incorporation of medieval romantic conventions, a central critical development emerges, namely a debate concerning the role of religion in *The Comedy of Errors*. To be sure, this area of inquiry encompasses a number of issues ranging from a general discussion of spirituality to more specific topics such as the religious significance of Ephesus within the play and institutional questions concerning the incorporation of Anglican doctrine on marriage. Twentieth-century criticism also exhibits, for the most part, an abiding appreciation for the rich development of characterization to be found in this early play. Still, in the earlier part of the century, there are those critics, such as Arthur Quiller-Couch and Mark Van Doren, who argue that *The Comedy of Errors* is a mechanical play lacking the depth of characterization that later critics have acknowledged. Beginning approximately at midcentury and opposed to a mechanical perspective of this play, there are several commentators who have been impressed with a multitude of important distinctions to be found between the Ephesian twins, both Antipholus and Dromio, in contrast with their Syracusan brothers. These distinctions include an analysis of the strongly contrasting personality traits exhibited between the worldly, prosperous, and self-centered Antipholus of Ephesus and his far more sensitive and romantic brother from Syracuse. Furthermore, as part of this comparison between the two masters, several critics likewise have noted the different relationships each has with his respective slave.

Another important area of investigation has been the extent to which Shakespeare improved on his sources in Plautus. Continuing an area of inquiry begun in the preceding century, later twentieth-century scholars provide a thoroughgoing analysis and acknowledgement of the many ways in which

Shakespeare far exceeded his ancient sources. While it is generally agreed that Shakespeare removed a great deal of the vulgarity and objectionable practices of Plautus's time, much of the discussion of this particular issue centers on Shakespeare's treatment of Adriana, which is in sharp contrast to that afforded the wife in the *Menaechmi*, and his decision to add a sister to the plot. Further on in the century, as proffered by such critics as Harry Levin, James Sanderson, and Thomas Hennings, a further historical contextualizing of the play manifests itself in an increasing interest in religious matters in regard to the Christian ethos that governs *The Comedy of Errors*. Douglas L. Peterson's essay presents us with a different perspective on Shakespeare's intermingling of ancient and medieval traditions, the latter including an important didactic dimension embedded within an entertaining story. According to Peterson, there are two distinct and fundamentally different types of comic "fictions" at work in *The Comedy of Errors*, one based on traditional notions of playfulness in the world of ordinary experience and the other presenting a "merry tale" of fantastic happenings, derived from medieval literary sources, with the intention of conveying a moral lesson. Other critics who have interpreted *The Comedy of Errors* from a historical context include Stephen Greenblatt, who finds it odd that the play does not include a scene of marital reconciliation given Shakespeare's obvious interest in the issue of the neglected or abandoned spouse.

Some critics, such as Eamon Grennan, introduce an ever-increasing line of inquiry into the tensions of the play, a trend that will continue into the twenty-first century. Focusing on Luciana as his paradigm of contradiction, Grennan argues that she offers contradictory advice on the subject of marriage and, consequently, sets a conventional, Elizabethan perspective of a divinely ordered universe in opposition to a more practical consideration that marriage is a human invention requiring a variety of stratagems. Citing the clothing metaphor as evidence for his argument, Grennan's essay also presents an interesting perspective on the superficiality of gender roles as expressed by Luciana's advice: "Apparel vice like virtue's harbinger."

To edify, indeed to pacify, her incensed sister, Lucian invokes the customary relationship between men and women in marriage as a manifestation of the cardinal law of nature. In doing so, she employs a traditionally sanctioned mode of analogy:

There's nothing situate under heaven's eye
But hath his bound in earth, in sea, in sky,
The beasts, the fishes, and the winged fowls
Are their males' subjects, and at their controls;
Man, more divine, the master of all these,

Lord of the wide world and wild wat'ry seas,
Indued with intellectual sense and souls,
Of more pre-eminence than fish and fowls,
Are masters to their females, and their lords:
Then let your will attend on their accords.

   (II.i.16–25)

This eloquent secular sermon on degree paints in miniature what
E.M.W. Tillyard has ensured will always be known as 'the Elizabethan
World Picture.' It represents a world of meticulous symmetries, as
esthetically rigid ('situate') as the solid couplets themselves. Fixture is
the defining marker of this world. By insisting that nature possess the
esthetic shapes it is the business of custom to impose upon the world,
Luciana implicitly identifies customary truths and the laws of nature.
The world and all that is in it run to the dictates of decorum, a single
principle governing all aspects of reality. 'Decorum,' as a recent critic
puts it, 'was thought to be natural order as perceived by the senses or
the aesthetic imagination.' The unitary mode of perception at work here
subsumes the human order of custom into the more comprehensive,
magisterial order of nature, 'that manner of working which God hath set
for each created thing to keepe.'

   When Luciana later lectures the man she assumes to be the husband
Antipholus on the same subject, however, the picture she provides is a
radically different one (III.ii.1–28). Now, what she calls 'A husband's
office' is a question less of cosmic determinism than circumstantial prag-
matism. Hortatory piety cedes to practical considerations:

If you did wed my sister for her wealth,
Then for her wealth's sake use her with more kindness,
Or, if you like elsewhere, do it by stealth,
Muffle your false love with some show of blindness.

   (4–7)

Mutability penetrates the fixed hierarchical picture of the world: marriage
may suffer seasonal fate ("shall Antipholus, / Even in the spring of love,
thy love-springs rot?" [2–3]). Without meaning to, Luciana severs the
institution of marriage from all external supports and leaves it the naked
human convention it is, a device to order in a decorous way, no matter
what the inner truth, the surface appearances of sexual relationships.

Finally, Harold Bloom argues that *The Comedy of Errors* is to be understood
as pure farce, which either raises our consciousness about ourselves or utilizes an

absurd plot to stage sincere human emotion. Bloom maintains that Shakespeare used a farcical situation as a vehicle for exploring the interiority of the play's most sympathetic and human character, Antipholus of Syracuse. In sum, above all considerations and opposing points of view, twentieth-century critics are unanimous in crediting Shakespeare for his ability to weave deep psychological insights into human behavior into an otherwise fantastical plot. This remains his most impressive and enduring achievement.

G. G. Gervinus's commentary is a tribute to Shakespeare's achievement in *The Comedy of Errors*. Describing the play as a complex work made up of both comic and tragic elements that operate in tandem to convey an important spiritual message, Gervinus refers to *The Comedy of Errors* as a "comedy of intrigue." Most significantly, Gervinus is impressed by Shakespeare's skillful management of a seemingly lighthearted plot into which the poet has injected a tragic background. From the start, Gervinus maintains that implicit themes of dark and foreboding events that lurk beneath the surface exist with respect to Egeon's plight as an imprisoned father in search of his long-lost sons and over whom the threat of execution remains until the last act. Because of the love manifested by the father and the eventual reconciliation of family and friends, Gervinus sees *The Comedy of Errors* as having far exceeded the characteristics of a mere farce and, instead, manifesting domestic love and an ability to transform suffering and misfortune into happiness and familial bonds. At the same time, Gervinus's essay provides a late-Victorian perspective toward women. Unlike some later twentieth-century critics who would fault Luciana for counseling Adriana to accept her subservient status in relation to Antipholous of Ephesus, Gervinus credits the sister with awakening Adriana's consciousness that in the "kingdom of nature" a woman is subject to the man.

In his introduction to Shakespeare's earliest comedies, Brander Matthews categorizes *The Comedy of Errors* as a play representative of Shakespeare's nascent talent and describes this early apprenticeship period in the bard's career as one in which he was producing "tentative experiments," favoring lyricism over dramatic effect and employing clever rimes and conceits. Nevertheless, Matthews has a deep appreciation for the play, in which he maintains that Shakespeare's skillful management of a complex and intriguing plot is the supreme element that makes *The Comedy of Errors* such a success. Comparing his handling of the plot to a skilled watchmaker, Matthews finds merit in the fact that the audience has the added pleasure of knowing that which is hidden to the characters of the play. Matthews also argues that Shakespeare far surpasses Plautus in his revision of the Latin play by removing the abundant vulgarity found in the *Menaechmi* and, further, that the actual audience for whom the ancient playwright was writing was made up of "ignorant freedmen who had to be amused at all costs." Most importantly, however, Matthews acknowledges the profoundly human quality of *The Comedy of Errors*, given the sympathetic nature exhibited most especially in the characterization of Adriana (whose portrayal Matthews believes is eminently realistic) as well as the dignity bestowed on Aegeon.

In his commentary on *The Comedy of Errors*, Arthur Quiller-Couch praises Shakespeare's choice of the shipwreck device as a romantic device that enables him to usher in an exciting adventure story with the added benefits that it bestows a sense of realism and verisimilitude to the world of actual experiences. Additionally, Quiller-Couch maintains that the shipwreck device enabled Shakespeare to append further tricks to his intriguing plot, such as the supposed demise of a long-lost mother who is eventually found alive and well. Nevertheless, despite these attributes, Quiller-Couch objects to *The Comedy of Errors* on the grounds that it is a mechanical play lacking in characterization. Quiller-Couch finds that neither the characters nor the events are credible and that, instead, Shakespeare increased the confusion among his two sets of twins by dispensing with masks rather than relying on the interactions between the characters to control events and make the play work.

A well-respected classical and Renaissance scholar, Cornelia C. Coulter traces elements of the Plautine tradition in a wide range of Shakespearean plays. While a direct comparison between Shakespeare and his classical antecedents in the individual plays is relatively straightforward, Coulter offers an overview of both the medieval romantic prose tales of Boccaccio and the Renaissance transformations of classical mythological themes into humorous scenes from real life woven into the French *fabliaux*. As Coulter argues, Shakespeare was likewise influenced by these various reinterpretations of the Latin classical playwrights and incorporated these later traditions into his plays. With respect specifically to *The Comedy of Errors*, Coulter identifies both intrinsic and extrinsic Plautine characteristics that are found in the *Menaechmi*. As to the larger issue of physical setting, Coulter points out that the ancient Roman stage normally represented a street with three house doors, an indispensable characteristic that Shakespeare retained as seen in the resulting confusion when Antipholus of Syracuse dines with Adriana while the true husband, Antipholus of Ephesus, is barred from entering. Another important external feature is the function of the prologue in Plautine comedy, which served to acquaint the audience with vital information such as a summary of the plot and setting, and which is reflected in Shakespeare's appropriation in Egeon's long speeches and explanations to the duke in the first scene of *The Comedy of Errors*. With respect to intrinsic aspects derived from Plautus, Coulter notes that it is significant that *The Comedy of Errors* is premised on the theme of mistaken identity, whether through natural resemblance or deliberate assumption of disguise, an issue popular with Roman dramatists. The play concludes with an invitation to dinner, a feature that imitates the Latin classical tradition of ending with a banquet either being mentioned or actually staged. Nevertheless, the similarities with the *Menaechmi* notwithstanding, Coulter acknowledges Shakespeare's additions and changes to his classical source, most importantly his use of a shipwreck as the inaugural event in the separation of Aegeon's family, rather than the incident related in Plautus when a son becomes lost in a crowd.

> It is evident, therefore, that Shakespeare typifies the influences which came into English both directly from Latin comedy and indirectly through German education-drama and Italian drama and romance. We see survivals of the tradition in a few externals, such as stage setting and the use of Prologue and Epilogue; in some devices of plot (which are common in the romances as well)—for example, mistaken identity and the restoration of long-lost children; in characters, drawn on conventional lines in Shakespeare's earlier plays, but rounded out and individualized in his mature work; and in stage-tricks like the perennial beating on the gate.

Mark Van Doren finds the plot of *The Comedy of Errors* to be based merely on the resolution of a "physical predicament" and sees the play as a whole sorely lacking in character development. In Van Doren's opinion, the physical aspects so dominate the play that the characters are relegated to being figures or gestures rather than existing as real people. Instead the characters merely respond as puppets to the circumstances of their immediate problems, while all of this is accompanied by a style wholly artificial and derivative. Nevertheless, despite his condemnation of the play, Van Doren finds commendable aspects of Shakespeare's artistry, stating that Shakespeare has enhanced Plautus's text, making special note of Dromio of Syracuse's refined wit in describing the servant woman. In the final analysis, however, Van Doren believes that the accidental premise on which the play is based, namely a shipwreck that has scattered the family, to be a weak basis for the ensuing multiplicity of errors.

Although Harold Goddard credits Shakespeare as an adept craftsman who aptly applied his skills in reworking Plautus's *Menaechmi*, Goddard is nevertheless of the opinion that *The Comedy of Errors* is pure farce rather than comedy, although he does not define these two terms. Instead, Goddard makes a distinction between intellect and genius and consigns the writing process of *The Comedy of Errors* to a mechanical procedure in which the playwright began with a preconceived plan as to its outcome rather than the method he employed in his later and far more accomplished works in which his imagination allowed the play to develop organically during the writing process. There is one point, however, for which Goddard praises Shakespeare, namely that he is making an implicit apology to his audience by having his bewildered characters repeatedly state that they must either be dreaming events or that some magic is at work. Goddard interprets this as an admission on Shakespeare's part that a "psychological or metaphysical explanation is demanded to reconcile with reality" the confusing events being enacted. Finally, Goddard compares *The Comedy of Errors* to the brilliance manifested in the great tragedies of *Macbeth*, *Hamlet*, and *Othello*.

In his essay on *The Comedy of Errors*, E.M.W. Tillyard expresses a deep appreciation for Shakespeare's creative adaptation of Plautus's *Menaechmi*. Tillyard provides a comprehensive analysis of the play, including an identification of multiple generic features and an edifying explanation of the rather sophisticated evolution of characterization within the play. Among the many observations concerning Shakespeare's sources and genres is Tillyard's argument that a strong element of romance exists in *The Comedy of Errors*, in its inclusion of such themes as shipwrecks and piracy as well as stories of travel and the search for lost children, derived from the ancient Greek novel.

The Greek novel is a prose narrative dating back to antiquity that told tales of love and seduction, separation, misfortune at sea, witchcraft, and other trials and tribulations of the characters, stories that in turn became popular during the Renaissance. More specifically, Tillyard states that Shakespeare incorporated aspects of the Greek romance of *Apollonius of Tyre*, a tale that was preserved in a Latin translation and retold by the medieval poet John Gower (ca. 1330–1408). Nevertheless, after identifying the existence of a romantic framework within *The Comedy of Errors*, Tillyard maintains that it would have no profound importance were it not for the fact that it enabled Shakespeare to fashion a complex story replete with layers of complications that would require a skillful manipulation of events to resolve a multitude of errors. Thus, according to Tillyard, fantasy and farce are thoroughly intertwined. Moreover, he observes that the character of Egeon is deliberately vague, for to have him more fully delineated would have introduced a strong element of tragedy into the play. Likewise, Tillyard sees the character of Aemilia as remaining somewhat imprecise for, although she is firm and resolute in discharging her authority, her characterization does not extend beyond this function. Indeed, he sees Aemilia as serving to interrupt the wild fantasy that heretofore has been unfolding. In Tillyard's opinion, what turns an otherwise farcical comedy into an enduring play is that which makes Shakespeare a master playwright, namely his ability to always present a penetrating understanding of human behavior no matter how fantastical the plot in which his characters must maneuver. Tillyard maintains that, in *The Comedy of Errors*, Shakespeare adroitly transcends mere farce by taking up the issue of how men live and interact with one another in Ephesian society, which for all its associations with sorcery and charlatans is simultaneously a small and ordinary town. Other realistic details that elevate the play beyond mere farce include Shakespeare's augmentation and differentiation in distinguishing the personalities of the twin Antipholuses, as well as his decision to add a sister for Adriana, a character who is not found in Plautus, to offer just a few examples. Given the extremes of illusion in which the characters become ensnared, Tillyard argues that Shakespeare is posing the question of what constitutes reality, for surely the young playwright was well aware when writing this early comedy of the different possible modes of human experience.

Harry Levin finds much to praise in Shakespeare's creative and sensitive revision of Plautus's *Menaechmi*. Levin identifies the existence of two closely intertwined narratives in *The Comedy of Errors*. He sees the predominant plot as the one concerning a highly charged and emotional series of domestic entanglements and estrangements that compel and produce a secondary plot based on extensive voyaging and the issues surrounding the varying experiences of strangers making their way through an alien land. In his discussion of how these dual plots are interwoven, Levin points out some of the more subtle aspects of familial imbroglios, such as the incomparable Nell, whose body parts are graphically transformed into a geographical representation of foreign countries.

> This heroine [Nell], invoked indifferently as Luce or Nell, is generically a Dowsabell or, for that matter, a Dulcinea—a kitchenmaid whose formidable proportions are vividly verbalized by the wrong Dromio, her brother-in-law, who is still quaking from the shock of having been claimed by her as a husband. This is the vulgar parallel to Adriana's claim upon her brother-in-law. Dromio's description of his brother's Nell, elicited by his master's queries as straight man, is a set-piece in the manner of Launce or Lancelot Gobbo, and may well have been assigned to the same comedian. With its geographical conceits, comparing the parts of her person to foreign countries, it might almost be a ribald reversal of Othello's traveler's tales when wooing Desdemona.
>
> But it is by no means a farfetched gag, since it embodies—on a more than miniature scale—the principal contrast of the play: on the one hand, extensive voyaging; on the other, intensive domesticity. In using an underplot which burlesques the main plot, Shakespeare employs a device as old as Medwall's interlude of *Fulgens and Lucres*, where the rival suitors have servants who court the mistress's maid under the diagrammatic designations of A and B. With Nell, as with the demanding Adriana, the normal approaches of courtship are reversed. The closest we come to romantic love is the sketchy relationship between her brother-in-law and her husband's sister-in-law. Yet that is a good deal closer than Plautus brings us; and though both masters are suitably mated in the end, the concluding dialogue of the servants emphasizes the pairing of twins, not spouses. Parents and children are united, family ties are reasserted; but Dromio of Syracuse remains a free agent. His greatest moment has been the midpoint of the play, when he acted as doorkeeper and kept out his fellow Dromio, as well as that Dromio's master, the master of the house.

Levin further contends that Nell's amorous and inappropriate overtures to the traveler, Dromio of Syracuse, are a replication of the excessively jealous and controlling Adriana, a wife who has driven her husband to the brink of sanity. Moreover, as he points out, in each instance, the conventional expectations of courtship and marriage are subverted. Levin also states that in his play Shakespeare is fulfilling an Elizabethan requirement for a double plot and that he does it with consummate skill. *The Comedy of Errors* begins with a newcomer, Egeon, entering the strange and threatening world of Ephesus. The old man is in turn seeking two other Syracusan travelers, namely his son and his servant, Antipholus and Dromio of Syracuse, both of whom were compelled to embark on a journey to reunite with their twin brothers. Once Egeon arrives in Ephesus, the entire play is then driven by an endless series of misidentifications, bewildering events, and erroneous accusations until the ultimate discovery that all family members are gathered in Ephesus and the source of the various confusions is finally explained. Among the many revisions of Plautus, Levin points out that *The Comedy of Errors* is governed by a Christian ethos far different from the ancient mores exemplified in *Menaechmi*. While the wife in Plautus's play receives no respect and is nameless and easily forgotten, Shakespeare augments Adriana's status by imbuing her with an excessively possessive conjugal love while, at the same time, diminishing the role of the Courtesan, who merely dines with an otherwise faithful husband. Furthermore, the addition of a sympathetic feminine personality in Luciana introduces yet another aspect of moderation while introducing a debate on marriage. In conclusion, Levin finds a great deal to admire in *The Comedy Errors*, including the highly individual and differentiated characterizations of the two Antipholuses. While the Syracusan brother, an endearing and benign being, is compelled to find his twin, Antipholus of Ephesus is wholly disinterested with his origins and, instead, has been reveling in his prominent social status and privileged relationship with the duke of Ephesus until he is at last reunited with his family.

> When Adriana and her husband appeal to the Duke, the stories they tell of their day's experience are mutually contradictory; but the discrepancies would disappear if the shadow of the interfering Antipholus were retraced through their reciprocal patterns. . . . It has been a lesson for Adriana, brought home by the gentle rebuke of the Abbess. For Antipholus of Ephesus, it has been an eye-opening misadventure. Apparently, he has never felt the impetus that has incited his brother and his father to sally forth in search of him. Unconcerned with his founding origin, he rejoices in the good graces of the Duke and takes for granted the solid comforts of his Ephesian citizenship.

James L. Sanderson commends *The Comedy of Errors* as a fully integrated work of art in its investigation of the theme of patience, an important issue for both the Middle Ages and the Renaissance from both a Christian and a humanist philosophical perspective. Beginning with an overview of a number of crucial instances in which impatience and irascibility are either acted out or counseled against, Sanderson presents a persuasive argument that the lack of patience is the root cause of all errors within the play, while the restoration of calm and emotional control becomes the solution to all its problems. As he points out, we are immediately confronted with the problem in act 2, scene 2 when Dromio of Ephesus unwittingly tests the forbearance of his supposed master, Antipholus of Syracuse, who in turn strikes his servant in anger. As Sanderson explains, this initial display of impetuous behavior is followed by numerous examples of intolerance and irritability, including Adriana's peevish attitude toward her husband's lateness and Antipholus of Ephesus's violent outburst in trying to force the door open after he is denied entry to his own home. However, the need to restore patience is evident in the abbess's (Aemilia's) speech in act 5 as she counsels all the contentious parties to remain calm and quiet. Both the abbess and her long-lost husband, Egeon, provide the solution to all the problems that beset Ephesus, in that they are paradigms of patience and thus can bring about the reinstatement of a happy family and harmonious society. Sanderson also sees the lack of patience as indicative of a weakness of character, while Egeon and Amelia become figures of charity and spirituality in their willingness to endure adversity. Finally, Sanderson points out that Shakespeare's chosen setting of Ephesus is deliberate for St. Paul's letters admonish the Ephesians to be courteous and forgiving to one another.

Eamon Grennan praises *The Comedy of Errors* for its imaginative exploration of the dialectic between nature and custom, a theme that he maintains Shakespeare pursues in his later plays. Grennan's contention is that such an argument exists based on the fact that Luciana is both a wholly Shakespearean invention and, more importantly, that she delivers contradictory speeches on marriage. In the first instance (II, i. 16–25), Luciana attempts to mollify her sister, Adriana, by explaining that men have a predetermined mastery over their wives and all other living beings, including women. Grennan attributes this tension to two opposing notions concerning marriage. The first concerns customary beliefs that in a marriage the man was master of both his wife and the natural world as opposed to the second, more practical understanding that marriage was a human invention intended to regulate sexual relationships and, as such, did not grant predominance of men over women but instead required skillful and sometimes deceptive manipulation. Citing Luciana as an exemplary character for his thesis, Grennan maintains that while she accepts the conventional tenet that marriage is an expression of the existence of a fixed order in the natural world and adherence to its principles are a matter of decorum and propriety, she nevertheless contradicts herself. In act 3, scene 2, lines 1–28, she simultaneously counsels a far different perspective to Antipholus, whom she believes to be the real husband of Adriana, in her explanation that marriage is a human invention and thus requires artifice in order to achieve power. Grennan cites the clothing metaphor as the preeminent image of superficiality and dishonesty in gender roles as expressed by Lucian's advice: "[a]pparel vice like virtue's harbinger." In delivering two mutually inconsistent lectures on marital relations, Grennan argues convincingly that Luciana is subverting the Elizabethan notion of a well-ordered, hierarchical world and supplants it with a perspective in which virtue is a slippery term, for through a skillful exercise of human stratagems one can easily seize control. In other words, the calmness of an ordered world can give way to violence and upheaval. As further proof of this systematic undermining of the "customary world," Grennan cites several instances throughout the play, including the fact that Antipholus of Ephesus, a customary man, quickly loses his grip on reality when confronted with his wife's "wayward mood." Grennan concludes that *The Comedy of Errors* is a rich and highly complex play that presents an inherent tension between an Elizabethan world-view and the far more random social order dictated by human nature.

Unlike so many other critics who have identified and discussed the importance of two thoroughly intertwined genres of comedy and romance, Ruth Nevo argues that *The Comedy of Errors* is to be understood precisely as a farce, the point ultimately being that the conundrum of two sets of dual identities is a parody of the human condition and each individual's quest for self-identity. Nevo begins with the premise that the dominant comic device of dual identities and the resulting errors that emanate from it, namely an inability to distinguish between the two sets of twins, is a wholly natural one rather than an artistic stratagem on Shakespeare's part. Furthermore, Nevo contends that Shakespeare is exploiting the *processus turbarum*, or absurd succession of commotion and uproar that follows from an inability to distinguish between the Ephesian and Syracusan twins, and that the solution to this riotous confusion of tumultuous events resides within the farce itself. One significant piece of evidence that Nevo offers is the ineffectuality of the medieval mountebank, Dr. Pinch, who fails to achieve any exorcism of Antipholus of Ephesus and instead reveals that he himself is possessed by devils. Thus, as Nevo argues, not only does Shakespeare achieve a hilarious comedy but, more significantly, he conjures a therapeutic resolution to the anxious search to find oneself only to realize that the quest for a separate and viable selfhood leads to a narcissistic web. As Dromio of Syracuse shows us, a quest for self-identity only leads to an understanding that the journey ends with a cheerful recognition of its impossibility, for "the contentment of Dromio with his ability to acquire a separate self at all is, our laughter tells us, the most reassuring antidote to insanity Ephesus could possibly supply."

Thomas P. Hennings extols *The Comedy of Errors* as a highly original comedy in which Shakespeare combines a wide variety of theatrical conventions of Latin farce, exemplary romances, and English and Italian comedy, while expanding on and augmenting his sources. Hennings's main contention is that Shakespeare's work is a deliberately Christianizing correction of a classical, pagan play, Plautus's *Menaechmi*, which celebrates the saturnalian values of unbridled merrymaking and a topsy-turvy social order in which the standard rules of behavior are overturned and even slaves are fully participant, a farcical inversion that bears no dire implications. In contrast to the Plautine paradigm, Hennings offers the competing later classical model of Lucretius (*De rerum natura*), which brings a far more disparaging perspective on humanity's place in the world, namely a belief in primitive humans' abuse of natural freedom. Having introduced the Lucretian challenge to Plautus's text, Hennings proceeds to build a case for Shakespeare having worked against the farcical elements of the *Menaechmi* in which repressed desires are simply given free range without having to face the consequences of such licentiousness and, further, that Plautus's notion of farce does not address the inherent moral values concerned with marriage and family found in Elizabethan comedy. Hennings states that, though Shakespeare exploited the farcical tradition, he did not ascribe to its immorality but, instead, incorporated the Lucretian perspective as compatible with the Renaissance notion of the "decay of nature."

> True to his native conventions of comedy, Shakespeare will gladly exploit the farcical mode of Saturnalian inversion, but he will refuse to indulge in its psychological escapism. In *The Comedy of Errors* the world of natural freedom or *licentia* involving the traveling twin, which Shakespeare deliberately associates with dreams (II.ii.182–83, V.i.377), is not the ingenuous Saturnalian ideal. That comic ideal, as well as its mode of inversion, is continually rebuked by the didactic mode, by serious discussions of moral values, and it is continually mocked by satiric ridicule precisely because its atmosphere is governed by the frightening Lucretian view of nature, which by Shakespeare's day had evolved into the celebrated Renaissance doctrine of the decay of nature. Consequently, the corruption of licentious release cannot be a desirable alternative to a severe gravitas, and as the action shuttles between the comic poles of release and restraint, Shakespeare concentrates on the problems of both twins, not just the citizen, and he associates both with physically and morally decaying "Time" itself. In *The Comedy of Errors* the tensions generated between the contrastive poles resolve themselves in the completion of the comic movement toward a just society founded on the institution of marriage and the family. And establishing the normative pattern of the marital roles is the Anglican doctrine of affectionate marriage.

Thus, Hennings identifies a fundamental tension in *The Comedy of Errors* between the carnivalesque nature of farce and the compulsion to seek resolution in the reestablishment of a proper society premised on the institutions of marriage and family. Such a remedy is to be found precisely in the Anglican Church and its teachings on matrimony. More specifically, while the *Menaechmi* promotes the belief that the wife is subservient to her husband, Hennings cites the precepts contained in the official Anglican sermon as being in complete disagreement, for it held that the double standard was wrong and, indeed, responsible for marital discord. Thus, Hennings offers a sympathetic interpretation of Adriana, whom he views as a victim of an unjust social order, while offering an in-depth analysis of the sermon as it relates to Luciana's destructive marital advice. In conclusion, though order is restored and the family reunited, Hennings maintains that this restoration in *The Comedy of Errors* is temporary, for Shakespeare is reminding us that there is a spiritual truth we must achieve before taking leave of the harmful effects of time and change.

> In the last moments of the play, Shakespeare reminds us that there is yet a higher reality of truth we must attain before we can escape from the imperfect world of time and mutability, appearance and illusion. It is a point brought out by the Duke's confusing the twins (V.i.365) and confirmed once again by the Syracusan Dromio's same error soon thereafter (410–12). Knowing there are two sets of twins may lessen but it does not eliminate the chance of error. Indeed, that the error is made twice in the space of a few minutes leaves the distinct impression that it will continue to be made—and often.

Douglas L. Peterson's essay identifies two distinct and fundamentally different types of comic "fictions" at work in *The Comedy of Errors*, namely a native tradition based on notions of joy and playfulness in the world of everyday experience and, at the same time, embedding a "merry tale" of marvelous events, derived from medieval theatrical conventions, in order to convey moral precepts. As to the first fiction, Peterson identifies the tradition of merriment as "ludic," wherein games of make-believe allow the audience to escape temporarily the frustrations and travails of common experience by laughing at the absurdities of their daily lives. The second fiction, on the other hand, which Peterson defines as "Ideal Comedy and which is concerned with staging extraordinary and awesome events," is derived from medieval miracle plays, which celebrated the martyrdom of saints or portrayed religious comedies, in either case with the intention of reinforcing ideas of "exemplary behavior." Furthermore, Peterson argues that the playful fiction of *The Comedy of Errors* surrounds and enfolds the more subtle moral fiction in a device known as interlacing. Thus, in applying his theory to the play, *The Comedy of Errors* provides a way of acknowledging Shakespeare's classical and medieval predecessors while appreciating his artistry in combining a rich variety of sources both ancient and English to create a unique comedy. Focusing on the tragic implications of Egeon's entrance and the treatment of his imminent execution, Peterson praises Shakespeare's ability to fashion a story of family and friendship that evolves in terms of both plot and emotional development into an exemplum of renewed vitality and happiness. Peterson contends that Shakespeare is questioning the effectiveness of recreation for, as the abbess's lecture to Adriana in act 5 suggests, to prevent another from indulging in "sports" and "sweet recreation" could have dire consequences for their mental stability and, further, that while recreation is essential for well-being, it must also serve a didactic function in order to bring true happiness.

As the title of his book *Shakespeare: The Invention of the Human* (1998) indicates, Harold Bloom praises *The Comedy of Errors*, stating that it is an early example of the bard's enormous imaginative powers in transcending the traditional boundary lines of genre. According to Bloom, Shakespeare uses the vehicle of a farce, a dramatic performance with the sole aim of producing laughter, to explore human emotion and interiority in the character of Antipholus of Syracuse. Caught in a compellingly desperate situation, Antipholus of Syracuse falls in love with Luciana and in his sincere confession to her thereby discovers who he really is at heart.

## 1903—G. G. Gervinus. From "The Comedy of Errors and The Taming of the Shrew" from *Shakespeare Commentaries*

Georg Gottfried Gervinus (1805-71) was a German literary critic and political historian. He is the author of *Geschichte Der Poetischen National Literatur Der Deutschen* (1835) and *Shakespeare* (1850).

If we may venture to number the Comedy of Errors and the Taming of the Shrew among the works of Shakespeare's early period, in which he appears dependent upon foreign originals, we see how the young poet, without any one-sided preference, equally tried his skill, in happy variety, upon all styles and subjects. He had worked at an heroic tragedy in Titus, at a romantic drama in Pericles, at a history in Henry VI.; in the Comedy of Errors he adopted a comedy of intrigue; and in the Taming of the Shrew a comedy in which plot and character equally engaged his attention. That the Taming of the Shrew really belongs to this earliest period, has hitherto been shown only by internal evidence; but the Comedy of Errors, as is proved by an allusion in the piece, was written at the time of the French civil wars against Henry IV. (1589–93), probably soon after 1591, when Essex was sent to the assistance of Henry IV., and it thus indisputably belongs to this early period.

The Comedy of Errors (a designation which, according to Halliwell, subsequently became proverbial) was, as is known, taken from the "Menaechmi" of Plautus, which Shakespeare may have read in an English translation, probably by Warner; the book, however, appears to have been written later than Shakespeare's play, and was printed in 1595; and, except as regards the groundwork of the subject, it had in language and execution no sort of similarity with Shakespeare's play. We know that a "Historic of Errors" had been acted at the English court about the year 1577 and later; possibly this was a remodelling of the "Menaechmi" of Plautus, which Shakespeare appropriated to himself and his stage. How far our poet's path may have been prepared by this precursor, we cannot of course say. But compared to Plautus, his play is superior both in form and matter; with him it is little more than a farce. Coleridge has even thus called Shakespeare's play, but it appears to us with by no means the same justice. We shall guard ourselves from imputing too profound a philosophy to a comedy the subject of which rests in a series of laughable accidents, lest we should build too massive a structure of explanation upon too light a basis of poetry. Nevertheless, in the Comedy of Errors, that great feature of Shakespearian profoundness, that power of obtaining a deep inner significance from the most superficial material, seems to lie before us in this one early example, in which the fine spiritual application which the poet has extracted from the material strikes us as all the more remarkable, the more coarse and bold the outwork of the plot. The errors and mistakes which arise from the resemblance of the two pairs of twins are carried still further, and are less probably the work of accident in Shakespeare than in Plautus. In Plautus' play there is only one pair of brothers, one of whom does not even know that they bear the same name, and neither knows that they are similar; thus the errors are more simple and possible. In Shakespeare's plot, on the contrary, the father must have told one child of the similarity which he bore to his brother at his birth. From this it certainly need not follow that this same similarity should have been preserved in mature years; but the sameness of name must ever have been prominently before the searching Syracusan; that the people at Ephesus know him and call him by name must have startled and struck him all the more as his recognition in Ephesus is combined with peril of life. To avoid the improbabilities found in the sources from which he drew, is everywhere else an effort which characterises most strikingly Shakespeare's knowledge of human nature; here, in the plot of the play, there is hardly a trace of this effort to be found. The scene of action, Ephesus, is represented at the very beginning as the corrupt seat of all jugglers and conjurors, mountebanks and cheats; and the good Syracusan Antipholus is driven, by the course of the intricacies which increase in a masterly manner up to the catastrophe, to such straits that he is inclined rather to consider himself bewitched than to arrive at the simple conjecture to which the very object of his journey must again and again have led him.

But whatever skilful management in respect to the plot may be wanting, this scarcely weighs in the balance when we see how the poet has given the extravagant matter of these mistakes and intricacies an inner relation to the character of the family in which he has placed them. These comic parts appear upon a thoroughly tragic background, which does not interfere at all with the extravagant scenes in the foreground, and perhaps only makes them the more conspicuous, but which nevertheless ever appears with sufficient importance to keep under the superficial and weak impression of a mere farce, the whole substance of which consisted in the mistakes of those similar twins. The hostilities between Syracuse and Ephesus form the farthest chiaroscuro background, upon which the whole picture is drawn, the comic parts of which can scarcely be considered more fascinating and exciting than the tragic. The fate of the imprisoned father who is seeking his lost sons, and who, engaged on a work of love, is condemned to death; whose mental sufferings at last increase to such a degree, that he sees himself unknown by his recovered son and believes himself disowned by him; all this raises the piece far above the character of a mere farce. This tragic part is united with the comic by the most delicate links—links which the poet has interwoven into the transmitted story, according to his subsequent habit, with that totality of his spiritual nature, that we are absolutely left in doubt as to whether he acted from blind instinct or with perfect consciousness. We look upon a double family and its earlier and present destinies, in which the strangest errors take place, not merely of an external, but of an internal character. In this family the strange contrasts of domestic love and a roving spirit are combined; these produce alternate happiness and misfortune; troubles and quarrels arise, in spite of inner congeniality of soul and family attachment, and estrangement and perplexity are occasioned, in spite of outward similarity. In the excellent exposition of the piece, the old Aegeon relates the history of the double birth of the two twins. Before their birth he had left his wife on a visit to Epidamnum; his wife, expecting to become a mother, hastened from Syracuse to join him. The inducement to this journey is left by the poet as a matter of conjecture; this only he has indicated, that if a loving, it was also a wilful step, and it is moreover evident in itself that the step combined at once those contrasting qualities of family affection and love of wandering. Was it the result of suspicion and jealousy—of that quality, which is itself of so contrary a nature, which destroys love, and yet has its source in love alone? We imagine so; for Aemilia subsequently warns her daughter-in-law so forcibly against this passion. Her twins are born at Epidamnum, and "not meanly proud of two such boys," she made, against the will of her husband, "daily motions for the home return;" during the journey that shipwreck befalls them which separates husband and wife, mother and father, and with each a pair of the twins, their own sons and foster-brothers and future attendants. The Syracusan family, the father and one son, feel again after the lapse of many years the workings of the same family character; the son travels for seven years in quest of his lost mother and brother, although he perceives the folly of seeking a drop in the ocean; similar love, sacrifice, and folly draw the father again after the son; a lively impulse works in them, as in the mother before, to unite the family, and this very impulse separates them more and more, and threatens at length to separate them forcibly and for ever. In the family at Ephesus, between the lost Antipholus with his mother and his wife Adriana, there is another error, the trace of which is to be found already in Plautus' "Menaechmi." The wife is a shrew from jealousy; she torments her innocent husband and robs herself wantonly of his love; her passion leads her to self-forgetfulness and a sacrifice of all that is feminine. And this moral error justly occasions other errors between the two brothers; until at last, by means of the mother Aemilia, the internal dissension is healed and the errors are cleared up, both at once, and with equal satisfaction. The reader feels indeed that these delicately veiled deeper relations invest the adventures and comic parts of the play with too high a value for the piece ever to bear the impression of a mere farce.

It is not impossible that not only an aesthetic emphasis was laid by the poet on the point that the discord of the family arose from jealousy and from the quarrelsome nature of the women, but that a pathological stress was given also to this fact, in consequence of personal sympathy. We advance this merely as a conjecture, upon which we would not place much value; it is also very possible that what strikes us from its unusual concurrence, is mere accident. We have before intimated that, in Shakespeare's early youthful writings especially, the impressions gathered from his own domestic circumstances, which he brought with him to London, seem to glance forth. In Henry VI. he has drawn the characters of the two masculine women, Margaret and Eleanor, more forcibly and with more expressive touches, than his predecessor; and how eloquently he makes Suffolk, at the close of the First Part, in a scene which we conjectured to be his writing, declaim against unloving marriages:

For what is wedlock forced but a hell,
An age of discord and continual strife?
Whereas the contrary bringeth forth bliss,
And is a pattern of celestial peace.

Here, in the Comedy of Errors, he awakens the conscience of the jealous shrew Adriana, when Aemilia lays upon her the blame of the believed madness of her husband, attributing it to her "venom clamours" and railing, with which she hindered his sleep and sauced his meat, and gave him over to "moody and dull melancholy." In contrast to her he has placed her mild sister, who "ere she learns love, will practise to obey," who draws a lesson from examples in the kingdom of nature that the woman is justly subject to the man, and who amid care and trouble procures the maintenance of life. In the Taming of the Shrew, a piece that stands in complete affinity, both in outline and idea, to the Comedy of Errors, Shakespeare describes how the shrew is to be educated on the threshold of marriage, and how she is brought by just discipline to the temper of mind which is natural to the mild Luciana. Her speech at the close of the piece strongly expresses the relation of a wife to her husband, as Shakespeare regarded it. This is quite conformable to the sentiments of that day; to our perverted feelings, it is an exaggerated picture; to the affected homage of the present day to the female sex, it will appear barbarity or irony. All that may seem in this speech of Katherine too energetic and strong, is to be explained by her spirit of contradiction, and the poet, in writing it, may have been spurred by his own bitter experience. It is certainly striking that Shakespeare has never again depicted this sort of unfeminine character in its conjugal relations; it seems as if he desired to disburden himself of his impressions in these pieces, just as he next exhausted his vein of love in a series of love plays. It is certainly possible that these early productions were the result of phases in the poet's personal existence, and that, like Goethe's "Mitschuldige," with its repulsive matter, they proceeded from the inner experiences of his own life.

The Taming of the Shrew bears a striking resemblance to the Comedy of Errors, especially in the parts which do not refer to the relation between Petruchio and Katherine. The Latin school, the mannerism which marked the Italians of the sixteenth century, Ariosto and Machiavelli, in reviving the comedies of Plautus, was justly perceived by Schlegel in this part of the play. This is simply explained by the fact that Shakespeare in this very part borrowed essential touches from the "Suppositi" of Ariosto, which in 1566 were translated into English by Gascoigne. Like the figure of Pinch in the Errors, those of the Pedant and the Pantalon Gremio are pure characters of Italian comedy, and the whole plot of the piece is perfectly carried out in the taste of this school. As in the Comedy of Errors, the long doggerel verse and the language of the old pre-Shakespeare comedy are here pre-eminent, as is the case only a few times besides in his earliest original comedies, the Two Gentlemen of Verona, Love's Labour's Lost, and others, and never happens again in the plays of Shakespeare's riper period. As in the Comedy of Errors, the diction is unequal, and the dialogue often clumsy; there are single passages, on the other hand, equal in good taste and in cleverness of verse and language to the matured style of the poet. As in that comedy, there is little regard paid to the probability of the story and its circumstances. As in the one the Ephesian Dromio, so in the other the little Grumio, is the coarser form of a clown, such as Shakespeare, in his early comedies alone, loves to introduce and to work out. As in the Errors, so here in the part which turns upon Lucentio's wooing of Bianca, the art of characterisation is imperfectly exhibited: the rich old wooer Gremio, the "narrow prying father" Minola, are superficial characters belonging to all comedies of intrigue; and so too in the Errors there is only a common distinction of character drawn between the violent Ephesian Antipholus, who usually beats his stupid servant, and the milder Syracusan, with whom his witty attendant stands more on the footing of a jester. In both pieces it is striking to remark how the poet lingers among his school reminiscences; no other undisputed play of Shakespeare's furnishes so much evidence of his learning and study as the Taming of the Shrew. In the address of the Syracusan Antipholus to Luciana (Act III. sc. 2), in which he calls her a mermaid, and asks her, "Are you a god?" there is a purely Homeric tone; the same passage, bearing the same stamp, is met with again in the Taming of the Shrew (Act IV. sc. 5), where Katherine, when she addresses Vincentio, uses a similar passage from Ovid, borrowed by him from Homer, the antique sound of which lingers even under the touch of a fourth hand. This pervading mannerism of his youthful writings ought long ago to have determined the position of this play as belonging to the earliest period of the poet. All critics have felt this: Malone, Delius, and even Collier, who thought that several hands had been engaged on the piece. Undoubtedly the poet's own hand was more than once employed upon it. In the form in which we now read the piece, it must have been subsequently embellished, as we assume with certainty of other plays. Very significant allusions point to later plays of contemporary poets, and the introduction refers to Fletcher's "Women Pleased," a piece not written before 1604. That the name Baptista in the Taming of the Shrew is rightly used as that of a man, and in Hamlet on the contrary as that of a woman, is a proof to Collier that the comedy was written later than Hamlet, in 1601. But whoever considers the refinement with which Shakespeare at this very period, in Much Ado about Nothing, repeated, as it were, in a higher sphere, the two characters of Petruchio and Katherine, will never believe that the same poet at the same time could have originally written this piece.

## 1907—Edward Dowden. "The Early Comedies," from *Introduction to Shakespeare*

Edward Dowden (1843–1913) was an Irish critic, university lecturer, and poet. His works include *New Studies in Literature* (1895), *The French Revolution and English Literature: Lectures Delivered in Connection with the Sesquicentennial Celebration of Princeton University* (1897), and *Shakespeare Primer* (1877).

The influence of Latin comedy is seen in the Comedy of Errors. While the main subject was derived from the Menaechmi of Plautus, some hints were also taken from his Amphitruo. But if Seneca was too heavy for Shakespeare,

Plautus was somewhat too light. Our dramatist, indeed, complicates the plot and diversifies the mirthful entanglements, making the fun fly faster by adding to the twin-brothers Antipholus their twin-attendants Dromio. But he adds also a serious background, and towards the close he rises for a little space from mirth to pathos. The ingenious construction of the play, its skilful network of incidents, its bright intricacy which never falls into confusion are remarkable; for Shakespeare is commonly credited with having paid but little attention to his plots.

⸺⸺ ⸺⸺ ⸺⸺

## 1913—Brander Matthews. Section 3 of "His Earliest Comedies," from *Shakspere as a Playwright*

Brander Matthews (1852-1929) was an American scholar and literary critic. Having become the first professor of dramatic literature, Matthews taught at Columbia University from 1892 to 1924, where he also created and curated a museum of costumes, scripts, and props in addition to dioramas of such important dramatic venues as the Globe Theatre. He is the author of *French Dramatists of the Nineteenth Century* (1881), *Aspects of Fiction and Other Ventures in Criticism* (1896), and *The Development of the Drama* (1903).

Yet there are few signs of this inexpert timidity in the 'Comedy of Errors,' which was probably the play Shakspere produced immediately after 'Love's Labour's Lost.' Plot, which is the special quality that the earlier piece lacks, is the special quality upon which he successfully concentrates his effort in the later piece. Hazlitt asserted that Shakspere "appears to have bestowed no great pains" on the 'Comedy of Errors,' a curiously inept comment when we consider the adroit complication of its action. Complexity of intrigue cannot be achieved without taking pains; and there is no play of Shakspere's, not even his major masterpieces of construction, 'Romeo and Juliet' and 'Othello,' to the plotting of which he must have given more conscientious labor. The skeleton of the action is articulated with a skill really surprising in a young playwright, working in a century when the principles of dramatic construction had been little considered. Perhaps its author had felt the emptiness of the story in 'Love's Labour's Lost' and had, therefore, resolved that the 'Comedy of Errors' should be free from this defect at least.

Taine once declared that the art of play-making is as capable of improvement as the art of watchmaking; and in this piece the art of the play-maker is closely akin to that of the watchmaker, since its merits are mainly mechanical. And the amusement which the 'Comedy of Errors' arouses even to-day when it is acted in the theater is the result of a dexterous adjustment of situations as one equivoke follows another and as one twin is confused with the other. There is an adroit crescendo of comic perplexity. Considered merely as a mechanism, as an artfully contrived imbroglio, due to a constantly increasing comicality caused by a succession of mistakes of identity, the 'Comedy of Errors' demands high praise even to-day, although the later pupils of Scribe have achieved farces of a more surprising intricacy. Entangled as the characters are in the deliberately devised complications, the action is transparently clear to the spectator, who gains an added pleasure from his superior knowledge hidden from the persons of the play, all of them lost in a puzzling labyrinth to which they have no clue.

Shakspere borrows the plan of his play from the 'Menaechmi' of Plautus; and he may have got the hint of doubling Dromio from the 'Amphitruo' of the same Latin author, although possibly he derives this idea from an earlier piece, the 'History of Error,' which is known to have existed, but which, like so many other Elizabethan dramas, is now lost. Yet Shakspere's play, even if its imbroglio is derived from the Latin play, is much more than a mere adaptation from Plautus. The English dramatist may lean heavily upon the Roman playwright, but he completely rehandles the material he takes over from the Latin; and he adds to it not a few of the most effective episodes. There are in Plautus twelve instances of mistaken identity; and in Shakspere there are eighteen. Furthermore Shakspere cleanses away most of the vulgarity flagrant in Plautus and perhaps to be explained by the fact that the Latin playwright wrote his pieces to be performed by slaves before an audience of ignorant freedmen who had to be amused at all costs.

Farce as the 'Comedy of Errors' frankly is—since our interest is aroused mainly by the plot itself and only a little by the characters who carry it on— none the less Shakspere has given it a human quality, due to the sympathetically drawn figure of the wife and to the delicately delineated figure of her sister. He has also stiffened the story by the early introduction of *Aegeon*, the father of the separated Antipholi. The exposition is a masterpiece of invention; and here the playwright had a difficult problem before him. For the spectators to enjoy the swift sequence of blunders they needed to know all about the two pairs of twins. How is this information to be conveyed to them before either pair of twins appears on the stage? Shakspere opens the play with *Aegeon* on trial for his life, than which nothing could more certainly arrest the attention of the audience. In his search for his lost sons the merchant has come to Ephesus, in defiance of the decree which forbade any Syracusan to land upon its shores under penalty of death. In self-defense *Aegeon* explains the potent reason for his rashness; and thus he not only puts the audience in possession of all the information they need for the comprehension of ensuing perplexities, but also awakens interest in his own sad plight, thereby strengthening the serious appeal of the comic story.

The reappearance of Aegeon toward the end of the play gives dignity to the final episodes. Indeed, Shakspere displays here for the first time his appreciation of the value of mounting up steadily to a climax. At first the equivokes are those of the Dromios and the merriment these arouse is plainly farcical; the later mistakes in which the two masters are involved are in a richer vein of humor; and when Adriana is led to believe that she has lost her husband's love, the fun has a serious lining and seems to point to an impending domestic catastrophe. In a plot relying wholly upon the elaborate ingenuity of its machinery there is little space for the portrayal of character, since the characters can be only what the situations require and permit. But Adriana is a genuine woman; she may be drawn in profile only, but the strokes are true, and they are sufficient to make us recognize her reality. It is in the elevation of Adriana that Shakspere most plainly reveals his superiority to Plautus. The English farce is funnier than the Roman; and it is also more human and more humane. Despite the frequent beatings of the two Dromios, the 'Comedy of Errors' is less callous than the 'Menaechmi'; it is in better taste; and it conforms to a finer standard of morals.

The charge has been urged that in putting twin servants into his play in addition to twin masters, Shakspere doubles the improbability of the theme. But even when there is only one pair of twins the improbability is a staring impossibility. That two brothers separated in boyhood, brought up in different countries, should as full-grown men be so alike in speech, in accent, in vocabulary, in manner, and even in costume that the wife of one should take the other for her own husband—this is simply inconceivable. It could happen to two pairs of twins just as easily as it could happen to one. Impossible as this may be, it is the postulate of the play. The audience must accept it or they debar themselves from enjoying the piece which is founded upon this impossibility. Experience proves that playgoers are always willing to allow the dramatist to start from any point of departure that he may choose, provided that the play which he erects upon this premise proves to possess the power of amusing them. They will yield this license even when the theme is serious, as in the 'Corsican Brothers,' and still more willingly when they are invited only to laugh. Coleridge was characteristically shrewd when he declared that "the definition of a farce is, an improbability or even impossibility granted at the outset, see what odd and laughable events will fairly follow from it."

# 1930—Mark Van Doren.
## "The Comedy of Errors," from *Shakespeare*

Mark Van Doren (1894–1972) was a poet, literary critic, and professor of literature at Columbia University, where he taught for thirty-nine years. His extensive list of works includes *American Poetry* (1932); *Collected Poems* (1939), for which he won a Pulitzer Prize; *The Noble Voice: A Study of Ten Great Poems* (1946); and *John Dryden: A Study of His Poetry* (1960).

"The Comedy of Errors" is not Shakespeare's only unfeeling farce. He wrote two others in "The Taming of the Shrew" and "The Merry Wives of Windsor," and a third if "Titus Andronicus" is one. In comedy, says Dr. Johnson, "he seems to repose, or to luxuriate, as in a mode of thinking congenial to his nature." If that is true, it is nevertheless not true of Shakespeare's comedies of situation: plays in which, obedient to the law governing such matters, he confines his interest, or almost confines it, to physical predicament—to things that happen to certain persons not because of who they are but because of what they are. In "The Comedy of Errors" they are not men but twins. The two Antipholuses and the two Dromios exist for no other purpose than to be mutually mistaken. They may groan and seem to go mad in their perplexity, but we only laugh the louder; for it is the figure that gestures, not the man, and our expectation indeed is that the playwright will strain his ingenuity still further in the invention of new tortures, provided new ones are possible. When no others are possible, or when the two hours are up, peace may be restored and the characters may cease to exercise that genius for misunderstanding the obvious which has distinguished. them to date. If Shakespeare's spirit reposed in comedy it was not in this kind of comedy. He could write it very well and be hugely funny; but the heart of his interest was elsewhere, and the poet had abdicated.

The poet in "The Comedy of Errors" puffs with unnatural effort, as when for instance he asks us to believe that Aegeon said:

Though now this grained face of mine be hid
In sap-consuming winter's drizzled snow,
And all the conduits of my blood froze up,
Yet hath my night of life some memory,
My wasting lamps some fading glimmer left.
     (V, i, 311–15)

His rhymes, surviving from an old convention in comedy, rattle like bleached bones. The long verse speeches, whether by Aegeon or by his twin sons, or by Adriana who is wife to one of them and for the most part nothing save the exclamatory wife to be expected in a farce, are stiff and prim and explicit, with no suggestion that their speakers have capacities beyond the needs of asseveration and complaint. Even wit is unnecessary in a play which counts on beatings and beratings to amuse us, and indeed counts rightly. The mental fooling between Antipholus of Syracuse and his Dromio at the beginning of II, ii, is among the dullest things of its kind in Shakespeare. But it does not matter, for to Plautus's idea of twin masters Shakespeare has added the idea of twin servants, and there are riches in the fourfold result which he can mine by manipulation alone. Dromio of Syracuse, to be sure, makes excellent verbal use of his fat kitchen wench: "She is spherical, like a globe; I could find out

countries in her." And Antipholus of Ephesus can call names almost as vigorously as Petruchio does in "The Taming of the Shrew":

> Along with them
> They brought one Pinch, a hungry lean-fac'd villain,
> A mere anatomy, a mountebank,
> A threadbare juggler and a fortune-teller,
> A needy, hollow-ey'd, sharp-looking wretch,
> A living dead man.
>
> (V, i, 237–41)

Yet there is no more need for such eloquence than there is for characters possessing qualities in excess of those required by the situation, or for verisimilitude in the plotted action. "What I should think of this, I cannot tell," says
Antipholus of Syracuse (III, ii, 184). What he should think of course is that his
twin brother has turned up. He does not so think for the simple reason that he
is in a conspiracy with Shakespeare to regale us with the spectacle of his talent
for confusion.

The minds of these marionettes run regularly on the supernatural, on
magic and witchcraft; but with the difference from "Henry VI" that there is no
suggestion of vast state intrigues, and with the still more interesting difference
from "A Midsummer Night's Dream" and "Othello" that no special atmosphere
is created, whether charming or terrible. "This is the fairy land," whines Dromio
of Syracuse (II, ii, 191); "We talk with goblins, owls, and sprites." Dromio is
consciously exaggerating; his world, like the world of the play, remains matter-
of-fact, however frequent the angry references to jugglers, sorcerers, witches,
cheaters, mountebanks, mermaids, wizards, conjurers, and the several fiends of
folklore with their drugs and syrups, their nail-parings and pinpoint drops of
blood. Cheaters is the word—pretenders to supernatural power, citizens in side
streets who prey on the gullible. The play itself is never tinctured; farce must
keep its head. So the ludicrous repetition throughout IV, i, of two plain words,
"the chain," achieves no effect resembling that achieved by two plain words, "the
handkerchief," in a scene to come; and Angelo the goldsmith's remark, "I knew
he was not in his perfect wits" (V, i, 42), carries no such burden of meaning as is
carried by Lear's "I fear I am not in my perfect mind."

Nor is the business of the shipwreck which has separated Aegeon from one
of his sons more than a hint of the shipwrecks which in the last plays will be
so beautiful and awful, and so important somehow to the life of Shakespeare's
imagination. This catastrophe occurs only as a device to get twins separated, and
to start the machinery of farce revolving. Yet it occurs. And Aegeon for all his
bad poetry wrings a few drops of pathos from it. So Adriana for one moment, if
only for one moment, outgrows her shrewish mold:

Ah, but I think him better than I say. . . .
Far from her nest the lapwing cries away.
My heart prays for him, though my tongue do curse.

    (IV, ii, 25–8)

There is a touch in her here of Beatrice, as well as of Shakespeare's silent heroines. And the lyric voice of her sister Luciana has perhaps no place at all in Ephesus, city of slapstick. Such elements, few and feeble though they are, point ahead to the time when Shakespeare will have found the kind of comedy in which his nature can repose, and to the year when he will have another try at twins but will make one of them a girl and give her the name Viola.

<hr/>

## 1951—Harold C. Goddard. "The Comedy of Errors," from *The Meaning of Shakespeare*

Harold C. Goddard (1878-1950) was professor of English at Swarthmore College and the University of Chicago. He is the author of *Studies in New England Transcendentalism* (1908) and *The Meaning of Shakespeare* (1951), the latter published posthumously.

*The Comedy of Errors*, it is agreed, is one of Shakespeare's very early plays, possibly his earliest. It is more nearly pure "theater" than anything else he ever wrote except perhaps *The Merry Wives of Windsor*. They are his two plays that have little more to offer the reader after two or three careful perusals. *The Comedy of Errors* especially evokes no sense of the inexhaustibility that characterizes Shakespeare's masterpieces.

And yet it is itself a masterpiece in its own kind. That kind, except for its enveloping action and occasional touches of nature in the main story, is, in spite of its title, farce and not comedy. Few better farces have ever been written, and there is something appropriate in the thought that Shakespeare so early came so close to perfection, even if it was perfection in what is commonly considered an inferior dramatic type. But, as is well known, the credit is not all his. The play is an adaptation from Plautus, and the young Shakespeare had the advantage of standing as it were on the shoulders of his Roman predecessor. However, he quadruples the ingenuity called for in managing the plot by introducing a second pair of twins. Plautus had had but one in *The Menaechmi*.

*The Comedy of Errors* leaves the impression that its author must have possessed this quality of ingenuity above all others. Yet ingenuity—not that he ever lacked it—is one of the last things we associate with the mature Shakespeare. It is an attribute of talent, not of genius.

The action of this play bears the marks of having been planned backward. Its outcome was plainly foreseen and worked up to. One can picture Plautus-Shakespeare making actual puppets or using bits of colored cardboard and moving them about on a table to keep the characters and situations straight—except that a mind endowed with skill of this particular order would probably need no external aids. As we saw in another connection, the intellect makes a plan in advance and works toward its fulfilment, while the imagination, like a living organism, "grows" a plan as it were as it goes along. That of course overemphasizes the contrast. Artistic creation is not quite as unconscious a process as the statement implies, and the intellect is needed to keep the creative impulse in restraint. But for practical purposes we may say that *The Comedy of Errors* is a product of Shakespeare's intellect rather than of his imagination. It was invented rather than created. It came out of the same side of the mind that makes a good chess player or military strategist, a successful practical architect or technically adept composer of contrapuntal music. (If anyone retorts that imagination is just what such activities call for, he is debasing the word from its proper sense when applied to the fine arts.)

We know little about the contemporary reception of *The Comedy of Errors*, but it is easy to fancy its being what we call today a "hit." It gratifies the essential theatrical craving. Why do we love the theater? For various reasons, but for one fundamental one. We live in the midst of a confusing world. We are forever making blunders ourselves and becoming the victims of the blunders of other people. How restful yet exhilarating it would be if for once we could get above it all and from a vantage point watch the blunders going on *below* us. Well, that is just what the theater permits us to do for an hour or two. For a brief interval it enables us to become gods. Stripped of all nonessentials, that, I think, is the ultimate nature of the theatrical *passion*, and that is why in one form or another practically everything that goes on in the theater is based on something misunderstood by some or all of the people on the stage that is at the same time clear to the people who are watching them. The spectator is thrilled to share a confidence of the dramatist at the expense of the actors. Hence the playwright's rule: Never keep a secret from your audience. Here is one explanation of the incessant concern of drama with the theme of appearance versus reality. And herein, too, lies the danger of the theater.

It is inspiring for a man to be put for a few moments in the position of a god. But it is an intoxicating experience, and much of it is as bad for him as a little is good. Too much will inevitably drive him mad. For the theater to be a food and not a drug, this purely theatrical quality must be mixed with and diluted by more terrestrial and substantial ingredients. "Theater" must become drama, and, if possible, poetry.

And there is danger to the playwright as well as to the audience, though of another sort. For the playwright who has once discovered the tricks whereby this theatrical effect is obtained is tempted to rely on them for the success of his invention. *Manufacture a misunderstanding and let the audience in on it* is a cheap but infallible recipe for making a play. It is one of the marks of Shakespeare's greatness that he apparently recognized this from the first and refused to be lured down the road to the easy success that has proved the ruin of thousands of promising young playwrights. He continued to make use of the popular appeal that lies in the ingenious plot and theatrical situation, but he subordinated these things progressively to other ends or transmuted them into something higher. The greatest scenes in his plays, however, like the play scene in *Hamlet*, the temptation scene in *Othello*, the murder and banquet scenes in *Macbeth*, along with their unsurpassed drama and poetry, continue to have in the highest degree this purely theatrical quality.

In proportion as they master them, men grow skeptical of their own professions. When they come to know them, they see through them. Shakespeare lived to see through the theater. He subdued it to himself rather than let it subdue him to itself.

There is one clear sign, even in *The Comedy of Errors*, that its author was not going to rest content with mere theatrical effect achieved by the mechanically made coincidences on which all farce relies. The characters of the play, in the face of the strange occurrences with which they are continually being confronted, keep declaring that they must be dreaming, that things are bewitched, that some sorcerer must be at work behind the scenes. In the aggregate these allusions amount almost to an apology to his audience by the author, an admission that a psychological or metaphysical explanation is demanded to reconcile with reality the unreal conventions of the stage. In that sense not only *A Midsummer-Night's Dream*, but *Macbeth* and *The Tempest* are already implicit in *The Comedy of Errors*.

<hr>

# 1965—E.M.W. Tillyard. "The Comedy of Errors," from *Shakespeare's Early Comedies*

E.M.W. Tillyard (1889–1962) was a classical scholar, literary critic, and master at Jesus College. The list of his scholarly works include *Shakespeare's Last Plays* (1938), his influential essay titled "The Elizabethan World Picture" (1943), *The Miltonic Setting: Past and Present* (1949), *Shakespeare's Problem Plays* (1950), and *The Nature of Comedy and Shakespeare* (1958).

---

## i. ITS ORIGINALS

The core of the *Comedy of Errors* is farce and it is derived from one play of Plautus and some scenes from another.[1] In the Menaechmi the motive of farce is the arrival in Epidamnus of a man, the identical twin brother of another man settled and married in the town. The incoming brother has been seeking his twin for many years in his own ship. Before the brothers meet and exchange news, a number of people in Epidamnus mistake one brother for another with various ludicrous results; and these results are the reason for the play's existence. The play is short and neat, and the farcical situations are well contrived. None of the characters excites our sympathy, nor does the play possess any other quality that might distract our attention from the purely farcical effect. Shakespeare appropriated the main motive and many of the details. For instance, his Adriana, wife of the established brother, is jealous in imitation of the wife of Menaechmus, while each wife has some cause for jealousy in the shape of a local courtesan. And if Menaechmus gives his Erotium a cloak and a gold chain Antipholus gives Erotium's opposite number a gold chain but no cloak. Both husbands are thought to be mad by their wives and incur or escape capture with a view to the proper medical treatment. So in a sense Shakespeare got the core of his *Errors* from the *Menaechmi*.

But he was not at all strictly bound to his original. Indeed, in his youthful ambition, he was not satisfied till he had added so much to the Plautine core as to make his version a totally different affair.

First, he went to another play of Plautus, the *Amphitryo*, for help in complicating the farcical situation. In the *Menaechmi* only the incoming brother has his confidential slave; but in the *Amphitryo* not only does Jupiter assume Amphitryo's form to promote his intrigue with Alcmena but he causes Mercury to take the form of Sosia, Amphitryo's slave, thus creating two pairs, masters and servants, of identical appearance. Shakespeare imitated this creation by adding to the identical brothers identical brothers' servants. He also borrowed from the *Amphitryo* the farcical situation of a citizen being barred out of his own house by his wife. By adding this second pair of twins Shakespeare embarked on a much more complicated task than Plautus had attempted, as it were choosing to play chess as against Plautus's draughts. The range of possible mistakes was greatly extended; and Shakespeare was able to set his prodigious powers of memory and intellect a satisfyingly exacting task.

But Shakespeare also went outside Plautus to enrich his theme. However stylized and matter-of-fact Roman comedy was, it retained some faint trace of its more romantic ancestry through its motives of recognitions of lost children, its closeness to the sea, its allusions to ship wreck and pirates. It thus connects remotely with the Greek novel, which had a common origin with Latin comedy however widely it diverged from it. Shakespeare exploited this connection by enclosing his Plautine farce in a framework derived from the Greek novel. In the *Menaechmi* the parents of the twin brothers figure among the characters; but they live in the town where the action takes place: and of the whole family it is only the second brother who does the travelling and the seeking. Moreover his travels are barely referred to. Shakespeare caused the parents to be separated, placing the father and one son in Syracuse and making them both search the world for the rest, who are living in the town where the action takes place, the mother as Abbess of a nunnery and the son a prosperous married citizen. And Shakespeare chose to recount both the events that led to the family's dispersal and the action of one separated part in seeking out the other. For this narrative he got his hints from the lost Greek romance of Apollonius of Tyre,[2] preserved in a Latin translation and retold by Gower. That Shakespeare read Gower's version is shown by his own dramatization of Apollonius's story, *Pericles*, with Gower speaking the prologue of each act. In the story a father seeks and finds a lost wife and daughter, the wife being priestess in the temple of Diana at Ephesus. It was this last detail that caused Shakespeare to change the Plautine setting of Epidamnus to Ephesus. Yet he had another reason to welcome this change. A crucial motive in the *Comedy of Errors* is that of the fairy world and especially witchcraft; and Shakespeare's audience, bred on the Bible, knew that Ephesus was noted for its magic arts. In the nineteenth chapter of the Acts of the Apostles it is recounted that 'certain of the vagabond Jews, exorcists,' tried unsuccessfully to compete with St Paul in the expulsion of evil spirits, with the results that many Ephesians who practised magic brought their handbooks to be burnt in public. Thus Shakespeare added to the farcical nucleus further examples of recognition after many years, episodes of storms, shipwrecks, rescues, separations, and hints of magical practice, all endemic in the world of romance.

Finally, Shakespeare did something which we need not connect with any precedent. He humanized his farcical nucleus and approximated it to comedy in a way Plautus never even began to do. First, he made his Ephesus a more living city than Plautus's Epidamnus. Ephesus became a place where not only ridiculous things happened but where men encountered the perennial problem of how to live together in a society. Second, he defined and contrasted his persons in a way Plautus never tried to do. His two brothers are quite different in temperament; to the citizen-brother's wife he added a sister, as different from her sister as he made brother from brother; father and mother differ somewhat as brother and brother do.

## ii. RHETORIC

As the content of the *Comedy of Errors* is far more varied than is often allowed, so is the vehicle. In the main, blank verse prevails; but in the scenes where the low characters figure there can occur prose, after the fashion of Lyly, or four-stress doggerel after the fashion of *Ralph Roister Doister* and of much comic stuff in the primitive Elizabethan drama. The scene of Antipholus of Ephesus along with his Dromio bringing the Goldsmith and Balthazar back home to dine and being barred out of his own house begins with Antipholus talking in blank verse and goes on to Dromio's replying in doggerel, with doggerel continuing throughout this broadly comic episode, till Balthazar turns to stately blank verse in his efforts to dissuade Antipholus from the scandal of breaking in at this busy time of day when half Ephesus may see him. The next scene, showing the other Antipholus courting Luciana and her attempts to reprove him, is in rhymed quatrains which suggest partly a sonneteering context, apt to the courting, and partly a sententious one, apt to Luciana's moralizing. Its rhetoric is perfectly fitting. But, if Shakespeare varies his blank verse with prose or other metres, that verse is more varied than it is reputed to be. True, it is largely end-stopped but within such a norm he can be extremely expressive; though only to an ear that is both attentive and unprejudiced. Take this example, from the opening scene, where Aegeon in calm and unhurried despair begins his tale of misfortunes:

> In Syracusa was I born, and wed
> Unto a woman, happy but for me.
> And by me, had not our hap been bad.
>     (I, i, 37)

Here not only does the verse depart from its end-stopped context, but the third line is unusual and most expressive in rhythm. And by me, had not our hap been bad, with *had* bearing a lighter stress than the other stressed words. Read thus, it suggests an afterthought following a long pause and serves to set up that feeling of the speaker's taking his time which is essential if we are to prepare ourselves for a long narrative. Or take the delicate adjustment of sound to sense in these two end-stopped lines (II, ii, 30–1):

> When the sun shines let foolish gnats make sport,
> But creep in crannies when he hides his beams.

Here the first line sounds gay and airy, the second low and earthy. And in final illustration, here is a passage end-stopped indeed yet so varied within its line-units as to give a sense of the most lively conversation. The context (IV, i, 52) is of the merchant to whom Angelo, the goldsmith, owes money, urging him to get from Antipholus of Ephesus his just debt for the chain.

> *Mer.* The hour steals on; I pray you, sir, dispatch.
> *Ang.* You hear how he importunes me—the chain!
> *Ant. E.* Why, give it to my wife, and fetch your money.
> *Ang.* Come, come, you know I gave it you even now.
> Either send the chain or send by me some token.
> *Ant. E.* Fie, now you run this humour out of breath!
> Come, where's the chain? I pray you let me see it.

Then there are the passages that, by sheer poetic eminence, are exceptions to the usual norm of metrical competence and aptitude. Take these few lines of soliloquy (I, ii, 33–8) spoken by Antipholus of Syracuse after the merchant has 'commended him to his own content' and left him:

> He that commends me to mine own content
> Commends me to the thing I cannot get.
> I to the world am like a drop of water
> That in the ocean seeks another drop,
> Who, falling there to find his fellow forth,
> Unseen, inquisitive, confounds himself.

Here there is not only the slow melancholy cadence that confirms the sentiment but the surprising collocation of *unseen* and *inquisitive*. Normally the inquisitive person does not worry whether he is seen or not. But Antipholus feels all the loneliness of a stranger at large in an alien city in which he is about to 'lose himself and wander up and down to view' it. Yet it is his duty to be inquisitive, and the surprising collocation of the two adjectives expresses both that duty and his despair of ever fulfilling it. It is a pleasant irony that as soon as he finishes his soliloquy he should cease to be unseen through being accosted by Dromio of Ephesus and prevented for good from taking his intended lonely walk round the town.

Then at the end of the same scene Shakespeare gives us a taste of his superb range of diction in Antipholus's account of what to expect in Ephesus:

> They say this town is full of cozenage;
> As, nimble jugglers that deceive the eye.
> Dark-working sorcerers that change the mind,
> Soul-killing witches that deform the body,
> Disguised cheaters, prating mountebanks,
> And many such-like liberties of sin;
>
> (I, ii, 97)

And the passage is matched by the other Antipholus's account of Pinch, the quack called in to treat him in his supposed madness. It is part of Antipholus's long appeal to the Duke to redress his wrongs (V, i, 237–41).

> Along with them
> They brought one Pinch, a hungry lean-fac'd villain,
> A mere anatomy, a mountebank,
> A threadbare juggler, and a fortune-teller,
> A needy, hollow-ey'd, sharp-looking wretch,
> A living dead man.

In sum, Shakespeare's rhetoric in the *Comedy of Errors* is good for something more than simple farce.

### iii. THE ROMANTIC FRAMEWORK

In my short discussion of Shakespeare's originals I began with the core of farce and worked outward. In going on to discuss the meaning of the different parts of the play I reverse this order, for I believe that it is in the core, as reinforced by the peripheries, that the main meaning of the play subsists.

In itself the romantic framework has no profound significance. It does not make us feel that either Aegeon or his younger son has surmounted an ordeal through the successful issue of his long wanderings; nor are we drawn anywhere near the feelings I have described as apt to the natural human routine of setting out from home, coping successfully with a task, and returning to relax. No, the romantic framework in itself does not go beyond arousing our simple feelings of wonder. Aegeon tells his story of marine adventures well enough, though not as well as Prospero was destined to tell his, and keeps our mind happily busy, yet not seriously extended, by its strangenesses. But in conjunction with the rest of the play the romantic framework weighs more. It helped to satisfy Shakespeare's craving for a rich subject-matter and in particular for an extreme complication of plot needing skilful disentanglement in the last scene. For the latter the added presence of Aegeon and Aemilia was essential. (Incidentally it is pleasant to reflect that not only does the first scene lead to the *Tempest* but the last scene to the grand finale of *Cymbeline*.) On the face of it, to graft remote romance on a crudely farcical plot was to court disaster; but it is precisely over such difficulties that Shakespeare was able to triumph. As it is, the fantasy of the romance leads easily to the fantastic shape which he caused the old farcical material to take on. When it comes to degrees of fantasy, there is nothing to choose between Aegeon and Aemilia tying one twin son and one twin slave to this end of the mast and the other son and slave to that, and Antipholus and Dromio of Syracuse going about Ephesus with drawn swords convinced that they are surrounded by witches and devils.

### iv. THE COMIC ELEMENT

Here, in the play that may be his first comedy, we find Shakespeare following what was to prove his permanent instinct: never to forsake the norm of social life. However distant he may get from that norm into inhuman horror, or wild romance, or lyrical fancy, or mystical heights, he always reverts, if only for a short spell, to the ordinary world of men and to its problems of how they are to live together. Even in the *Winter's Tale*, where the proportion of the remote and the fantastic may be the highest, Shakespeare recalls us to the gross life of ordinary folk with the entry of the old shepherd and his 'I would there were no age between ten and twenty-three' and the rest. You may say that he was forced to do this to please his public; but he was also following his instincts, which insisted on connecting, on demonstrating the unity of all experience. It is an instinct that has made Shakespeare so widely loved and the lack of which explains the comparative neglect of Spenser. The extent to which he indulged that instinct in the *Comedy of Errors* has not been fully recognized.

Take the setting. Though Henry Cuningham, in his preface to the Arden *Errors*, may be right in identifying the abbey in Ephesus with Holywell Priory near two of the London playhouses, the Curtain and the Theatre, Ephesus itself is a small ordinary town where everyone knows everyone else's business, where merchants predominate, and where dinner is a serious matter. The last item suggests an illustration of how Shakespeare added normal life to farce. Though we hear plenty about Antipholus of Ephesus before, he does not appear on the stage till the beginning of the third act. But when he does his first words show we are in the very central area of comedy:

> Good Signior Angelo, you must excuse us all;
> My wife is shrewish when I keep not hours.
> Say that I linger'd with you at your shop
> To see the making of her carcanet.
> And that tomorrow you will bring it home.
>
> (III, i, 1)

Antipholus has indeed been laying up trouble for himself, for not only is he shockingly late for dinner but he is bringing with him two guests, probably unnotified and certainly offensive to the housewife as eating a dinner that through over-cooking does an injustice to her domestic competence. No wonder Antipholus tries to excuse himself on the ground that it was his solicitude for his wife's chain that made him late and seeks further safety by getting Angelo to father the lie. So, in their way, his sins are great, but how ludicrously different from the sins Adriana imputes to him. Or take a touch like this one. The second scene of the second act begins with Antipholus of Syracuse meeting his own Dromio and their immediately getting at cross purposes. Antipholus loses his temper and beats his slave; but his good nature asserts itself, and he tells Dromio to be more sensible and watch his master's mood before he talks nonsense to him.

> Because that I familiarly sometimes
> Do use you for my fool and chat with you,
> Your sauciness will jest upon my love.
> And make a common of my serious hours.
> When the sun shines let foolish gnats make sport,
> But creep in crannies when he hides his beams.

If you will jest with me, know my aspect.
And fashion your demeanour to my looks,
Or I will beat this method in your sconce.
     (II, ii, 26)

Neither of these very human touches or the many others like them I could cite
have any bearing on the purely farcical situations; but, as I shall explain, they
may have a great deal of meaning if, not attempting to integrate comedy and
farce, we set one in contrast to the other.

Then there are the characters. For the farcical effect, Shakespeare did not need
to diversify them. Situations he must of course diversify even to extravagance;
but the characters of those who find themselves in the situations hardly count.
It would not matter if the two Antipholi were identical not only in appearance
but in character. The primary need is that they should be subjected to a variety
of accidents. But Shakespeare could not be content simply to satisfy this primary
need; his nature insisted on his giving the two brothers different characters. The
elder brother, Antipholus of Ephesus, is the more energetic, the more practical,
the more choleric; the younger Antipholus is in comparison melancholy,
sensitive, and of a livelier imagination. Barred from his house, Antipholus of
Ephesus proposes to break in by force and has to be reminded by Balthazar
of the scandal this would cause, before desisting. And after he has broken his
bonds and escaped his confinement in the dark room he vows that he will scorch
his wife's face and disfigure her. With his different temperament Antipholus of
Syracuse is pessimistic about finding his brother, open to the notion that the
Ephesians are queer folk and that there is witchcraft abroad, and slow in the
practical matter of drawing the right conclusion from the way many people seem
to know who he is and salute him. The contrast between the brothers is not thrust
on us but it is there in all clarity, as it is there in *Cymbeline*, where, although the
plot does not demand it, Shakespeare made Guiderius, the elder brother, the
more practical and trustful and Arviragus, the younger, more imaginative.[3] By
distinguishing between the Antipholi in this way Shakespeare adds the comic
to the purely farcical.

The parents, Aegeon and Aemilia, on the other hand, are hardly characterized
at all. Aegeon is little more than a humour of aged melancholy; rightly, because, if
fully animated, he would have introduced an element of tragedy that the farcical
core could not have sustained. Aemilia, a symbol of severe and stately authority,
but again hardly characterized, serves the play substantially. Her unexpected
appearance (and we can picture her as tall and commanding, and conspicuous
in her black habit among the excited particoloured folk that throng the stage) is
one of the great moments of the play; an abrupt check to the wild fantasy that
has been accumulating through the previous acts and a sign that the resolution
is at hand. She is also the agent of the final drawing out of Adriana's character,

when she 'betrays her to her own reproof'. Yet, though thus an agent of normal human action, she is hardly humanized herself.

It is on the two sisters that Shakespeare expends his power of making ordinary, living people. Bradley noted how few lines Cordelia speaks in comparison with the impression she leaves behind. To a smaller extent this is true of Adriana and Luciana, to whose vivid characterization justice has hardly been done and whose natures, I venture to think, have not been properly understood. Shakespeare's study of the two sisters ranks, indeed, with other studies of that classic theme: with those found in the *Antigone*, *Arcadia*, the *Heart of Midlothian*, *Sense and Sensibility*, *Middlemarch*, and the *Old Wives' Tale*. In all these the sisters are different, sometimes opposed, in temperament, but loyal one to the other, however much their principles may differ and their actions in life diverge.

It is usual to describe Adriana as a jealous woman and to leave it at that. But this is too simple a description and indeed it heads us off the truth. It must be granted that she keeps on professing jealousy but her nature need not contain an excess of it. The root of her trouble is stupidity,[4] and lack of reflection and restraint that makes her her own worst enemy. She belongs to a higher rank in life than Mrs Quickly, but in her stupidity and her garrulousness she is like her. She is also good-natured at bottom and quick to forgive. All these qualities save the last are evident in the scene (II, i) in which she first appears. Here she is shown in distraction because her husband is late for dinner and Dromio, sent to fetch him, has not returned. And Luciana's sensible advice—

Perhaps some merchant hath invited him,
And from the mart he's somewhere gone to dinner;
Good sister, let us dine, and never fret.

    (II, i, 4)

Most people get a sense of pleasant and reassuring solidity from their everyday occupations. If their nerves are in good order, they find such acts as buying writing-paper, catching a train, or answering an invitation, to be parts of a substantial core of existence. Virginia Woolf has summed up this state of things with perfect vividness and conciseness in the words, 'Tuesday follows Monday' . . . It cannot be doubted that Shakespeare, with his eye for detail and his healthily slow development, fully shared this way of feeling. . . . There are, however, times when in the realm of action even the simplest and the most normal people find their scale of reality upset. Under the stress of war, or love, or remorse, or a strong disappointment, the things that seemed solid, the acts that seemed to proceed so naturally and without question from one's will, appear remote. Eating and buying writing-paper become rather ridiculous acts which you watch yourself, or rather yourself appearing not yourself, proceeding to do. . . . Once the equipoise is disturbed, the real things are not everyday acts but passionate mental activities. . . . No great poet can be unaware of these and other planes of reality, and in one way or another he has to make his peace with them. . . . The normal poetic method of dealing with them is to try to unite them by referring to a single norm; but there is another method: that of communicating the sense of their existence without arranging them in any pattern of subordination.

And I cite *A Midsummer Night's Dream* as an example of the first method, everything in the end being subordinated to the comic, social, norm; and *The Waves* as an example of the second.

In transcending mere farce as I think it to do, the *Comedy of Errors* raises the question of what is the norm of reality. One need not suppose that, at any rate at this stage of his career, Shakespeare had consciously formulated any opinions on such matters; but it is certain that he was aware of many modes or standards of experience well before he came to write his play; and what literary kind more than farce, with its congenital bent to the fantastic, was likely to express that awareness? I have said what I think to be the culminating moment of the play: namely when Antipholus of Syracuse and his Dromio enter with drawn swords, and Adriana and the rest think them her husband and servant broken loose and fly in terror. Both parties suffer from an extremity of illusion, one as it were ratifying the illusion of the other. Moreover the states of mind have been arrived at by gradual and entirely logical processes. And we conclude that the state of violence presented has somehow acquired its own solidity and thus stands for a way of experiencing, alternative to the way common in the plain working world.

On the whole things go right in the *Comedy of Errors*. The pathos of Aegeon in the last scene, when his younger son apparently refuses to recognize him, is too turgid to carry conviction:

> Though now this grained face of mine be hid
> In sap-consuming winter's drizzled snow,
> And all the conduits of my blood froze up,
> Yet hath my night of life some memory,
> My wasting lamps some fading glimmer left,

>      (V, i, 310)

(But note how the last line frees itself from the turgid and carries conviction.) The backchat in II, ii, between Antipholus of Syracuse and his Dromio is excessively dreary to a modern, however pleasing the word-play was in its time. But these are mere details and are exceptions. It is worth noting here that Dromio of Syracuse's account of the kitchenmaid in III, ii, succeeds by modern as well as by contemporary taste. It is as near to us as a music-hall turn and builds up a convincing picture of a monster. Having built it up, Shakespeare was wise not to bring her on the stage but to trust to our imaginations. Ignoring the blemishes, I find that the play is about as good as the verse allows. The verse has its limits and probably would not have reached to some subtle development of character, for instance. But it reaches to the things attempted; and the play has not been rated a major success only because it is Shakespeare's.

NOTES

1. For an exhaustive account of the sources see T. W. Baldwin, op. cit, chap. XVIII.

2. He may have got hints from Greene's pastoral romance, *Menaphon*. See Baldwin, op. cit., p. 794. But Shakespeare's sobriety is unlike Greene's froth.

3. See my *Shakespeare's Last Plays* (London, 1938), p. 35.

4. It is surprising that E. P. Kuhl, who has written some of the sanest criticism on *The Shrew*, should call Adriana and Kate 'two mischief-making women—women much alike'. On the contrary Kate differs in being highly intelligent; and part of her education is for her to be made to use an intelligence overlaid by violent passions. See *P.M.L.A.*, 1925, pp. 611–12.

5. In the light of this scene I just fail to see how Charles Brooks in *Shakespeare Quarterly* (1960), p. 351 can say, 'Both Adriana and Kate are admirably intelligent women.'

6. Boston, Mass., 1928, p. xxxii.

7. London, 1945, pp. 85–92.

8. pp. 60–8.

## 1995—Douglas L. Peterson. "Beginnings and Endings: Structure and Mimesis in Shakespeare's Comedies," from *Entering the Maze: Shakespeare's Art of Beginning*

Douglas L. Peterson is professor emeritus at Michigan State University. He is the author of *English Lyric from Wyatt to Donne: A History of the Plain and Eloquent Styles* (1967) and *Time, Tide and Tempest: A Study of Shakespeare's Romances* (1973).

My concern is with a way of beginning and concluding which Shakespeare develops in *The Comedy of Errors*, *Love's Labour's Lost*, and *A Midsummer Night's Dream* and continues to use throughout his career as a compositional schema in plays as different as *As You Like It*, *Measure for Measure*, and *Cymbeline*. In each instance a threat of death initiates the main action. Egeon in *The Comedy of Errors* faces execution for having violated a law barring all citizens of Syracuse from Ephesus. In *A Midsummer Night's Dream* Hermia must be prepared to die or live the barren life of a votaress of Diana if she continues to refuse to marry according to her father's wishes. In *Love's Labour's Lost* the threat is "devouring time," itself. Each threat is followed, in turn, by a sudden and radical shift in dramatic focus. Egeon is left behind, "hopeless and happless . . . to procrastinate his liveless end" (I. i. 157–58),[1] while we follow his son, Antipholus of Syracuse, into what seems to him to be a strange and dream-like world of inexplicable occurrences. In *A Midsummer Night's Dream* we leave Theseus' court to follow the young lovers into a forest of moonlight and enchantment. The shift of focus in *Love's Labour's Lost* is not so immediately obvious. We join a king and his friends and guests in what amounts to an interval of holiday until a packet of documents on its way from the King of France arrives. Finally, in the closing moments of each play the focus suddenly shifts again and the characters in the play-world must again confront the mortal threats which since the opening moments have been put aside.

The result in each instance is a play consisting of two distinct and radically different kinds of action, each with its own beginning and ending, and with one enframing the other. The enframing actions are recognizable as common to the world we leave behind when we enter the theater to be free for a time of its claims—where fathers are unreasonable, laws inequitably administered and even unjust, and where we confront the demands of everyday. The enframed actions, on the other hand, are playful and even farcical and are set in places where the laws of verisimilitude and probability, along with clocktime itself, have been set aside.

Each action, in short, is presented in a distinct kind of fiction which, in turn, invites a different kind of response from the audience. The fictions of the enframing actions, however extraordinary the events they depict, are mimetic and invite identification and empathy—recognition that the problems encountered by those who are involved in them are of the kind that touch our own lives, whereas the enframed fictions are "ludic" and invite the opposite kind of response. They are games of make-believe which the audience is invited to join as a way of escaping temporarily from the very kinds of problems with which the enframing fictions invite the audience to identify. Participation requires only that the audience accept the hypothetical situations they present—two sets of long separated identical twins on the loose in the same city, or a fairy-enchanted forest. Having accepted the hypothesis, we are free as members of the audience to laugh at situations which the characters find utterly incomprehensible and even frustrating because we are in on the fun. The playmaker has taken us into his confidence, "distancing" us from those situations by sharing with us his perspective. We laugh at the bewildering situations the Antipholus brothers and the runaway lovers encounter because we know they are only temporary and will be happily resolved for all. For the plays of which they are a part are comedies and comedies always, or almost always—*Love's Labour's Lost* being the obvious exception—have happy endings.

The result in each instance is a play which really consists of two plays in one: one which is mimetic, involving dangers to life and inviting audience identification and empathy; and another which is "ludic," devoted to the improbable and offering the audience an interval of fun in which to escape for a time the problems that engage us all.

The native traditions of comedy provide long-established precedents for Shakespeare's enframing of an interval of "mirth and game" within a fiction representing the world of everyday. The practice of providing audiences with two kinds of entertainment is at least as old as the secular drama itself. Henry Medwall, for instance, at the close of *Fulgens and Lucrece* (1497) indicates that he has mingled "mirth and game" of an old and familiar kind with exemplary instruction:

That all the substaunce of this play
was done specially therfor
Not onely to make folke myrth and game,
But that such as be gentilmen of name
May be somewhat mouyd
By this example . . .

   (II, 888–93)[2]

John Rastell, too, when describing *The Nature of the Four Elements* (1517) as a "philosophical work" in which he has "mixed . . . merry conceits to give men comfort,"[3] indicates that he has provided his audience with two different kinds of entertainment—something of substance for those who are looking for profit and edification and "merry conceits" for those who want simply to be entertained.

As a practice guaranteeing the broadest range of potential patrons of public playhouses, the mingling of "substance" with "merry conceits" and "toys" was one which professional playwrights were quick to take up. William Wager advertises *The Longer Thou Livest the More Fool Thou Art* (1559–68) as a play in which he has "interlaced" "honest mirth" with "wholesome lessons" (Prologue, ll. 6470).[4] Nathaniell Woode explains in his Prologue to *The Conflict of Conscience*[5] that its story of suicidal despair is so unremittingly painful he has introduced intervals of "honest Mirth" to "refresh the minds" of his audience. Robert Wilson, too, promises the audiences of *The Three Lourdes and Ladies of London* (1584) both "comic" and instructive entertainment when describing it as "A Pleasant and Stately Morall . . . Commically interlaced with much honest mirth, for pleasure and recreation, among many moral observations, and other important matters of due Regard."[6]

"Interlacing" instructive examples with "mirth and game," in short, was a practice which patrons of the public theaters of London had come to expect, and one which an ambitious apprentice-playwright, who must have known only too well from his own experience as an actor that his success would depend upon entertaining commoners as well as royal patrons, might be expected immediately to adopt as his own.

There are also equally well-established native precedents for the particular way he combined these two kinds of theatrical entertainment in *The Comedy of Errors*.

Contrary to the view prevailing among historians of the drama, the humanist notion of comedy as a Mirror (Imitatio vitae, Speculum consuetudinis, Imago veritatis), which Donatus in his commentaries on Terence attributes to Cicero, was not the only one available to Tudor playwrights. Nor was it the most influential in the native comedy's formative stage of development. However useful the notion proved to be to pedagogues as a means of exemplary instruction, a reading of Tudor comedies indicates that playwrights who were actually writing plays to be performed found two other notions, both of medieval origin, more immediately useful to their purposes. One is of comedy as a "merry tale" or *ioca* whose "iocose materia" serves simply to provide "solas," "comfort," or "recreation" on appropriate festive occasions. The other is of comedy as an extraordinary or "wonderful" history beginning in sorrows, ending in joy and celebrating the restorative power of divine and human love.[7]

Comedy as an ioca or "merry tale," which "recreates" by providing its audience with an interval of sport and mirth in which to escape temporarily from the claims of everyday,[8] has its origins in the native festive drama of the Middle Ages. As V. A. Kolve and others have shown, the native drama is "ludic" rather than mimetic, a form of "play" or game of make-believe rather than an imitation of life.[9] While it may instruct, its chief purpose, according to its early advocates, is to provide the mirth and sport which are as essential as rest and proper food to one's mental and physical well being.[10] Affording a temporary escape from the claims of the world of earnest, it is a healthy alternative to idleness and tedium, a source of relaxation, and (as a cure for melancholy) even a preventative of madness.[11]

The apprentice-Shakespeare's familiarity with the notion of comedy as a recreational game of make-believe is easily demonstrated. References to the recreational value of sport, play, and theatrical entertainment are frequent throughout *The Comedy of Errors*, *Love's Labour's Lost*, and *A Midsummer Night's Dream*. In fact, the Introduction of *The Taming of the Shrew* contains a definition of comedy as a form of "mirth and game" whose purpose is purely recreational. Sly is told that his physicians have recommended he see a comedy, "a kind of history" whose purpose is to cure melancholy:

> Your honor's players, hearing your amendment,
> Are come to play a pleasant comedy,
> For so your doctors hold it very meet,

Seeing too much sadness hath congeal'd your blood,
And melancholy is the nurse of frenzy.
Therefore they thought it good you hear a play,
And frame your mind to mirth and merriment,
Which bars a thousand harms and lengthens life.

> (Ind. ii. 129–86)

The other notion of comedy—as a "rare" and wonderful history beginning in sadness and ending in joy, and which I have identified elsewhere as "Ideal Comedy"[12]—has its origins in the miracle plays celebrating the martyrdom of saints and in religious comedies in imitation of Terence. In its formative stage, its exemplary actions are presented as historically true. The imitations of life it presents are "rare," "most perfect," and "wonderful"[13] and its method precisely the opposite of Mirror Comedy. Whereas Mirror Comedy is successful to the extent that it provides audiences with examples of behavior with which they can readily identify, Ideal Comedy is devoted to the exceptional case. It presents examples of extraordinary actions which arouse wonder, admiration, and reflection. Beginning in perturbations occasioned by threats of death and ending in familial and communal concord and joy, it celebrates love as the authentic source of recreation.

Ludic and Ideal Comedy are distinguished, then, not only by purpose, but also by the kind of fiction in which each is cast. The fictions of Ludic Comedy are non-representational—games of make-believe offering their participants recreation in the form of a temporary escape from the world of everyday. Those of "Ideal Comedy" are mimetic, "figuring forth," to borrow Sidney's terms, "perfect patterns" which renew hope and inspire emulation.

To approach *The Comedy of Errors* by way of the precedents identified above is to appreciate Shakespeare's innovativeness as well as his indebtedness to his predecessors. His *conflation* of a farcical tale of mistaken identities adapted from Plautus and a tale of an aging father's *reunion* with wife and sons appropriated from medieval exemplary romance is perfectly consistent with the practice of *mingling* "mirth and game" with matters "substantial."[14] Each is inherently "comic" and, in fact, an example of the kind of comedy with which he had experimented in *The Two Gentlemen of Verona* and *The Taming of the Shrew*. Plautus's plays had been read in the Middle Ages as *iocae* providing recreation,[15] and more recently, as the prologues to *Jack Jugeler* and *Ralph Roister Doister* indicate, exploited as sources of stage "mirth and game" whose chief and occasionally only purpose is to provide recreation.[16] The Egeon narrative, on the other hand, is a "rare" and "wonderful" fiction, comic in its symmetry and emotional progression. Beginning in sorrow and the threat of imminent death and ending in the joyous celebration of a "new nativity," it depicts a full cycle in the lives of Egeon and his family.

The result is two comedies in one, a diverting interval of ludic "recreation" and a "rare and wonderful" fiction which offers, as we shall presently see, a more substantial form of recreation in the form of an exemplary pattern. Each comic action, moreover, as a result of Shakespeare's enframing the ludic within the mimetic, serves the purpose of the other. Once underway, the interval of "mirth and game" completely engages the audience's attention until the errors out of which it develops have been discovered. For this ludic interval of escape from the world of everyday the story of Egeon serves simply as a frame or "transitional" fiction.[17] Once the Egeon story comes full circle in the final reunion scene, the relationship between the two is reversed. Now the merry tale of mistaken identities is not only subordinate; when viewed from the perspective established by the reunion scene, it actually serves the purpose of the exemplary tale of loss and recovery by serving as a parodic opposite for the "perfect pattern" that is "figured forth" in the reunion.[18]

As a compositional method, the enframing scheme Shakespeare works out in the course of conflating two kinds of comedy in *The Comedy of Errors* is grounded in sound epistemological and psychological theory—and shrewdly practical. "Mirth and game," whether of the old festive kind or newly introduced as *iocae* borrowed from Plautus, is immediately engaging and the reason for the play's perennial success on the stage. It requires neither schooling nor reflection, and when well-performed always fulfills its purpose as a diverting recreation. The other comedy is conceptual. It requires disengagement from the immediate— that is, from the play as experienced in performance—and then wonder and reflection. Reflection leads, finally, to a recognition of the "recreational" value of Egeon's reunion with his wife and sons. A father, assured of heirs, no longer despairs. His sons in being "reborn" have regained fully their identities and are ready, in turn—one through an impending marriage, the other through a marriage restored to harmony—to participate in the communal life of Ephesus and Syracuse.

But closure has been won only within an ideal fiction. Closure to the play itself remains for the audience to determine. The rejuvenation Egeon enjoys through a strange and wonderful turn of events, the audience is offered in the form of a "rare" and "wonderful" fiction. In the closing moments of that fiction the silent figure of Egeon bowled over by the unexpected revelations and recovery of wife and sons is a reminder to the audience that begetting children is a way of defeating mortality. For those who embrace the solution it offers, the Egeon story will have been authentically recreative. For those who do not, the merry interval provided by the action it enframes may at least have proved a relaxing pastime.

In presenting the audience with these alternatives Shakespeare also invites its members to consider a question which he raises again to explicitly address in both *A Midsummer Night's Dream* and *Love's Labour's Lost*. It is a question concerning the recreational efficacy of the two forms of comedy the play has offered them. He introduces the question in *The Comedy of Errors* in the moment of closure of the merry game of make-believe by employing the Abbess's speech on "sweet recreation" reflexively to call attention to the very purpose for which it was conceived and then immediately reintroducing the threat of death which remains to be met if closure to the Egeon story is to be won.

Turning to Adriana, the Abbess blames her for her husband's apparent madness. By shrewishly interfering with his sports, she has denied him the recreation that is essential to his mental and physical well-being:

> Thou sayst his sports were hind'red by thy brawls;
> Sweet recreation barr'd, what cause doth ensue
> But moody and dull melancholy,
> Kinsman to grim and comfortless despair,
> And at his heels a huge infectious troop
> Of pale distemperatures and foes to life?
> In food, in sport and life-preserving rest
> To be disturb'd would mad or man or beast;
> The consequence is then, thy jealous fits
> Hath scar'd thy husband from the use of wits.
>
> (V. i. 77–86)

Because we are "in" on the game, we recognize and enjoy the superficiality of the diagnosis. We know, too, that although Adriana may have nagged her husband, his preoccupation with his own world and disregard for hers has given her cause. In any event, diverting sports are no cure for their marital problems. Nor would they cure S. Antipholus' brooding melancholia. Only the recovery of what he searched for so long will finally revive his spirits.

The ludic interval is suddenly over when the First Merchant notices the time—"By this I think the dial points at five" (V. i. 119). We are back in the world of time. The First Merchant, serving as a kind of prologue, announces the setting for the action remaining to be resolved:

> Anon I'm sure the Duke himself in person
> Comes this way to the melancholy vale,
> The place of death and sorry execution,
> Behind the ditches of the abbey here.
>
> (V. i. 119–28)

The figure of Egeon who now enters, manacled and on his way to his execution, serves to point up explicitly the limited efficacy of "mirth and game" as a source of recreation. For some sorrows diversion and gaiety are simply no remedy. On the other hand, what of plays which end happily? Are comedies that celebrate the recreational power of love in the face of death any more substantial? Are they finally anything other than escapist illusions or wishful thinking?

As we have seen, the answer offered in the story of Egeon is implicit in the way in which it finally comes full circle. The action in which Egeon has been involved, thanks to chance and Socinius's compassion, has been truly recreative. Beginning with a threat of death, it has concluded with the assurance of renewal metaphorically affirmed by both the setting and language used by Amelia to describe the "wonderful" event: a "place of death and sorry execution" has been transformed by the reunion into a setting for a "new nativity." Father, mother and wife, and sons and brothers have been re-created and hope and joy born out of melancholy and despair.

But the recreation Egeon enjoys through a wonderful turn of events, the audience is offered only in the form of an exemplary fiction. The silent figure of the aging father, bowled over by the unexpected revelation and recovery of wife and sons, is a reminder to the audience that begetting children is a way of defeating mortality. To embrace the solution offered is to find the Egeon story authentically recreative and, in effect, to join the on-stage community in its celebration of the "new nativity." If not, we remain outsiders for whom the action it enframes may at least have been a merry and relaxing pastime. It is also, finally, to affirm the legitimacy of Ideal Comedy as an authentic source of recreation.

## NOTES

1. All citations from Shakespeare are from the *Riverside* edition.

2. Edited by F. S. Boas and A. W. Reed (Oxford: Oxford University Press, 1926).

3. *A Select Collection of Old English Plays*, originally published by Robert Dodsley, 4th ed., 15 vols, ed. W. C. Hazlitt, vol. 1 (London, 1874–76), p. 10

4. Ed. Alois Brandl, *Shakespeare Jahrbuch* 36 (1900), pp. 14–64.

5. Dodsley, *Old English Plays*, vol. 6.

6. Dodsley, *Old English Plays*, vol. 6.

7. See Douglas L. Peterson, "*The Tempest* and Ideal Comedy," *Shakespearean Comedy*, edited by Maurice Charney (New York: New York Literary Forum, 1980), pp. 99–110.

8. I have discussed this notion of comedy in "Princes at Play in Lyly, Greene, and Shakespeare," *Shakespeare Studies*, 20 (1987), 20–33.

9. *The Play Corpus Christi* (Stanford: Stanford University Press, 1960, pp. 8–32).

10. See, for instance, Nicolas Udall's Prologue to *Ralph Roister Doister*, in *Chief Pre-Shakespearean Drama*, edited by Joseph Quincy Adams (Cambridge, Mass.: Riverside Press, 1924, 1952) and the Prologue to the anonymous *Jack Jugeler*, in *Three Tudor Classical Interludes*, edited by Marie Axton with Introductions and Notes (Cambridge: D. S. Brewster & Littlefield, 1982).

11. For a discussion of the origins and development of the recreational theory of play, see Glending Olson, *Literature as Recreation in the Later Middle Ages* (Ithaca, New York: Cornell University Press, 1982). Chapters 1–3.

12. "*The Tempest* and Ideal Comedy."

13. Typical examples include *Apius and Virginia* (1564) and *Conflict of Conscience*, and *Damon and Pithias*. The former, "a new tragical comedie . . . wherein is lively expressed a rare example of the virtue of Chastitie," celebrates martyrdom as a victory over death; the latter presents in its protagonist's last-minute recovery from suicidal despair "a strange example done of late which might . . . stir minds to godliness." Richard Edwards also stresses the extraordinary action of *Damon and Pithias*, describing it in his prologue as "*a rare example of friendship true*" (my italics).

14. For a discussion of the political ramifications of this mingling of familiar forms of popular entertainment with the new humanistic learning see Robert Weimann, *Shakespeare and the Popular Dramatic Tradition* (Baltimore and London: Johns Hopkins University Press, 1978), pp. 110–112.

15. See Mending Olson, *Literature as Recreation in the Later Middle Ages*, pp. 27, 128–30.

16. See footnote No. 10 above. Thomas Heywood, writing of the comedy performed on the public stages of his day, indicates that recreation continues at end-century to be one of its principal functions:

> If a Comedy, it is pleasantly continued with merry accidents and intermixt with apt and witty iests, to present before the Prince at certaine times of solemnity, or else merrily fitted to the stage. And what is then the subject of this harmlesse mirth? either in the shape of a Clowne, to shew others their slouenly and unhansome behauior, that they may reforme their simplicity in themselues, which others make their sport, lest they happen to become the like subject of general scorne to an auditory; else it intreates of loue deriding foolish inamorates, who spend their ages, their spirits, nay themselues on the seruile and ridiculous employments of their Mistresses: and these are mingled with sportful incidents, to recreate such of themselues are wholly deuoted to Melancholly, which corrupts the bloud; or to refresh such weary spirits as are tired with labour, or study, to moderate the care and heauiness of the minde, that they may returne to their trades and faculties with more zeale and earnestnesse, after some small soft and pleasant retirement.

*An Apology for Actors* (1612), edited by Richard H. Perkinson with introduction and notes (New York: Scholars Facsimiles and Reprints, 1941), F. 80.

17. Dennis Huston provides a good account of the effects achieved by the sudden shift in focus from the earnest world introduced in the opening scene to the ludic world of pastime into which S. Antipholus leads the audience:

> The members of Shakespeare's audience, attending a play, temporarily put aside their own problems, frustrations, and sorrows. They enter the theater, there to be entertained, and so to escape, for the space of an afternoon, the often harsh and arbitrary laws of nature and society which hold sway over their lives. The parallel is not, by any means, exact. Egeon is delivered from immediate execution, while Shakespeare's audience, if it thinks on death at all, view it from a great distance; no one ever went to a comedy for the express purpose of delaying his execution. But an audience which attends a '*Comedy of Errors*' at least partly goes to the theater in order to find temporary reprieve from the problems of everyday. Against such problems the play provides refuge by transporting that audience for a time to a realm of imaginative play . . ." (*Shakespeare's Comedies of Play* [New York: Columbia University Press, 1981], pp. 30–1).

Huston's remarks here and elsewhere on "play" in Shakespeare's comedies are those of a sensitive and intelligent spectator.

18. This use of parody in the interest of definition is an instance of what Robert Weimann, when discussing the parodic enframing plot in Henry Medwall's *Fulgens and Lucrece*, calls "Mimetic inversion" (*Shakespeare and the Popular Tradition in the Theater*, pp. 106–107). For another early example see the sub-plot of Robert Bauer's *Apius and Virginia*. See also, for a brilliant example in the later plays of Shakespeare, the sheep-shearing festival in *The Winter's Tale* in which Autolycus functions as parodic opposite first to Perdita in her role as Flora and then to Camillo as counsellor. For an analysis of Autolycus' role as parodic agent see Douglas L. Peterson, *Time, Tide and Tempest* (San Marino Calif.: Huntington Library Press, 1973), pp. 169–171.

---

## 1998—Harold Bloom. "The Comedy of Errors," from *Shakespeare: The Invention of the Human*

Harold Bloom is Sterling Professor of the Humanities at Yale University and is the author of more than 30 books, including *Jesus and Yahweh: The Names Divine* (2005), *Genius: A Mosaic of One Hundred Exemplary Creative Minds* (2002), *Where Shall Wisdom Be Found?* (2004), *How to Read and Why* (2000), and *The Anxiety of Influence: A Theory of Poetry* (1975).

The Ephesian Antipholus is not a very interesting fellow, compared with his Syracusan twin, upon which Shakespeare chooses to concentrate. Partly, the Antipholus of Syracuse benefits in our regard from what bewilders him: the strangeness of Ephesus. Since St. Paul's Epistle to the Ephesians makes reference to their "curious arts," a Bible-aware audience would expect the town (though clearly Shakespeare's London) to seem a place of sorcery, a kind of fairyland where anything may happen, particularly to visitors. Antipholus of Syracuse, already lost to himself before entering Ephesus, very nearly loses his sense of self-identity as the play proceeds.

Perhaps all farce is implicitly metaphysical, Shakespeare departs from Plautus in making the uneasiness overt. *The Comedy of Errors* moves toward madcap violence, in which, however, no one except the charlatan exorcist, Dr. Pinch, gets hurt. It is a play in which no one, even the audience, can be permitted to get matters right until the very end, when the two sets of twins stand side by side. Shakespeare gives the audience no hint that the Ephesian Abbess (presumably a priestess of Diana) is the lost mother of the Antipholuses until she chooses to declare herself. We can wonder, if we want to, why she has been in Ephesus for twenty-three years without declaring herself to her son who dwells there, but that would be as irrelevant as wondering how and why the two sets of twins happen to be dressed identically on the day the boys from Syracuse arrive. Such peculiarities are the given of *The Comedy of Errors*, where the demarcations between the improbable and the impossible become very ghostly.

Exuberant fun as it is and must be, this fierce little play is also one of the starting points for Shakespeare's reinvention of the human. A role in farce hardly seems an arena for inwardness, but genre never confined Shakespeare, even at his origins, and Antipholus of Syracuse is a sketch for the abysses of self that are to come. Even when he contemplates sightseeing, the visiting twin remarks: "I will go lose myself, / And wander up and down to view the city." You do not lose yourself to find yourself in *The Comedy of Errors*, which is hardly a Christian parable. At the play's close, the two Dromios are delighted with each other, but the mutual response of the two Antipholuses is left enigmatic, as we will see. Nothing could be more unlike the response of the Ephesian burgher, so indignant that his assured self-identity should ever be doubted, than the Syracusan quester's appeal to Luciana, sister-in-law to his brother:

> Sweet mistress, what your name is else I know not,
> Nor by what wonder you do hit of mine;
> Less in your knowledge and your grace you show not
> Than our earth's wonder, more than earth divine.
> Teach me, dear creature, how to think and speak;
> Lay open to my earthy gross conceit,
> Smother'd in errors, feeble, shallow, weak,
> The folded meaning of your words' deceit.
> Against my soul's pure truth why labour you
> To make it wander in an unknown field?
> Are you a god? would you create me new?
> Transform me then, and to your power I'll yield.
> But if that I am I, then well I know
> Your weeping sister is no wife of mine,
> Nor to her bed no homage do I owe;
> Far more, far more to you do I decline;
> O, train me not, sweet mermaid, with thy note,
> To drown me in thy sister's flood of tears;
> Sing, siren, for thyself and I will dote;
> Spread o'er the silver waves thy golden hairs,
> And as a bed I'll take them and there lie,
> And in that glorious supposition think
> He gains by death that hath such means to die;
> Let Love, being light, be drowned if she sink.

    (III, ii, 29–52)

# THE COMEDY OF ERRORS
# IN THE TWENTY-FIRST CENTURY
### ❧

Twenty-first century critics have continued the essential debates from the prior century, namely a further investigation into the distinct personalities between the two sets of twins and, most especially, a further attempt to define the true genric identity of *The Comedy of Errors*. In this second area of inquiry, scholars exhibit an abiding interest in the inherent tensions within the text between the competing literary styles and conventions of farce and romance. Additionally, there is close attention paid to the often contrary nature of magic within the play and the ways it functions to the detriment of the characters. Among other issues, critics such as Marjorie Garber (*Shakespeare After All*, 2005) argues that Egeon's narrative clearly introduces an element of tragedy, while the play as a whole contains a stronger element of romance than it does farce. She adds that the setting of Ephesus, while functioning as a magical world rather than consistently benign, is in many ways a source of anxiety for many characters, especially Antipholus of Syracuse and his Dromio. Similar to Garber's contention that the magic of the play has a definite malignant component, Stephen Orgel discusses the historical context of *The Comedy of Errors*, written in the 1590s when Elizabethan statutes against witchcraft were being vigorously prosecuted. He argues that the basis for humor within the play resides in the characters' misinterpretation of strange events rather than in the subject of fantastical events themselves. On the other hand, Orgel maintains that the abbess has a unique function within this world of forbidden magic and its negative associations with Catholicism, in that she occupies a place of reverence and authority at a time when nuns were treated as comic figures in Reformation England. Kent Cartwright argues that Shakespeare is here attempting to establish a space in which Protestant rationalism co-exists with medieval fantasy to present its own version of truth.

> If the magical in *The Comedy of Errors* privileges the Providential, then treating it as an error is itself an element in the comedy of errors. But my point is not simply to valorize magic—or amplification or the carnivalesque—against their opposites. I think, rather, that Shakespeare is

attempting to mark out a suggestive, mutual terrain somewhere between religion and magic, and the literal and the metaphoric.

Charles Whitworth, whose essay is included in this volume, argues for a critical generic shift within the play whereby the farcical antics and physical appeal of low comedy, such as visual gags, large gestures, and embarrassing mistakes, are gradually replaced by the more refined features of romance, in both their classical and medieval versions. According to Whitworth, the visual and aural effects of farce that appeal to the audience's sense of humor are eventually supplanted by more sophisticated interests such as the psychological status of the characters and the ways in which their individual stories evolve, by themes and features that situate the play squarely within the romance tradition dating back to such classical works as Homer's *Odyssey* and the wanderings of Odysseus into the dangerously enchanting world of Circe. Whitworth also takes exception to those critics who easily categorize *The Comedy of Errors* as simply a farce from beginning to end and, instead, traces the evolutionary process by which this generic transformation takes place. His analysis begins with representational issues revolving around these two opposing genres and makes an important distinction between them in stating that farce is essentially a dramatic art designed for the stage, whereas romance belongs to the literary realm and is therefore reliant on the narrator's descriptive skills in presenting time, place, setting, and the characters' states of mind. Accordingly, Whitworth focuses on Egeon as representative of the tragic suffering hero who must endure many hardships in pursuing his quest to be reunited with his family. With respect to the Syracusan twins, Whitworth also raises an important issue concerning the connection between mental instability and the romantic genre in *The Comedy of Errors*, most especially with respect to the vulnerability of Antipholus and Dromio of Syracuse, wherein the fear of losing one's mind and being isolated in the midst of a world where others have taken leave of their senses is a predicament commonly found in classical and medieval texts, from Odysseus to Lancelot du Lac. Ultimately, Whitworth sees time itself being reversed from the everyday, mundane concerns of farce to the distant land of "once upon a time" on which romance is predicated.

Carol Neely continues Whitworth's discussion regarding mental illness and instability but argues from a wholly different perspective. Neely contends that an inherent tension exists within the play between two competing modes of comedy, namely the farcical and the festive. In her discussion of the critical consensus of the different types of Shakespearean comedies, Neely applies C. L. Barber's distinction between the festive, which celebrates unrestrained merrymaking, and the farcical, as exemplified in such early works as *The Comedy of Errors*, in which the "unfestive" and disturbing elements of restriction, violence, and punishment against transgression wrestle with a world of ungoverned license. In a word, Neely contends that farce "creates the conditions of nightmare" and that its ultimate goal is to seek retribution against its targets, rather than releasing individuals from any accusations of wrongdoing, thereby promoting the restoration of peace and communal harmony. Thus, the dark elements of farce, a comic mode that presents a disturbing connection between mental instability and dire social consequences, are opposed to the more "festive" type of comedy, which celebrates unbridled happiness and social license. Neely provides an insightful analysis of the genric characteristics of farce and the particular ways in which mental illness is treated as a vehicle of social utility and "comic" resolution of the problems and obstacles that encumber happiness and familial reunion in the play. To this end, Neely contends that in *The Comedy of Errors*, mental instability and mental illness are imposed on certain unruly characters by others who are unfit to render judgment and, thus, insanity here can never be credibly substantiated. Unlike such characters as Ophelia in *Hamlet*, Lady Macbeth, and King Lear, who truly lose sanity in their roles, the characters of farce do not elicit our sympathy for the simple reason that their mental status is misdiagnosed by incompetent doctors and spiritual advisers. In Neely's analysis of the two supposed healers in the play, Dr. Pinch and the abbess, she makes several interesting and original insights, especially with respect to the latter. As to Dr. Pinch's ineptitude, he renders a false judgment of bewitchment and a fake exorcism of Antipholus of Ephesus's questionable behavior and, accordingly, makes a mockery of both the Catholic Church and Puritan exorcists who subscribe to this cure of demonic possession. On the other hand, Neely sees the abbess, whom many critics have praised for her guidance and ability to restore stability to the disputants, as yet another incompetent healer, for she diagnoses the wrong man, Antipholus of Syracuse, and compels Adriana to admit that she is a nagging wife. Moreover, the abbess extracts a "confession" from her and uses it to accuse her of causing her husband's insanity. Neely argues that at the end of the play, Amelia's authority is undermined in that she proposes a "gossip's feast," thereby mocking her spiritual authority within the Catholic Church while becoming herself another nagging wife.

Comparing Shakespeare's rendition of insanity to Plautus's, Neely states the following in regard to the two healers in *The Comedy of Errors*:

In the *Comedy of Errors*, this brief episode [of madness in Plautus] is exuberantly doubled and exaggerated. First, instead of the twins sharing the diagnosis of madness made by family and doctor, they are treated by different healers. Their differentiated 'cures' fit their contrasted situations and characterizations. Antopholus E. in Shakespeare the more 'choleric' and misogynist of the twins, is represented as beating his servant, raging at his wife, and genuinely acquiring debt for a chain bought for his Courtesan. He attributes madness to all those who misrecognize him, never for a moment doubting his own rectitude and sanity. So his punishment is to be accused of madness, an extreme of the choler he exhibits; he is treated violently as he treats others. Dr. Pinch diagnoses possession; he has Antipholus E. bound and carried to his own house, where his exorcism causes "deep shames and great indignities" at the site of his misdemeanors—"in a dark and dankish vault at home" (5.1.254, 248). Antipholus S., his part greatly enlarged from that of the Traveller, becomes the more sympathetic of the two brothers. He is represented as habitually 'melancholy' (1.2.20), yearning, and dissatisfied, not settled and self-satisfied like his twin. He seeks his mother and brother; he befriends his servant rather than beating him; he is a romantic lover not an irascible husband. Rather than regularly attributing madness to others he fears for his own stability—both in the early soliloquy when he falls in love (1.2.33–40) and in his amazed responses to mistaking. Believing Epehsus to be a town of 'nimble jugglers that deceive the eye, / Dark-working, sorcerers that change the mind, / Soul-killing witches that deform the body' (1.2.98–100), he fears he may be possessed or bewitched or that he and his servant are 'distract' (4.3.40). Although he himself attempts to exorcise the Courtesan (3.3.46–75), his anxious melancholy is promised treatment with soothing potions by an Abbess in a Priory.

But both therapies take the form of farcical punishments that beget more confusion. Luce, the Police Officer, and Dr. Pinch represent the punitive conscience that must have its way before reconciliations can occur . . . and the Abbess can be added to this list. Both healers are also caricatured and themselves subjected to their own medicine. The farcical retribution against Pinch exacerbates rising tensions. While Pinch may partly represent the punitive superego, he has more material and historical resonances. His representation is a mockery of three early modern male authority figures—a Doctor, a 'Schoolmaster' (following 4.4.37), and a Catholic exorcist; any of these might use 'pinches' to diagnose or treat their hapless clients. (pp. 141–42)

* * * * *

The Syracusan pair, mistaken for their local counterparts and declared mad too, seek succor in a prior where another spurious diagnosis is proffered by a nun, a similarly anachronistic Catholic authority figure. Like Pinch, the Abbess diagnoses without evidence and insistently claims her prerogative to treat the 'distraction' she inaccurately interprets and cannot heal.

Ultimately, it is Neely's contention that these episodes of misdiagnosis make a mockery of Elizabethan society and its cherished institutions. For all this, she maintains that Shakespeare has far outdone Plautus in that he has left us with the difficult question as to who is in a position to diagnose insanity.

Martine van Elk likewise examines the dual genres of farce and romance as two very different modes of representing subjectivity (self-identity and awareness), the former producing nothing but absurdities and the latter offering the reassurance of physical and spiritual identification. The result of this competition with the play is that a Christianized version of romance ultimately prevails by suppressing the absurdities, confusions, and errors of farce. In analyzing the genric differences in presenting the characters' identity and self-awareness, van Elk maintains that a character's identity in farce is random, unstable, and dependent on one's social, political, and economic status, thus lacking a sense of individuality, while subjectivity in the romance genre is predicated on one's physical and spiritual essence and allows for reflection and a stronger sense of self. A crucial aspect of van Elk's argument is a thorough investigation of the complexities of the romance genre, and to this end, she emphasizes the importance of John Gower's Christianized romances such as the Apollonious story in the *Confessio Amantis*. Van Elk argues that in *The Comedy of Errors*, the characters at first lose themselves. They roam aimlessly and confused until their ultimate return to a secure self-identity fixed within a divinely determined world order. Van Elk maintains that Shakespeare is equally interested in exploring issues of selfhood and psychological renewal. She places Egeon's character and situation squarely within the confessional mode of Christian romance. Though he is compelled to wend his way through a secular world fraught with problems, his narrative is replete with pathos and somber reflection and even begins with the word *fall*, a term loaded with spiritual connotations. Furthermore, as van Elk points out, Egeon's capacity for suffering and melancholy places him in the context of the medieval notion of consolation, while the duke's response is in stark contrast as he advises the old man to cease pleading his case for it will not help him. Ultimately, she maintains that the harmonic restoration of community in *The Comedy of Errors* rests firmly on issues of faith and morality that are outside the traditional comic settings. Thus, the farcical problems are resolved through the medieval romance and, furthermore, the romantic mode is the predominant genre in *The Comedy of Errors*, for the play is predicated on issues of faith and morality that place it outside the boundary lines of comedy. Instead, van Elk contends that *The Comedy of Errors* must be read entirely according to the confessional mode of Christian romance.

The different uses of genre are present from the outset. In romance terms, the opening scene establishes the initial separation between the protagonist and his former social identity, to prepare him for the test of faith that must follow. The play places Egeon in the mercantile setting expected in farce or other types of urban comedy. But hints of a secular dramatic setting and comic plot are offset by the language. Egeon opens with a line that ends in the loaded word 'fall' to set the tone: 'Proceed, Solinus, to procure my fall, / And by the doom of death end woes and all' (1.1.1–2). The Christian theme of original sin, the alliteration ('doom of death'), and the finality of the rhyme show how religion informs the language, and thus identity, in the frame. Egeon's first words are poetic, somber, unequivocal, and infused with spiritual meaning. Language, this moment suggests, has a one-on-one relationship with the world in romance—for it to have proper religious significance it must claim to describe the world perfectly, but the opening shows that it does not so much describe a preexisting world as *create* one. The Duke's immediate response seems curiously, even comically, out of touch with these lines: 'Merchant of Syracusa, plead no more" (1.3). The play's first strange moment of generic merger occurs here: the Duke believes he is in a different generic world, one in which deceitful merchants try to talk their way out of an execution. It is not until Egeon's second response is given in a style similar to his first words that the play moves more decisively into romance. Egeon's narrative represents a break with, and can only be uttered in disregard of, the legal situation in which he has been placed by the trade laws of Ephesus.

   Generically, Egeon's speeches construct the realm of Christian romance, a realm in which Egeon's status as a merchant must be discarded before his gradual redemption can begin. Although he is labeled 'merchant' in the opening scence in the First Folio, Egeon's self-presentation is much more conflicted about his social status than his citizen-son's and, as seen in the Duke's initial response to him, out of touch with his legal situation, which identifies him only on the basis of his economic position. Egeon comes to Ephesus as a father, not a merchant; but his goods are never again mentioned in the play. While his impending execution results from an unexplained failure to access his capital, we can infer that even if he had the money, he would forgo the opportunity to buy his way out. His sense of doom precedes the family separation, we learn, since he says that he 'would gladly have embraced' (l. 69) death during the storm, if not for his weeping wife and children. . . . Egeon's sadness indicates that there are other forces at work beyond the purely secular mechanics of trade and law, forces that will test him on a deeper level of faith and patient suffering. (p. 53)

Richard Dutton's essay takes the position that the crux of *The Comedy of Errors* resides in the dissimilarities between the two sets of twins rather than the romantic entanglements that prior critics have focused on. More particularly, Dutton is especially focused on the character of Antipholus of Syracuse, who he contends unwittingly unleashes a chain of slanderous statements to his brother, his brother's wife, and his brother's creditors. Dutton arrives at this interpretation based on his discovery that the character of Antipholus is derived from a famous essay in classical antiquity by Lucian known as the *Calumnia non temere credendum*, translated as "On not believing rashly [or: being too quick to put faith] to slander" and, further, that within Lucian's essay is a description of a painting on the theme of the slander of Appelles, a famous artist of his time who was himself a victim of malicious misrepresentation. In support of his premise, Dutton also notes that several famous Renaissance painters were likewise interested in re-creating Appelles's painting based on Lucian's account. Dutton uses slander as an interpretive tool for reading *The Comedy of Errors*. Moreover, he maintains that slander is readily apparent in Balthasar's warning to Antipholus of Ephesus that slander once initiated can have wide-ranging and long-lasting effects once it takes root. Dutton then applies this thesis to all the principal characters: "For slander lives upon succession / For e'er hous'd where it gets possession." However, Dutton maintains that the issue is never directly about whether one has behaved properly but, rather, a matter of public opinion in a world in which gossip rules and scandal, a closely related issue, is created. The fact that the two Antipholuses share the same name is a slanderous predicament, for they are held to be the same person and, while in fact there is a sharp distinction in their respective characters, the Syracusan brother is victimized by the financial and sexual slanders that his Ephesian twin has brought on himself. Having established the way in which a bad reputation can be unjustly earned, Dutton moves his argument to another non-Plautine context, namely a discussion of the religious implications that he suggests Shakespeare intended, most especially since the action was moved to Ephesus, the seat of sorcery and trickery and the playwright's chosen venue for a multiplicity of slanders. Nonetheless, the ultimate movement of the play, replete with errors "literal, theological and slanderous," is to an enchanting realm where the errors no longer exist.

> *The Comedy of Errors* is a play about identities and selfhoods: the collision of two long-separated pairs of identical twins undermines the comfortable, conventional certainties the four of them have enjoyed about themselves and their places in the world. For the twins are not only physically indistinguishable, they also share the same names—socially, the signifiers by which identity and individuality are primarily conferred. The uneasy farce which this generates may be understood as figuring forth a number of deep-seated psychological insecurities, which in this play are to be resolved in the reconstruction of the lost nuclear family—unlike the action of most of Shakespeare's Elizabethan comedies, where resolution at least notionally lies in the construction of new families by marriage.

As part of this *regressive* process there is an important sense in which the two Antipholuses (like the two Dromoios) *are* the same person, are undifferentiated versions of the same selfhood. Or, as the Duke puts it: "One of these men is *genius* to the other" (5.1.332).

In that identity lie the seeds of slander and scandal: in simply existing as they do, they as it were slander *him*self. By being in the same place, and being the-same-but-not-the-same, Antipholus of Syracuse repeatedly (if unwittingly) slanders Antipholus of Ephesus, giving rise to a scandal in which his brother denies receipt of a precious object and fails to pay his debts. At the same time he compounds a sexual slander which Antipholus of Ephesus has largely brought upon himself, with some assistance from Adriana's jealousy: that he is shunning her and being unfaithful. . . . (pp. 18–19)

* * * * *

The fact that this process [towards reconstruction of the nuclear family] is conducted under the aegis of the Abbess/Mother, so redolent of the Virgin Mary in Ephesus, perhaps points us towards the Catholic faith as the vehicle of redemption. But it is more psychologically compelling in this context that the Catholic was the Old Faith, the faith of an undivided Christendom, where brother did not slander brother just by what he believed, or was thought to believe, or where he lived. The errors of the play are wanderings, literal, theological and slanderous; the comedy lies in a magical regression to a state where they no longer exist. (p. 27)

## 2002—Charles Whitworth. "Farce, City Comedy and Romance" from the introduction to *The Comedy of Errors*

Charles Whitworth is professor of English literature and director of the Centre for English Renaissance Studies at Université Paul Valéry, Montpellier, France. He is the author of *"Love's Labour's Lost*: Aborted Plays Within, Unconsummated Play Without" (1990), "Wooing and Wedding in Arden: Rosalynde and *As You Like It*" (1997), and "Reporting Offstage Events in Early Tudor Drama" (1998).

E. M. W. Tillyard, in his generally sympathetic if not unequivocally enthusiastic discussion of *Errors* [*The Comedy of Errors*], followed the well-established tradition, in both criticism and stage production, of assuming its 'core' or essence to be farce and its comedy as being that exaggerated kind peculiar to farce. The critical tradition dates from the time of Coleridge at least. He insisted on the uniqueness of the play in the Shakespeare canon, defining it as 'a legitimate farce', distinct 'from comedy and from other entertainments' by 'the licence . . . required . . . to produce strange and laughable situations': 'A comedy would scarcely allow even the two Antipholuses . . . but farce dares add the two Dromios'.[1] While on the page, farce may be conveyed by vigorous dialogue and in stage directions and a sympathetic reader may react to it, only on the stage does it come into its own, there for all to see. From the low comedy that crept into the Restoration theatre and was decried by Dryden and other guardians of dramatic decorum, to vaudeville and the popular French farces of the late nineteenth century by masters like Labiche, Feydeau and Courteline, to the slapstick of early American cinema, farce has always had to be seen to be (dis)believed. It relies on visual gags, facial expressions, large gestures, exaggeration, repetition, grotesque business such as pratfalls, ear-wringing and nose-pulling. That generations of literary critics, many of whom rarely or never went to the theatre, could have affirmed so emphatically that *The Comedy of Errors* is a farce is just one of the misfortunes of its critical and theatrical history.

What critics usually have in mind when they label the play as farce is the increasingly hectic and crazy action in the middle acts generated by the presence in Ephesus of two sets of identical twins, and in particular the physical violence of which the two servant Dromios are the main victims. Their increasingly irritated and uncomprehending masters, the Antipholus brothers, resort to beating and threats of such punishment on several occasions—there are specific directions in the Folio only at 2.2.23 and 4.4.45—and there is much talk of beating, especially by the Dromios. *Beat, beaten* and *beating*, always in the primary sense of physical blows (as opposed to the beating of the heart, for example, or of the sea upon the rocks), occur a total of fourteen times in *Errors*, more than in any other play in the canon. There is further vigorous action in 3.1 when Antipholus and Dromio of Ephesus and their dinner guests try to enter their own house, where their Syracusan twins are already ensconced, and in 4.4 when the exorcist Pinch and his assistants catch and bind the supposedly possessed Ephesian master and servant. But to categorize the *whole* play as 'farce', even 'the only specimen of poetical farce in our language, that is intentionally such', as Coleridge did, solely because there are twins and people mistake them or because masters sometimes beat servants, would seem to be wilfully to ignore its other facets. Perhaps critics' uneasiness about its authenticity, dating from Pope, could be resolved by isolating it in a separate genre from all of Shakespeare's other plays. After all, there are apparently identical twins, of opposite sexes, in *Twelfth Night*, one of whom is married to a woman who thinks she has married the other, who is in fact a girl—yet few critics have called that wonderful comedy a farce. Beatings are administered and characters are otherwise physically assaulted in a comical context in many other plays: *The Taming of the Shrew*, *The Two Gentlemen of Verona*, *Love's Labour's Lost*, even *The Tempest*, but those plays have not generally been relegated to the literary outer darkness connoted by the term 'farce'. As for improbable or 'unbelievable' endings, if that is what some may have in mind as justifying the label, one need look no further than some of Shakespeare's other comedies—*Twelfth Night*, *As You Like It*, *Much Ado About Nothing*, *Measure for Measure*—or any of the late plays, with their multiple, complex, truly incredible revelations and resolutions—*The Winter's Tale*, *Pericles*, and above all, *Cymbeline*.

Farce is essentially a dramatic genre, viewerly, spectator-friendly; romance is essentially literary, readerly, a narrative genre, making large demands upon the imagination whereas farce leaves little or nothing to it. In performance, drama occurs in the present, is immediate, visual as well as aural, shows as much as or more than it tells. Narrative is usually in the past tense, most often in the third person, and the narrator must supply descriptions of places, actions, persons and their states of mind; such work is done by actors, directors, designers, composers and set-builders in the theatre. Romance in particular relies on the scene-setting, mood-making, spell-binding voice of the narrator. 'Once upon a time, long ago' is the romance narrator's typical opening gambit, but not the dramatist's, whose action begins in the present, *in medias res*. Even if a narrator does not start his story at the beginning, as many authors of prose romance have done, from the Greeks Chariton and Xenophon of Ephesus to the Elizabethans Sidney, in his original *Arcadia*, and Lodge, in his *Rosalynde*, but rather at a decisive moment in the plot, as both Heliodorus in his *Ethiopian Story* and Sidney in his partially-revised *Arcadia* did, he must eventually go back and fill in, in his own voice or in that of one or more characters, the prior history necessary to the hearer's or reader's understanding of all that will occur. And of course he is free to move from one place and one character or group of characters to another and back again—the *entrelacement* of French medieval romance—confident that the hearer/reader will follow. Both the time-scale and the geographical space of romance can be vast.

But the task is much more difficult for the dramatic author who, as Shakespeare so persisted in doing, attempts to put romance matter on the stage. There is not time for all that scene-setting, back-tracking, gap-filling, digressing and explaining, and there is normally, in the dramatic mode, no narrator on hand to do it. Consider some of Shakespeare's ploys to resolve the problem of the intractability of romance story: he uses prologues, epilogues, choruses, frames, or simply great lumps of narrative within the play. The forward action stops, and someone tells the story or the necessary part of it that is supposed to have taken place previously and/or elsewhere, up to the present moment, when the present-tense of drama resumes: Orlando at the beginning of *As You Like It* and Oliver in Act 4, Scene 3 of the same play, Othello with his striking story about story-telling in Act 1, Scene 3, Prospero in the second scene of *The Tempest*, the succession of Gentlemen in Act 5, Scene 2 of *The Winter's Tale*. Samuel Johnson complained that in his narrative passages Shakespeare

> affects . . . a wearisome train of circumlocution, and tells the incident imperfectly in many words, which might have been more plainly delivered in few. Narration in dramatic poetry is naturally tedious, as it is unanimated and inactive, and obstructs the progress of the action; it should therefore always be rapid and enlivened by frequent interruption. Shakespeare found it an encumbrance . . . [2]

If that is so, Shakespeare repeatedly brought it upon himself by choosing to dramatize romance material. Only once did he (and his collaborator) simply put a narrator on stage and leave him there throughout, to sort out for the spectator/ auditor the tangled threads of the too-complicated plot, that of the Apollonius of Tyre story: Gower in *Pericles*. It is a striking recognition of the peculiar nature of the material that in the most quintessential romance in his entire dramatic canon, Shakespeare and his colleague in effect handed the famous story back to a story-teller, and a real, historical one besides. Gower refers repeatedly to his tale or story, calling it a play only in the very last line: 'Here our play has ended'. (Then George Wilkins, who was probably Shakespeare's collaborator, wrote his prose version, 'being the true history of the play of *Pericles*, as it was lately presented by the worthy and ancient poet, John Gower', thrusting the romance firmly back into its more natural, narrative mode.[3]) The Apollonius story was simply too much to handle in conventional theatrical terms. As we have already seen, just that story, or one very like it, is told by Egeon in the first scene of *The Comedy of Errors*. Furthermore, the denouement of that story, its concluding chapter as it were, constitutes the final three hundred lines or so of the play.[4]

The farcical action is framed, overarched and subsumed by the romance plot, as the latter absorbs the characters from the former: in the family romance finale, both sets of twins as well as a husband and wife are reunited, two sons are restored to their parents, the misunderstandings between another husband and wife are resolved, as is a potential rivalry between sisters, a new pair of lovers is formed, legitimately now (and Dromio of Syracuse gratefully escapes a snare set for him by a man-hungry kitchen wench). Egeon himself, the narrator of his and his family's tragic mishaps in the first scene, becomes a character in the dramatic conclusion to his own story, absorbed in the stories told by others, suffering errors and confusion and anguish as they have done, then being saved from death, then rejoicing with them in the rescues and reunions. The language of the final scene both recalls Egeon's account of the twins' birth in his opening narrative, and anticipates that of the finales of other, later family romances: both Pericles and

Cymbeline, for example, like the Abbess in *The Comedy of Errors*, use images of rebirth when they are reunited with children whom they had believed dead.[5] And the last *coup de théâtre* of all looks forward to the 'resurrection' of Hermione in the final scene of *The Winter's Tale*: the revelation of Emilia as Egeon's wife. We had known that both sets of twins were in Ephesus since the first of the 'errors' in Act 1, Scene 2. Their eventual reunion was just a matter of time. But Shakespeare keeps from us the fact that the Abbess, who does not appear until the final scene anyway, is Emilia, Egeon's wife, mother of the Antipholus twins, alive and safe; the last we heard of her was in Egeon's tragic tale of their separation at sea years before. Even in *Pericles*, we witness the rescue of Thaisa from the sea well before the end when she is reunited with her husband. But the romance ethos and atmosphere seep into the rest of the play too, infusing even the 'farcical core' and the city comedy with mystery, weirdness and awe. Indeed, this early comedy is much more nearly kin to the true romances and the romance-based comedies of Shakespeare's later career than has usually been acknowledged.

Egeon's seemingly interminable narrative, 'the wearisome train of circumlocution', ends, and he is led away to await his fate: the past has caught up with him. The dramatic present of theatre succeeds the narrative past of romance, and the second scene opens in the midst of a conversation, in mid-sentence in fact ('Therefore . . . '), begun before the three characters, Antipholus and Dromio of Syracuse and the First Merchant, burst upon the scene and into the story. 'Once upon a time' gives way to *in medias res*. The very verbs and temporal indicators change, from the past, mostly distant, of Egeon's story, to the immediate present, indicative and imperative: 'Therefore give out' (1.2.1), 'This very day' (3), 'Is apprehended' (4), 'not being able' (5), 'Dies' (7), 'There is' (8). The shift is radical—plot, mode, time-scale, everything. Nevertheless, we soon begin to understand that the two apparently unrelated plots *are* related, and also that the threat of death to the weary old man with which the first scene ended will not be carried out, as the elements necessary to forestall it and bring about the happy denouement begin immediately to assemble: tragicomedy (or romance), not tragedy, will be the genre. The very subject of the conversation into which we intrude in the second scene is what we have just witnessed in the first, the dire sentence pronounced against Egeon. The frequent reminders of the time of day—in eight of the play's eleven scenes—keep Egeon and his impending doom on the edge of the spectator's consciousness while he is absent from the stage, from the end of 1.1 to well into Act 5, just under a third of the way through the final scene. Shakespeare's pointed observation of the unity of time—all of the action occurs between late morning and late afternoon of the same day—signals the end of the romance, its final chapter.

In the only other Shakespeare play whose time-scale is explicitly limited to one day, *The Tempest*, Prospero interrupts in the second scene the dramatic action begun by the storm in the first to tell Miranda the story of their lives and misadventures up to that moment. His narrative serves exactly the same purpose as Egeon's in the first scene of *Errors*. It is very nearly the same length (about 150 lines; *Tempest* 1.2.37–187) as Egeon's 'sad stories of [his] own mishaps', and like his, it is punctuated by questions and remarks from his auditor. In the later play too, the action that unfolds constitutes the final chapter of the story related by the father to his daughter, and that action begins with the arrival on the scene of the first of the other characters from the story who must together act out its conclusion. A similar strategy is evident in the early comedy. This is just one of the ways in which the Egeon romance plot 'overarches' the inner plot drawn from Plautus. Coincidences and links begin at once to appear: Antipholus and Dromio are from Syracuse, which provides the opportunity for the Merchant to tell them about their fellow countryman who has just been condemned to death (and to suggest that they 'give out' they are from somewhere else). Within a few minutes, the amount of money returned to Antipholus by the Merchant in the opening lines—'There is your money that I had to keep' (1.2.8)—and entrusted by the master to his servant, is mentioned: a thousand marks (1.2.81). That sum, we just heard, is exactly what is needed by Egeon to pay his ransom (1.1.21).

Money and trade will be prominent motifs throughout the play: Ephesus, for all its reputation as a strange and dangerous place, is also a working commercial centre, where the making of profit and the doing of deals is everyday and everybody's business. The enmity between Ephesus and Syracuse has arisen from a trade war: merchants are in the thick of it. The Duke defends the business interests of his subjects with terrible rigour. No sooner does the old merchant Egeon leave the stage to seek the pecuniary means to save his life than another merchant ostentatiously hands over just that sum to Egeon's son. The First Merchant excuses himself from accompanying Antipholus on a visit of the town because he has an appointment with 'certain merchants' of whom he hopes 'to make much benefit' (1.2.24–5). Antipholus himself proposes to 'Peruse the traders' (13) while on his sightseeing tour, presumably because they are one of the things the city is famous for. Several merchants, a goldsmith and a businesswoman (the Courtesan) figure among the dramatis personae. Buying and selling seem to be going on all the time. Creditors repeatedly demand payment of bills, people get arrested in the street for debt, send for money to pay fines, pay officers to arrest others. Money, purses and articles of barter (a chain, a ring) are prominent properties in any production of the play. Dromio of Syracuse's first exit is on an errand to put his master's money away safely at their inn; his absence is the occasion of the first 'error' when his twin comes to call his supposed master home to dinner. The word *money* occurs twenty-six times in Shakespeare's shortest play, more than in any other work in the canon. *Marks* (the amount of money) and *mart* also occur more times than in any other play. *Gold* and *golden* are found more often only in *Timon of Athens*, *ducats* and merchant(s) more times only in *The Merchant of Venice*. The rare *guilders* occurs only in *Errors*, where it appears twice. This extraordinary density of vocabulary relating to financial and commercial affairs, with the busy to-and-fro of the marketplace, makes *The Comedy of Errors* a true city comedy. The city itself, Ephesus, has a personality, is not just a setting, but a presence in the play's world, like Venice in *The Merchant of Venice*, Vienna in *Measure for Measure*, or Rome in *Julius Caesar*.[6] But the comparison should be made also with such romance never-never lands as the wood outside Athens, the Forest of Arden, Illyria, or Prospero's island. Whatever moved Shakespeare to replace Plautus' Epidamnus with the Ephesus of romance and the New Testament, it gave him two cities in one, a twin: the bustling, mundane metropolis of urban comedy, and the weird and wonderful setting of romance.

The imagery of romance also carries over from the first scene to the second and thence to the rest of the play, binding the separate plots and the broken family together. Egeon's tale is of the sea and shipwreck, of a family torn apart, carried away from one another, helpless before the stupendous powers of nature. The motif, expressed in imagery of the sea and the loss of oneself in that vast element, is the theme of Antipholus' first soliloquy:

> I to the world am like a drop of water
> That in the ocean seeks another drop,
> Who, failing there to find his fellow forth,
> Unseen, inquisitive, confounds himself.
> So I, to find a mother and a brother,
> In quest of them unhappy, lose myself.
>
> (1.2.35–40)

The objects of his hopeless search and subjects of his despairing meditation, his mother and his brother, are those very ones who were lost to Egeon and his remaining son, this same Antipholus. In fact, Egeon in his long tale in the first scene, and Antipholus in his short reflection in the second, speak of the same lost members of their family, and both speak the language of the sea, the former referring literally, in his factual narrative, to a particular large body of water, the latter, in his dramatic soliloquy, likening himself, in simile, to a single drop in an even vaster gulf, the ocean. *Errors* has more occurrences of the word *sea(s)*— plus one compound, *seafaring* (also *ocean* and *gulf* once each)—than any of the comedies and romances except the obvious sea-story ones, *The Tempest*, *The Winter's Tale*, *Pericles*, and *The Merchant of Venice*, which has the same number; *Errors* has one more than *Twelfth Night*. The *bay* is mentioned three times in dialogue and once in a Folio stage direction. Only in *Pericles* in the entire canon do *ship(s)* and its compounds occur more often. *The Comedy of Errors* is not just farce, not just adapted Roman domestic or city comedy, it is also romance, sea-romance, family romance, and not only in the Egeon frame plot.

Adriana, the scolding but devoted wife of Antipholus of Ephesus, echoes the other Antipholus when she addresses him, mistaking him for her wayward husband:

> For know, my love, as easy mayst thou fall
> A drop of water in the breaking gulf,
> And take unmingled thence that drop again
> Without addition or diminishing,
> As take from me thyself, and not me too.
>
> (2.2.128–32)

The conjugal conflict of domestic comedy is expressed by the distressed wife in the same terms as her unknown brother-in-law's anguish in his isolation and despair. Storm, shipwreck and loss at sea, the very stuff of romance, become metaphors for spiritual and emotional incompleteness, hopelessness, self-doubt, loss of one's identity. The sea/water motif swells and surges into all corners of the play, in floods, tears, streams, waves. In an unexpected passage of formal verse in cross-rhymed quatrains and couplets, which set it off from the blank verse and prose on either side of it, Antipholus of Syracuse, infatuated by Adriana's sister Luciana, imagines that she is a mermaid, enticing him to perdition, to lose himself in a watery bed:

> O, train me not, sweet mermaid, with thy note
>   To drown me in thy sister's flood of tears.
> Sing, siren, for thyself, and I will dote.
>   Spread o'er the silver waves thy golden hairs,
> And as a bed I'll take them, and there lie,
>   And in that glorious supposition think
> He gains by death that hath such means to die.
>   Let love, being light, be drownèd if she sink.
>
> (3.2.45–52)

Later in the scene, in a grotesque prose counterpart to Antipholus' lyrical wooing, Dromio tells him of his terror at the advances of the immense kitchen wench, the spherical 'Nell'. Her sweat and grime are too much even for Noah's flood to wash away (106–9). In his geographical anatomization of her, the English Channel and its chalky cliffs, armadas of Spanish treasure ships, and such faraway lands across the seas as America and the Indies, are evoked (116–44). The scene ends with Antipholus' resolution to take the first ship available and flee this increasingly disturbing place. Salt water washes over and through the whole fabric of the play.

Sinking and drowning, dissolution, transformation, metamorphosis, madness—these and related processes and states constitute a central motif, running through the play from beginning to end. They occur and recur, weaving a dense web of associations and allusions, criss-crossing and bridging the various plot elements, making one whole. Words such as *changed* and *transformed* echo throughout. The mood is sometimes humorous, sometimes fearful, sometimes anguished. Adriana wonders if age is diminishing her beauty, causing her husband to seek his pleasure with other women (2.1.88–102). When old Egeon's son does not know him, he supposes that grief and 'time's extremity' must have changed him beyond recognition (5.1.297–9). Both use the rare word *defeatures*, its only two occurrences in Shakespeare. Dromio of Syracuse is convinced he is an ass in the scene with Antipholus just mentioned (3.2.77), and that the 'drudge', 'diviner', or 'witch' who claims him for her betrothed would, had he not been resolute and fled, have turned him into another kind of beast:

> And I think if my breast had not been made of faith, and my heart of steel,
> She had transformed me to a curtal dog, and made me turn i'th' wheel.
>
>      (150–1)

'I am transformèd, master, am not I?' wails the same bewildered Dromio earlier (2.2.198), convinced he is an ape (201). Luciana tells him that he is merely an ass (202), having already called him 'snail' and 'slug' a few lines before (197), as he muttered nonsense about goblins, elves, sprites, and being pinched black and blue (193–5). He even *feels* like an ass: ''Tis true: she rides me, and I long for grass. / 'Tis so, I am an ass' (203–4). In the very next scene, the other Dromio is told by his master 'I think thou art an ass', and replies in much the same way as his brother: 'Marry, so it doth appear / By the wrongs I suffer and the blows I bear' (3.1.15–16); he confirms his metamorphosis a few scenes later: 'I am an ass indeed. You may prove it by my long ears' (4.4.30–1). The workaday city of Ephesus itself is curiously animate: its buildings and houses bear the names of exotic fauna—Centaur, Phoenix, Tiger and Porcupine. More than thirty names of animals, real and legendary, generic and specific, occur in the play.

The Duke makes explicit the idea of metamorphosis (and in so doing looses its hold upon fevered imaginations) in the final scene when he exclaims 'I think you all have drunk of Circe's cup' (5.1.270). No one has, of course. But the allusion to the goddess-enchantress of ancient legend recalls her transformation of Odysseus' men into swine in Book 10 of the *Odyssey*, most famous of all classical sea-romances. It also recalls the 'siren' and 'mermaid' of Antipholus' rhapsody in 3.2 when he was under the spell of Luciana's 'enchanting presence and discourse', and his subsequent determination to 'stop [his] ears against the mermaid's song' (169): it was Circe who gave Odysseus advice on how to avoid the deadly Sirens' song by stopping his men's ears with wax so they could not hear it as they sailed past (*Odyssey*, Book 12). Apart from one in Act 5 of the First Part of *Henry VI* (a passage which may not have been written by Shakespeare), this is the only allusion to Circe, by name at any rate, in the canon.

Madness, the fear of it in oneself and the conviction of it in others, is a closely related theme, as are magic and conjuring. Even before anything bizarre or distressing happens to him, Antipholus of Syracuse voices in his first soliloquy his trepidation at finding himself in Ephesus, with its renowned 'libertines of sin', eye-deceiving, body-deforming, mind-changing, soul-killing (1.2.98–102). The lexical group of words formed from and including *mad*—*madness, madly, madman*, etc.—are more frequent in Shakespeare's shortest play than in any others except his longest, *Hamlet*, and *Twelfth Night*, a play which has more than that and a pair of twins in common with the earlier comedy. The theme was already there, of course, in *Menaechmi*: the local brother's relations and acquaintances think he is mad as he seems not to know any of them, and a doctor is sent for to cure him, the ancestor of Shakespeare's schoolmaster-exorcist Dr Pinch. The treatment prescribed for the supposedly mad Ephesian master and servant is exactly that imposed upon the allegedly mad Malvolio in *Twelfth Night*: 'They must be bound and laid in some dark room' (4.4.95). The furious frustration of Antipholus of Ephesus is exactly that of Malvolio: to those who are convinced that one is mad, nothing one can say—especially 'I am not mad' (4.4.59)—will change their minds. The frantic comic tension that has built up in *The Comedy of Errors* prior to Act 4, Scene 4, creates a quite different atmosphere from that in *Twelfth Night* when Malvolio's tormentors insist that he is mad, but the utter conviction and deadly earnestness of everybody (including, particularly, the grieving wife Adriana) give the underlying theme of supposed madness a potential gravity and disquieting edge missing from the later play. In *Twelfth Night*, Malvolio's alleged madness is a prank, which deteriorates into a cruel joke. He is the unfortunate butt. Everyone knows that Malvolio is not really mad (not in the way the conspirators pretend he is anyway), the threat ends with the joke, though the distasteful impression of mental cruelty may remain, as is seen in much modern criticism and many modern productions, in which Malvolio is made an almost tragic figure. Feste's Sir Topas is a much more sinister exorcist than the pompous mountebank Pinch. Everyone concerned *does* believe that Antipholus and Dromio of Ephesus are mad, no one is pretending or playing a game. Only the denouement resolves that problem and saves the two from further attempts at 'curing' them. Of course, the farcical frenzy has reached such a peak, and Pinch is so inept, that any real threat remains well below the surface in performance. It is there nevertheless, part of the pervasive romance atmosphere.

Still another aspect of the madness theme, different from both the supposed madness of Antipholus and Dromio of Ephesus and the alleged madness of

Malvolio, is the fear that one is mad, or going that way, oneself. This is the predicament of the Syracusan pair from early on in the action. It reinforces strongly their isolation in a strange country, particularly that of Antipholus, who is given several soliloquies in which he expresses his fears. Such fears, such isolation, generating self-doubt, failure of the will, the temptation to surrender, and sometimes madness itself, are common to romance heroes from Odysseus of Ithaca to Apollonius of Tyre to Lancelot du Lac to Frodo Baggins of the Shire, struggling on in his lonely mission in the hostile Land of Mordor, and Luke Skywalker facing the evil forces of the Empire. For some of those heroes, as for Antipholus of Syracuse, the absence of family, the uncertainty even that he has a family any more, is a main factor in their despair and sense of isolation. Antipholus is peculiarly vulnerable because he is lonely, and is susceptible to the least suggestion that he may be losing his senses and his self. Ephesus is definitely not the place to be when one is in that frame of mind. Egeon is not the only one who finds danger in that strange, hostile city. For Antipholus too is a romance hero, wandering, searching, isolated, fearful, half-believing already the things he has heard about Ephesus and resolved to be gone as soon as possible, yet held there as if by magnetism. Before the end of Act 2, Scene 2, though he suspects some 'error' that 'drives our eyes and ears amiss' (2.2.187), he is ready, until he knows 'this sure uncertainty', to 'entertain the offered fallacy' (188–9), that is Adriana's insistent invitation to be her husband and come in to dinner, though he may wonder: 'What, was I married to her in my dream?' (185). In just such terms, another twin, Sebastian in *Twelfth Night*, a stranger in Illyria, when enjoined by Olivia to go with her to her house, marvels 'Or I am mad, or else this is a dream', and resolves still to sleep (4.1.60–2). Later, while he hopes that 'this may be some error but no madness' (4.3.10), he is driven to conclude the contrary: 'I am mad, / Or else the lady's mad' (15–16). In any case, 'There's something in't / That is deceivable' (20–1).[7] The close parallels between the predicaments and reactions of Antipholus of Syracuse and Sebastian, even to the very language and images in which they express themselves, illustrate well the kinship between the 'early' and the 'middle' comedy written some seven years later. Surely the twinship of Sebastian and Viola in the later play, whichever source he may have drawn it from and despite the differences in plot (and gender), triggered recollections and produced echoes in Shakespeare's mind of passages composed for the earlier one. We do not hesitate to affix the label 'romance' to *Twelfth Night*. The fear-of-madness motif is common to both plays.

The vulnerability of Antipholus is strikingly emphasized by the scenes in which he is seen in the company and under the spell—as he believes—of a woman. These imagined enchantresses succeed each other in a sequence of neatly distributed scenes, one per act: Adriana in 2.2, Luciana in 3.2 (in which we also hear of Dromio's encounter with the terrible 'Nell', another sorceress), the Courtesan in 4.3, the Abbess (his mother) in 5.1; another element in the play's tight and tidy structure. And as prelude to the sequence, there is the soliloquy in 1.2 in which Antipholus voices his fear of sorcerers, witches and the like. His case is similar to that of a hero of Arthurian romance, Perceval, one of the Grail knights. Brought up by his mother in ignorance of chivalry (his father, the famous King Pellinor, had been killed, and the widow tries to protect her sons from a similar fate), his encounters with women—his mother, his saintly sister, the fiend in female guise several times—underline his naïvety and his susceptibility to error. During his Grail quest, he narrowly avoids succumbing to temptation on several occasions when beautiful women, always of course fiends in human form, attempt to seduce him. When Antipholus of Syracuse, convinced that he and Dromio are bewitched, calls for divine aid—'Some blessèd power deliver us from hence' (4.3.44)—the Courtesan appears, not a heavenly rescuer, but the fiend herself. In Adrian Noble's 1983 RSC production, she rose spectacularly from beneath the stage floor, scantily and seductively clad in red, black, and white. The terrified Antipholus recognizes her immediately: 'Satan, avoid! I charge thee, tempt me not!' (48); then, to Dromio, emphatically: 'It is the devil' (50). Epithets such as 'Satan', 'devil', 'fiend', 'sorceress', 'witch', ten or more of them in a thirty-line passage, are hurled at the supposed 'devil's dam' (48–79). In the very next scene, 4.4, Satan is hailed again by the would-be healer Pinch, who exhorts him to leave his abode in the allegedly mad Antipholus of Ephesus. The madness theme is now given expression in satanic terms. One brother sees the devil in the woman standing before him, the other is believed by all who know him to have the devil in him. Divine aid will come, and in female form, bringing safety and relief from the fear of madness, when the Abbess appears and gives her unknown Syracusan son and his servant sanctuary. In contrast to his brother, Antipholus of Ephesus is always seen in the company of men only— his servant (or the other, wrong, one), friends, business associates, creditors, the officer who arrests him—until the conjuring scene (4.4), when at last he *is* surrounded by women—his wife, his sister-in-law, the Courtesan—who insist that he is mad. The same woman, the Abbess, mother to this Antipholus also, will resolve that error too. The two brothers are further distinguished by the fact that the Syracusan has no fewer than six soliloquies and asides, totalling fifty lines, while the Ephesian has none. The one, isolated, fearful, impressionable, is the vulnerable romance protagonist, the other, irascible, defiant, impetuous, the jealous husband of domestic comedy.

A complex of related motifs, made up of opposite or complementary states or processes, underlies and reinforces the more prominent and explicit ones, such as metamorphosis, loss of identity and madness. Losing and finding, closing and opening, binding and freeing, spellbinding and spellbreaking, condemning and pardoning, separating and uniting, beating and embracing, dying and being (re)born, and other such pairs are the play's thematic sinews. And binding all of *them* together, ensuring that the positive, hopeful one of each pair—finding, freeing, pardoning, uniting, embracing—prevails in the end, is Time. 'The triumph of Time', the subtitle of Robert Greene's short romance *Pandosto*, published in 1588 and used by Shakespeare as his main source for *The Winter's Tale*, could well stand as a subtitle for all romances, including *The Comedy of Errors*. Time, of which we are repeatedly made aware as it ticks away, bringing the happy end of the story ever closer, and its nevertheless ineluctable ravages, the work of its 'deformèd hand', are the subject of two comic exchanges, between Antipholus and Dromio of Syracuse (2.2), and between the same Dromio and Adriana at the end of 4.2. Dromio is Time's spokesman, and at the very end of the play, he defers to his brother, his 'elder', in acknowledgement of its inexorable rule over all persons and things, despite such apparent anomalies as twinship. It was noted earlier that the time of day is mentioned frequently, some ten times, in eight of the play's eleven scenes, and that does not include the two comic duologues just referred to and a few other general references to the hour, clocks, sunset, etc. In only two other plays in the canon, *As You Like It* and *Henry IV*, *Part One*, both considerably longer than *Errors*, does the word *clock* occur more often, and in only a small number of plays, a half-dozen or so, does *hour(s)* occur more often.

As the time of day, five o'clock, set for Egeon's execution, is announced—'By this, I think, the dial point's at five' (5.1.118)—the Duke and the old man return to the stage for the first time since the end of the first scene. The Abbess has just withdrawn into the abbey into which the Syracusan pair had fled (5.1.37). The Ephesian pair had previously been forcibly removed into the Phoenix to be bound and laid in a dark room (4.4.131). Both pairs of twins are hidden away, the farce is suspended, and the main romance plot resumes. A new order intervenes in the person of the Abbess, one of genuine divine authority, not Pinch's sham, and the solemn temporal authority of the Duke reasserts itself after the anarchic disorder of the previous scenes. The farce is suspended, but the comedy continues and bridges the two plots: Adriana throws herself prostrate at the Duke's feet, impeding his progress towards the place of execution, literally halting the tragic progress in its tracks. At this moment the two plots meet and merge, for Adriana pleads with the Duke to intercede on her behalf with the Abbess to get her husband, whom she believes to be in the abbey, restored to her. Just as the First Merchant in 1.2 links the Egeon frame and the inner play by informing the newly arrived Antipholus and Dromio of Syracuse of another Syracusan's fate, so now another member of the city's thriving commercial community (Angelo the goldsmith in the present edition) announces the arrival of the Duke and Egeon at the appointed time, signalling the opening out of the action to embrace both plots. His interlocutor is sure that they are to witness the final act of a tragedy: 'See where they come. We will behold his death' (5.1.128). But this is romance, not tragedy. To be sure, the unravelling will take some three hundred more lines, and there will be further supposes, surprises, reversals and irruptions, even some pathos, as when Egeon pleads with the wrong son and servant, the ones who have never known him (286–330). Again, the parallel with *Twelfth Night* is evident: in the later play, Antonio, under arrest and in mortal danger, pleads desperately with the supposed Sebastian whom he had befriended earlier. But it is the uncomprehending Viola in her disguise as Cesario whom he addresses (*Twelfth Night* 3.4.325–64). The finale of *Errors* is one of Shakespeare's most eventful and complex, a true romance denouement, anticipating those of later plays such as *As You Like It, Twelfth Night, All's Well that Ends Well, Cymbeline* and *The Winter's Tale.*[8] At 430 lines, it is considerably longer than the final scenes of all but three of the other comedies and romances in the canon: *Love's Labour's Lost, Measure for Measure* and *Cymbeline.*

Time, which Dromio claimed had gone back an hour (4.2.53), has in fact gone back years, to when the family of Egeon and Emilia was whole, before the tragic events narrated by the husband and father a couple of hours earlier took place, thirty-three or twenty-five years ago, it matters little. The boys, all four of them, were infants then, new-born. It is, fittingly, the Abbess, the holy mother, who gives explicit utterance to the metaphor of nativity, describing this moment as one of rebirth:

> Thirty-three years have I but gone in travail
> Of you, my sons, and till this present hour
> My heavy burden ne'er deliverèd.
> The Duke, my husband, and my children both,
> And you the calendars of their nativity,
> Go to a gossips' feast, and joy with me.
> After so long grief, such felicity!
>
>     (5.1.402–8)

The imminent death with which the play began is transfigured into birth; then we met with things dying, now with things newborn. The stern, death-dealing Duke of Act 1, Scene 1, becomes the generous, life-giving magistrate, refusing the ransom offered by Antipholus of Ephesus for his new-found father: 'It shall not need. Thy father hath his life' (392)—so much for Ephesian law which he had been so scrupulous to enforce in the opening scene. Patron already to one Antipholus, the Duke becomes godfather to both at their re-christening. The ever-moving clock in Theodor Komisarjevsky's famous 1938 Stratford-upon-Avon production . . . should have been whirling furiously backward at this point, turning back the years, for in the biggest and best of the comedy's errors, Time has indeed gone back, all the way from death to birth, from the intense dramatic denouement to the expansive romance narrative 'Once upon a time', from the end of the play to the beginning of the story. That, essentially, is what happens in romance.

## NOTES

1. From *Samuel Taylor Coleridge: Shakespeare Criticism*, ed. Thomas Middleton Raysor, 2 vols. (1960), i. 213; quoted by Miola, p. 18.

2. Preface to Johnson's edition of Shakespeare (1765); reprinted in Brian Vickers, ed., *Shakespeare: The Critical Heritage, 5: 1765–1774* (1979), 67.

3. Shakespeare's exploitation of the differences and tensions between the telling/hearing function peculiar to narrative, and the showing/seeing one peculiar to drama, particularly in the late romances but with reference also to *The Comedy of Errors* among other plays, is the subject of a published lecture by the present editor, *Seeing and Believing in Shakespeare* (Rome, Ga., 1993). Stanley Wells's 'Shakespeare and Romance' (in *Later Shakespeare*, ed. John Russell Brown and Bernard Harris, Stratford-upon-Avon Studies, 8 (1966), 49–79) contains a suggestive reading of *The Tempest* as romance, with Prospero as a romance narrator (pp. 70–8).

4. The similarities and differences in Shakespeare's handling of very similar if not identical romance narrative material in *Errors* and *Pericles*, and the narrators' respective roles in the two plays, are discussed in some detail in Charles Whitworth, '"Standing i' th' gaps": Telling and Showing from Egeon to Gower', in *Narrative and Drama*, vol. 2 of *Collection Theta: Tudor Theatre*, ed. André Lascombes (Bern, New York and Paris, 1995), pp. 125–41.

5. 'Thou that begett'st him that did thee beget, / Thou that wast born at sea, buried at Tarsus, / And found at sea again!' (*Pericles*, 21.183–5); 'O, what am I? / A mother to the birth of three? Ne'er mother / Rejoiced deliverance more' (*Cymbeline* 5.6.369–71).

6. Gail Kern Paster has a stimulating section on *Errors* as city comedy in her *The Idea of the City in the Age of Shakespeare* (Athens, Ga., 1985), pp. 185–94.

7. Menaechmus Sosicles in Plautus' comedy thinks that Erotium the courtesan is either 'mad or drunk' (*aut insana aut ebria*) when she hails him as her lover (Warner, Act 3).

8. Stanley Wells compares details in 'Reunion Scenes in The Comedy of Errors and Twelfth Night', *Wiener Beitrage sur Englischen Philologie*, 80: *A Yearbook of Studies in English Language and Literature 1985/86*, pp. 267–76.

# BIBLIOGRAPHY

Arthos, John. "Shakespeare's Transformation of Plautus." *Comparative Drama* 1 (1967): 239–53.

Austen, Glyn. "Ephesus Restored: Sacramentalism and Redemption in *The Comedy of Errors. Literature and Theology* 1 (1987): 54–69.

Baldwin, Thomas Whitefield. *On the Compositional Genetics of* The Comedy of Errors. Urbana: University of Illinois Press, 1944.

Berry, Edward I. *Shakespeare's Comic Rites.* Cambridge: Cambridge University Press, 1984.

Berry, Ralph. *Shakespeare's Comedies: Explorations in Form.* Princeton: Princeton University Press, 1972.

Cacicedo, Alberto. "'A Formal Man Again': Physiological Humours in *The Comedy of Errors. The Upstart-Crow* XI (1991): 24–38.

Candido, Joseph. "Dining out in Ephesus: Food in *The Comedy of Errors.*" *Studies in English Literature*, Vol. 30 (1990): 217–41.

Cartwright, Kent. "Language, Magic, the Dromios, and *The Comedy of Errors.*" *Studies in English Literature*, Vol. 48, No. 2 (Spring, 2007): 331–54.

———. "Surprising the Audience in *The Comedy of Errors.*" In *Re-Visions of Shakespeare: Essays in Honor of Robert Ornstein.* Edited by Evelyn Gajowski. Newark, DE: University of Delaware Press (2004): 215–30.

Champion, Larry S. *The Evolution of Shakespeare's Comedy.* Cambridge, MA: Harvard University Press, 1970.

Christensen, Ann C. "'Because Their Business Still Lies out a' Door': Resisting the Separation of the Spheres in Shakespeare's *Comedy of Errors. Literature and History*, Vol. 5, No. 1 (Spring 1996): 19–37.

Crewe, Jonathan V. "God or The Good Physician: The Rational Playwright in *The Comedy of Errors.*" *Genre* 15 (1982): 203–23.

Dutton, Richard. "*The Comedy of Errors and The Calumny of Apelles:* An Exercise in Source Study." From *Religion and the Arts*, Vol. 7: Nos. 1–2 (2003): 11–30.

Elliott, G. R. "Weirdness in *The Comedy of Errors.*" *University of Toronto Quarterly* 9 (1993): 95–106.

Fineman, Joel. "Fratricide and Cuckoldry: Shakespeare's Doubles." In *Representing Shakespeare: New Psychoanalytic Essays.* Edited by Murray M. Schwartz and Coppelia Kahn. Baltimore: Johns Hopkins University Press (1980): 70–109.

Freedman, Barbara. "Errors in Comedy: A Psychoanalytic Theory of Farce." *New York Literary Forum*, Vols. 5–6 (1980): 233–43.

Garber, Marjorie B. *Shakespeare After All.* New York: Pantheon Books (2004): 160–74.

Garton, Charles. "Centaurs, The Sea, and *The Comedy of Errors.*" *Arethusa* 12 (1979): 233–54.

Gibbons, Brian. "Erring and Straying Like Lost Sheep: *The Winter's Tale* and *The Comedy of Errors.*" *Shakespeare Survey*, Vol. 50 (1997): 111–23.

Gill, Erma. "A Comparison of the Characters in *The Comedy of Errors* with those in the *Menaechmi.*" *Texas University Studies in English* 5 (1925): 79–95.

———. "The Plot-Structure of *The Comedy of Errors* in Relation to Its Sources." *Texas University Studies in English* 10 (1930): 13–65.

Glyn, Austen. "Ephesus Restored: Sacramentalism and Redemption in *The Comedy of Errors.*" *Literature and Theology*, Vol. 1, No. 1 (March 1987): 54–69.

Godman, Maureen. "'Plucking a Crow' in *The Comedy of Errors.*" *Early Theatre*, Vol. 8, No. 1 (2005): 53–68.

Greenberg, Marissa. "Crossing from Scaffold to Stage: Execution Processions and Generic Conventions in *The Comedy of Errors* and *Measure for Measure.*" In *Shakespeare and Historical Formalism.* Edited by Stephen Cohen. Aldershot, England: Ashgate (2007): 127–45.

Grennan, Eamon. "Arm and Sleeve: Nature and Custom in *The Comedy of Errors.*" *Philological Quarterly*, Vol. 59, No. 2 (Spring 1980): 150–64.

Hart, Elizabeth. "'Great is Diana' of Shakespeare's Ephesus." *Studies in English Literature*, Vol. 43, No. 2 (Spring 2003): 347–74.

Hennings, Thomas P. "On the Anglican Doctrine of the Affectionate Marriage in *The Comedy of Errors. Modern Language Quarterly*, Vol. 42, No. 2 (June 1986): 91–107.

Hughes, Ian. "Dromio of Syracuse in *The Comedy of Errors.*" In *Players of Shakespeare 5.* Edited by Robert Smallwood. Cambridge, England: Cambridge University Press (2003): 29–42.

Kehler, Dorothea. "*The Comedy of Errors* as Problem Comedy." *Rocky Mountain Review* 41 (1987): 229–40.

———. "Shakespeare's Emilias and the Politics of Celibacy." In *In Another Country: Feminist Perspectives on Renaissance Drama.* Edited by Dorothea Kehler and Susan Baker. Metuchen, NJ: Scarecrow Press (1991): 157–78.

Kinney, Arthur F. "Shakespeare's *Comedy of Errors* and the Nature of Kinds." *Studies in Philology* 85 (1988): 29–52.

Landau, Aaron. "'Past Thought of Human Reason': Confounding Reason in *The Comedy of Errors*." *English Studies*, Vol. 85, No. 3 (June 2004): 189–205.

Lanier, Douglas. "'Stigmatical in Making': The Material Character of *The Comedy of Errors. English Literary Renaissance* 23 (1993): 81–112.

Leggatt, Alexander. "The Comedy of Errors." From *Shakespeare's Comedy of Love*. London: Methuen & Co. Ltd. (1974): 1–19.

Levin, Harry. "Two Comedies of Errors" from *Refractions: Essays in Comparative Literature*. New York: Oxford University Press (1966): 128–50.

———. *Playboys and Killjoys: An Essay on the Theory and Practice of Comedy*. New York: Oxford University Press, 1987.

Luxon, Thomas H. "Humanist Marriage and *The Comedy of Errors*." *Renaissance and Reformation*, Vol. 25, No. 4 (Autumn 2001): 45–65.

Lyne, Raphael. "Shakespeare, Plautus, and the Discovery of New Comic Space." In *Shakespeare and the Classics*. Edited by A.B. Taylor. Cambridge, UK: Cambridge University Press (2004): 122–38.

Maguire, Laurie. "The Girls from Ephesus." In *The Comedy of Errors: Critical Essays*. Edited by Robert S. Miola. New York: Garland (1997): 355–91.

McJannet, Linda. "Genre and Geography: The Eastern Mediterranean in *Pericles* and *The Comedy of Errors. In *Playing the Globe: Genre and Geography in English Renaissance Drama*. Edited by Virginia Mason Vaugham. Madison, NJ; London: Fairleigh Dickinson University Press; Associated University Press (1998): 86–106.

Miola, Robert S. *Shakespeare and Classical Comedy: The Influence of Plautus and Terence*. Oxford: Clarendon Press, 1994.

Neely, Carol Thomas. "Confining Madmen and Transgressing Boundaries" in *Distracted Subjects: Madness and Gender in Shakespeare and Early Modern Culture*. Ithaca and London: Cornell University Press (2004): 136–45.

Ornstein, Robert. "*The Comedy of Errors*." From *Shakespeare's Comedies: From Roman Farce to Romantic Comedy*. Newark: University of Delaware Press (1986): 25–34.

Pandit, Lalita. "Emotion, Perception and Anagnorisis in *The Comedy of Errors*: A Cognitive Perspective." *College Literature*, Vol. 33, No. 1 (Winter, 2006): 94–126.

Parker, Patricia. "Shakespeare and the Bible: *The Comedy of Errors*." *Semiotic Inquiry*, Vol. 13, No. 3 (1993): 47–74.

Parks, Patricia. "Elder and Younger: The Opening Scene of *The Comedy of Errors*." *Shakespeare Quarterly* 34 (1983): 325–27.

Petronella, Vincent F. "Structure and Theme Through Separation and Union in Shakespeare's *The Comedy of Errors*." *Modern Language Review* 69 (1974): 481–88.

Raman, Shankar. "Marking Time: Memory and Market in *The Comedy of Errors*." *Shakespeare Quarterly*, Vol. 56, No. 2 (Summer 2005): 176–205.

Riehle, Wolfgang. *Shakespeare, Plautus and the Humanist Tradition*. Cambridge: D.S. Brewer, 1990.

Salgado, Gamini. "'Time's Deformed Hand': Sequence, Consequence, and Inconsequence in *The Comedy of Errors*." *Shakespeare Survey* 25 (1972): 81–91.

Segal, Erich. *Roman Laughter*. New York: Oxford University Press (1987).

Shelburne, Steven R. "The Nature of 'Error' in *The Comedy of Errors*." *Explorations in Renaissance Culture*, Vol. 18 (1992): 137–51.

Tannenbaum, Samuel A. "Notes on *The Comedy of Errors*." *Shakespeare Jahrbuch* 68 (1932): 103–24.

Taylor, Gary. "Textual and Sexual Criticism: A Crux in *The Comedy of Errors*." *Renaissance Drama* 19 (1988): 195–225.

van Elk, Martine. "'This sympathized one day's error': Genre, Representation, and Subjectivity in *The Comedy of Errors*" from *Shakespeare Quarterly*, Vol. 60, No. 1 (2009): 47–72.

Weld, John S. "Old Adam New Apparelled." *Shakespeare Quarterly*, Vol. 7, No. 4 (Fall 1956): 453–56.

West, Gilian. "Lost Humour in *The Comedy of Errors* and *Twelfth Night*." *English Studies* 71 (1990): 6–15.

Williams, Gwyn. "*The Comedy of Errors* Rescued from Tragedy." *Review of English Literature* 5 (1964): 63–71.

Yang, Sharon R. "*The Comedy of Errors*: Variation on a Festive Theme." *The Upstart Crow*, Vol. 14 (1994): 11–27.

# ACKNOWLEDGMENTS

❧

### *The Comedy of Errors* in the Twentieth Century

Mark Van Doren, "The Comedy of Errors." From *Shakespeare*, pp. 33–36. Copyright © 1939 by Mark Van Doren. Published by Henry Holt and Company, republished by New York Review of Books, 2005.

Harold C. Goddard, "The Comedy of Errors." From *The Meaning of Shakespeare*, pp. 25–28. Copyright © 1951 by The University of Chicago. Reprinted with permission of the University of Chicago Press.

E.M.W. Tillyard, "The Comedy of Errors." From *Shakespeare's Early Comedies*, pp. 45–70. Copyright © Stephen Tillyard 1965. Republished by Athlone Press, 1999.

Douglas L. Peterson, "Beginnings and Endings: Structure and Mimesis in Shakespeare's Comedies." From *Entering the Maze: Shakespeare's Art of Beginning*, edited by Robert F. Wilson Jr., pp. 37–59. Copyright © 1995 Peter Lang Publishing Inc.

Harold Bloom, "The Comedy of Errors." From *Shakespeare: The Invention of the Human*, pp. 21–28. Published by Riverhead Books. Copyright © 1998 by Harold Bloom.

### *The Comedy of Errors* in the Twenty-first Century

Charles Whitworth, "Farce, City Comedy and Romance." From *The Comedy of Errors*, pp. 42–59. Copyright © 2003 Oxford University Press.

# INDEX